By Jwaundäce Belcher and Marchella Bell

Copyright © **Another BOMB Production**, 1998
All rights reserved

First edition

Front Cover Design: Michael Hodge
Back Cover Layout: Alberto Chacon
Photographs: Vincent Johnson

Published by Another BOMB Production
2480 Briarcliff Road #166
Atlanta, Georgia 30329

ISBN: 0-9662377-0-6

Printed in the United States of America
Gilliland Printing

Distributed by Lushena Books
Chicago, Illinois

This is a work of fiction. It is not meant to depict, portray, or represent any particular gender, real persons or group of people. All the characters, incidents, and dialogues are products of the author's imagination and are not to be construed as real. Any resemblance to actual events or persons, living or dead, is purely coincidental.

All rights reserved. No part of this book may be reproduced in any form without written permission from the publishers, except by a reviewer who may quote brief passages in a review to be printed in a newspaper or magazine.

ACKNOWLEDGMENTS

Being the direct person I am, I'm going to try to make this short enough to not get me into any kind of trouble by saying something I may regret in my future but detailed enough to get my point across.....So, check it.

I must give thanks to my Creator, who is also my Best Friend, my Provider, and my Comforter. Thanks for rescuing me at the times I needed you to and not at the times I wanted you to. 'Cause you know it always pays off when you call the shots. I'm blessed you have introduced positive energies into my life so that I can take advantage of what life really has to offer. All that I have accomplished, achieved and am working toward is all because of my strong faith in YOU. Please help the blind to see that to believe is the key...

I give thanks to my family-The Belcher's (my right hand), The Bray's (my left hand).

Grandma (Dear), I love you, and my late grandfather, Bug, boy, I miss him, for raising me, nourishing my body with food and water and a roof over my head. This one's for you.

Mama, thanks for delivering my body to Earth. I will always love you, no matter what.

Dad, thanks for assisting mama with the procreation process. I owe you.

Andrea, I always will love you, sis, even when you think I don't. I'm glad Fred and my beautiful niece, Aisha, has brought you peace.

Dedrick, my little brother, I love you for bringing happiness into Daddy's life. Thank you, too, Lorna.

Aunt Deb, always was there when I needed you the most. Lynn and Stacie I love you.

To my late grandfather, Isaiah, I miss your guidance.

To my late uncle, Reginald, I miss your wit.

Tara and Tajuana Jefferson, I wouldn't trade you two for any other cousins in the world. We grew up together and thanks for always supporting me and making me feel special.

ACKNOWLEDGMENTS

To my life long friends-Shauna, we had fun..didn't we? thanks for my godson, Colby; Tanesha, you still swole? I love ya though; Melissa, out of touch and out of sight; Nicole, thanks for putting up with my moods when we were roommates; Gayle, mi amiga; Jennifer, thanks for an exciting social life in Dallas; Anne, my spiritual buddy; Temeka, my homegirl to the end; Kris, my AC pal; Harry; my confidant, my...; Johnny, thanks for always making me laugh; Felonte, thanks for listening to me, buddy; Dalton, what's up, partner?; The Blows, you know; Terry, Kimberly, Keisha, Donnis, Rita, Trish, Miesha, Michael, Tony, Tiy-e, Uncle Pete, Uncle Tyrone, and my cuzs--TJ, LA, and Darryl, Mike, Big Sweepie, Frank, and Netta, I haven't forgotten about ya either.

I would especially like to thank my sorors of the Delta Iota Chapter who were my friends before, during and after Delta--Marshal, Paula, Charie, Carla, Aundrea, Shaunie, Netta and Shannon and I haven't forgotten about ya Renee, Denise, Deidra, Cheryl, Dawn, Lisa and Angie.

I'd like to give a shout out to my roots in Birmingham, Alabama...to my out of touch but unforgotten friends who attended Grambling State University, including my mentor--Mr. Norman and the crazies in Theater Guild...my former graduate colleagues and co-workers in Dallas, Texas...and to all of the positive and talented brothas and sistas at The Palace who made me feel welcomed when I moved to my newfound home in Atlanta, Georgia.

To my soul mate and friend--William Metz IV, I love you!!!

I would like to thank the people whose names were unintentionally forgotten but whose spirits I will never forget. But most importantly, I thank the people, whom I believe were angels, yeah, you, whom came in and out of my life blessing me with words of wisdom, inspiration and praise.

Much love and many blessings for your support,
jwaundace belcher

ACKNOWLEDGMENTS

Everyone who knows me, knows that I like to do things dramatically. I like big Texas hair, big jewelry, and I definitely love big, fine, brothers! So this thank you is going to be no different. To do such a tremendous project in such a short amount of time, and during one of the most tumultuous times in my life, has taken the support of so many people. My family, my friends, my classmates, my co-workers, and my church family have all been extremely supportive and enthusiastic about the book and the direction of my life. So to them all I say thank you which barely scratches the surface of my indebtedness. A few special people I would particularly like to thank are:

My Mother--Thanks for being the knot at the end of my rope..no one will ever know the scope of our relationship. And just when we thought it couldn't be stretched any further....here we go again. I'm so glad my soul chose you to be my mother and I'm delighted that you have chosen me to be your friend.

My Daddy--Thanks for telling me to reach for the sky and for knowing that the stars weren't good enough. Thanks for my name which means 'to love or please God', and for teaching me the importance of being a good communicator and marketing myself. And thanks, daddy for all the little things you do that make such a huge difference in my life.

My sister, Barbra--Thank you for helping me to find the place in me that is kneeling at the foot of the rainbow Praising God! And Kevin for recognizing Aretha, Gladys and Whitney living in a remote corner of my mind. Miss Brianna, thanks for being a prissy little mimic whose presence sheds so much light on my life and who keeps me youthful and fun. And of course, Desmond--Thanks for being as cool as Santa Claus on a hot July day. Thanks for your bright little countenance shining and showing what all this is about.

My brother, Lance--We've been through so much together, thanks for being a true big brother. As much as I hate to admit it-- you've helped me to keep on course and protected me from trillions of knuckleheads. I love you dearly and I'm proud to be called Lance's Lil Sister.

ACKNOWLEDGMENTS

To Tanika-- Thanks for being my big sister during the trying college years when our slogan was 'when we gon' get paid?'. And thanks for teaching me those 'Mack' skills--some day I'm gonna get around to applying them!

To Kendra--Thanks for whispering my size when my heart was carrying the weight of my life. Thanks for sharing your pain and enduring with me through mine. You and Nikki are truly like sisters! Also thanks for the home away from home Mr. and Mrs. G.

To Pastor Haynes--Thanks for teaching me how to make a hole-in-one without ever lifting a club. And to my Friendship West church family thanks for your words of encouragement and for constantly inquiring about my schooling. To Joyce, one of my surrogate sisters, you are a jewel amongst God's precious gems-- thanks for always listening and challenging me to rise beyond the glow and face the truth.

And to Darrell--You know you my boy! Thanks for reminding not to take life so seriously. To Marvin--Thanks for setting off the hunger pains that led to the revolution of my true self. Ruth, thanks for stripping down to nothing so that I could see what a real soul looks like and for our times in prayer which showed me the power of two voices calling out to God in harmony! And to Tonette, John, Ara, and Karen, To Mighty Mike and the Power Angels, Nicole and the Barryer family, The Criddales, The Traylors, Janet, Contius, Carnisha, Becca, Leon, Patrick, Mark, Bobby, Vincent, Scotty G., Kina, Monique, sorors Paulette, Cassandra, and Nicole, your encouragement was paramount.

To Gloria--Thanks for caring enough to share your phenomenal peace of mind with the world. And to my hypnotherapy colleagues may each of you find your place in the revolution against 'crazy-making'. Thanks for your support!

And to my Heavenly Father--Thanks for being the ribbon at the finish-line that took so long to get to and such a short, but sweet time to break through. Thanks for the rain cause without it there would have been no rainbows. Thanks for every emotional push-up that I did outside in the cold, dark dreary nights

ACKNOWLEDGMENTS

overlooked by the captain of my soul. Thanks for the tears--tiny and tall; their fall built a bridge for still others to cross. Thanks for the tragedy of one grandmom's life and of another's death that left a legacy of 'try-umph' for me to gain. Thanks for setting the alarm time and time again when I chose to snooze. Thanks for letting my little light shine!

Thank you all for your love, time and patience.
May God be as generous with you, as you have with me.
marchella bell

♋

ACKNOWLEDGMENTS

Our thanks to the following Professionals that loaned us their eyes, ears, and minds:

Michael Baisden--Thanks for helping us get the information we needed when we needed it.

Chris Hill and Vincent Johnson--thanks for patiently picturing these two meticulous sisters. Our best to you!

And to the Circle of Friends Book Club II (Atlanta, GA)-- our grateful appreciation to you for reading our manuscript and offering your literary advice.

Marshal and your creative husband, Mike, for blessing us with Second Millenia.

Alberto Chacon--keep up the good work coming.

Metropolitan Dallas Alumni--thank you for allowing us to share our services and talents.

To all the radio stations who allowed us to share this gift to their listening audiences, especially V103 in Atlanta, GA; Soul 73 105.7 and 100.3 in Dallas, Texas; and WPGC 95.5 in Washington, D.C. A special shout out to Yvonne St.John in Dallas.

To Emma Rogers and the *Black Images* crew for undying commitment to black literature.

To Tariq & Geneva Jones--thanks for going out of your way to help us in so many ways.

Thank you Nia and Francine, Janice, Fanta and Sarita for being one of the first to support us along with others great works to come.

To all of our contributors--who made all of this possible.

The Journey

Deep Throat 1

Doing the Nasty 8

Eatin' Out 17

*Sixty-Nine 21

Entering the Backdo' 28

Master-Baiter 37

It's On When the Club Close 48

A Fire in the Hole 60

In and Out 71

Silent Cream 82

Four-Playing 94

Face Down .... .112

Booty Call 130

I'm Coming Out .... .145

Sometimes You Feel Like a Nut 167

Midnight Snack 181

Hand-Cuffs 202

StripTease 229

Treasure Hunt 238

Freak Nic 266

Ass-Out 288

Fortitude..302

Chapter 1
Deep Throat
♋

Fuck Men! Fuck God and definitely fuck OA! Fuck everybody who want something from me and ain't willing to give me nothing. I'm tired of being everybody's helping hand --where is my damn helper? Why do I always have to be alone? Why am I always trying to improve myself--for what? --so I can help someone else get married, have a family and live happily ever after--without me? Where is my thank you-- not the words, but the love, the man, the family I need? What about me? When am I going to be happy? free? settled? I don't want to get better, I want to get laid. When will I stop dreaming about and start living? I'm sick of this shit! I'm sick of praying, crying, begging for the life I dream of. I'm sick of being so damn good, of trying to look just right, and be just right, and of being there for everyone. How am I supposed to have the faith to help others when I don't believe that I will ever have anything more than a boring meager existence? Why have I been punished with this fucked up life-- if you can call it a life? I don't know where to turn now. I've tried everything to no avail...even God don't give a damn about me. I guess I'll just keep on until I drown in my tears.

June 11 at 9:30 am

Shoot, look at the time, this is the third time this week... Thank God for an understanding boss. Speaking of, I'd better get my fatass up and call in.

But first, let me just lay here for a few minutes. Ahhh! relaxation, now that's what I deserve. When I lose this weight I'm gonna go to Cancun and wear a bikini so small that all the men will be looking at me and begging me for some of this. They don't know what the hell they are missing--nice tight little stuff just dripping with anticipation for a man like..like LaRon. Man is he fine. What a sista wouldn't do to be riding a man like that night after night! Now that would be worth getting all fine for. His tight rippling ass against my plush velvety thighs... Just the thought makes me wanna...uhmm! Now here's something those hard-ass carrots could do some good for.....

Ring!
Riiiinnng!
Oh Shit! It's ten o'clock...and who the hell is this calling me? I better check the I.D. box. oo-oh!
"Hello," I said making sure to sound as drained as I felt.
"Hey girl. You up? This is Nicolette."
"Yea I'm up, but I'm not feeling so well."
"What's wrong??!"
"I guess I've just got a bug or something."
"Are you coming in?"
"Girl, I..."
"Well the only reason I asked is because according to this schedule I'm supposed to spend some time with you going over the intake process this week, and I've done everything else on the schedule for this week, and part of next week, so I guess that leaves you."
"Oh Nic, I'm sorry. I forgot. I'm gonna be right there."
"Well, it's okay if you can't make it because I've been helping out with the phones since Vicky is out on maternity leave...I'm learning a lot out here."
"Girl, you know working those phones is probably the quickest way to learn the ropes. But I'm still comin' right over, I know how it feels to be the new guy, I'm not going to leave you hangin'...besides you haven't done all this schooling to be no receptionist."
"Are you sure you are up to it?"
"Sure...I'll be there in about 30 minutes."
"Alright...thanks girl...see ya in a minute. Bye."
"Bye-Bye."
Nic is so sweet, and I would die to have her life...lawyer's kid, second generation Howard grad, long pretty hair, a bad-ass figure, and a vette to match. The only reason she don't have a man is that she too picky. LaRon would drop

his teeth if he saw her sassy twinkling green eyes, and he would absolutely die if he tried to get up in there because she don't take no shit, and ain't giving up no play for no hard nigger like him. She likes'm rich and educated, and her daddy wouldn't let his ghetto ass sniff their freshly manicured, always-smelling-like-watermelon lawn. I can just see his buff, 'I-wish-I-made-the-team' ass standing at their gate looking like a nigger in prison. It's almost worth introducing them so I can see his reaction...but naah, cause I know I'd be pissed off to the highest degree of pisstivity if they hooked up.

Ring!

NOW, who is it?

Riiiinng!

You know, people don't want you until you busy. If I was laying here doing nothing the phone wouldn't...

It's Evelyn...I surely wouldn't want to talk to her right now.

Riiiinng!

"Hello."

"Hi. Dana??"

"Yes."

"This is Evelyn, your Overeaters Anonymous sponsor."

Thank you for reminding me warden. Yes, I've put the refrigerator on lock down.

"Yes, Evelyn. How are you?"

"I'm too blessed to be distressed. And how about yourself?"

I feel like throwing up yesterday's healthy slop in your happy face.

"Oh, I'm doing great. I stuck strictly to my plan on yesterday." Except for the 1/2 gallon of Ben and Jerry's that was on sale at the grocery store.

"And what goodies are on your plan for today?"

How about a double-crust, Mexican pan pizza with extra sauce from del Sol's, an ice cream Slushie, and peach cobbler, by Weight Watcher's, of course.

"Well, a friend of mine called this morning with an emergency, and I just finished helping her out with it, is why I hadn't called you yet. And now I'm really late to work. So could I gather up my things and call you from there?"

"Sure! I have to pick up Little Anthony at noon so I'll be out around that time, but other than that, I'll be right here."

Okay, Mrs. Cleaver. And don't forget to wash behind the Beaver's ears and tell him a night-night story.

"Okay, thanks for reminding me. My friend really threw me off this morning...You know how it is with friends, you just can't say no."

"Well, call me Dana if you need to talk about anything."

"Thanks. I'll call you from work. Good-bye."

"Oh, and don't forget the meeting tonight..the speaker is going to be my old sponsor..she's so inspirational..she's the one who everyone talks about..you know she was on Oprah for loosing over two hundred..you will just love her..I really adore her..."

Did she not hear me say I was in a hurry?

"Yes, yes...I remember. I'll call you from work about my plan. I've got to go now, I have a meeting at 11:30."

"I'll expect your call."

"Good-bye."

"Good-bye."

If there are two people in the world who shouldn't ever have a weight problem, it's Evelyn and Oprah Winfrey. I mean, how you gon' be rich and fat? All Evelyn does is sit at home all day and wait for her little boy to need her for something. Shoot, if I was her, I'd just have myself tied to the stairmaster. I would have gotten a cook and a personal trainer a long time ago, and instructed everyone on the staff not to eat around me, not to talk about food and to absolutely not--no matter how I begged or threatened to fire them--give me any food.

I think I'll catch up on my soaps and Oprah tonight. Oh yeah, after the meeting with Evelyn. I mean, maybe the fat bitch will inspire me to loose this extra 35 pounds I've put on since I left home. And afterwards, I can drop by the gym, and maybe get a glimpse of LaRon's hot, sweaty body on the basketball court. I love how his body gets straight and hard and curves just a little as he bumps off his opponent street-ball style and takes it all the way to the hoop..jamming it in as if he's winning the State championship all over again. It reminds me of when I used to daydream that I was Kelly, the cheerleader he gave the game ball to after making a fast break and saving our asses in the playoffs. He was skinnier then, that was before he got into this health stuff and started doing those pin-ups, and before Kelly broke his heart. Personally, I think he's still frustrated over her--after all I did to try to console him. He coulda had a *real* woman, but he just couldn't see it. But he's still my boy, and I'll always be there for him. Maybe I'll run into him today. If not, there's always my pin-ups.

♋

It feels great outside today! I'm glad I had a good cry this morning. That's one thing Evelyn *was* right about--getting it out, does help me feel better. But I hate it while I'm going through my little mood swings--no man is gonna want to deal with me when I'm like this, so I'd better straighten up my act, or I'll never get a man.

    Nicolette really needs my help. So I'm going to leave all these demons behind today, and focus on teaching her how to work this joint. She really doesn't seem to have a heart for this kind of work...well, I don't know, maybe I just haven't given her a chance. We'll see if she's doing any better with her clients this week. She kind of treats therapy like fuckin': you get yours, I get mine, and we all get paid, and live happily ever after. She'll learn quick that people ain't like that. People are weird, and though they come to us to get fixed, there's no real cure to just make them better. We are not like locksmith's figuring out their combination, but we are more like juggling instructors, helping them to understand and juggle life as it comes to them without dropping all the balls. And helping them to pick them up, and start all over again when they do. That sounded kinda good--I really am good with words. One day I'm gonna write a book and put all my juicy fantasies, and my intellectual prowess into it. Until then, I'd better get my ass on the j-o-b, before I *really* be juggling for a living.

CHAPTER 2
Doing the Nasty
♋

Today was a pretty productive day. I helped Dana with the intake process and I saw two clients who got on my nerves with their problems. I'm sick of seeing these crazy people everyday who don't have real problems. They are always whining or crying. I'll be glad when I see real people with real issues.

Nicolette, June 11

I was about to leave work about a quarter after six, after my last client phoned that she would not be able to make it-- again. This is the second time she has called in the past two weeks canceling her appointment. I've only seen her twice and her presenting problem is that she gets into arguments with her husband when he comes home from work. She volunteered that he always initiated the arguments for reasons like dinner not being ready, or the house is not clean. She added the fact that he's always horny, and wants to screw, and she's never ready when he wants it. Then, she blamed his behavior to stress on his job. She also told me that she tries to please him in any way possible because she doesn't want to lose him. See, her husband is a cop, and from what she tells me he is very dominating, aggressive and likes everything his way or no way. But, she said 'he does have a sensitive side that no one sees but herself'. Sounds co-dependent to me, but I wouldn't tell her that. That's when I asked her what has she tried to resolve this so-called marital conflict. She told me that she tried everything from ignoring him, to going in another room, to agreeing with what he says (even though she may disagree). She also tried making silent and verbal gestures like nodding her head at him while saying 'un-huh', 'you right', 'okay honey' to 'whatever', 'here you go again', 'you say that every day'.
    I tried this paradoxical situation with her that Dana taught me. So in our last session I told her word for word: "Go home, and the minute your husband walks through the door from work, I want YOU to start an argument with him, about something that he's not doing to satisfy you, or something that he does that you don't like. Then, I want you to log every time it occurred, including what happened before, during, and after the argument, what it was about, and how you felt, and thought about it. Try this for one week, and

when you come back for therapy, we can both sit down, analyze and challenge the problem from a different perspective".

She looked at me like I'd lost my damn mind. And you know what--that was my last time seeing or hearing from her. Dana told me that it was supposed to have worked even without the husband being present to hear all of this. She told me that she just needs to learn how to take up for herself, and if he realizes this, he may back down. I didn't think it would work without him being present to get his side of the story. But Dana always thinks she is right, with her smart, fat ass. Maybe that's why my client didn't come back--Dana's technique did work to solve her so-called problem which to me was never a real problem. She would not have the problem if she left that sorry-ass, narcissistic child. I will never stoop down to her level. But huh, like most people think, at least she got a man. And I'm patiently waiting for my Prince Charming.

As I was packing up and collecting all of my things out of Dr. Hemminger's office, knowing one day I'll have my own, I heard Dana's footsteps from a distance. I yelled,

"Hey, slim!"

"I told you never to call me that," Dana whined.

"Stop whining, sista, you can't take a joke?"

"You know how sensitive I am."

"Yeah, whatever...come with me to the mall. I want to catch the sale at Macy's."

"Oh, and what am I supposed to do, just sit around and watch yo' skinny ass buy every sale article without trying them on. You make me sick with your perfect body."

"Come on, silly girl, we'll find something for you, too, and then afterwards we can get some of that homemade ice cream that tastes so good it'll make you not want to have sex no mo'."

"I don't know about that. If anything, it'll make me want to put it in between my thighs to cool my ass down to get over the fantasies that I have about smokin' black LaRon. Hell, I don't think enough ice cream in the world would cool me off."

"Well, since you can't have him right away, we'll just get your ice cream topped off with nuts and cream."

"Damn, Nic, you gonna have me masturbating myself in a minute."

"Let's get out of here, slim--I mean, silly girl, before I have to counsel you on Dr. Hemminger's couch."

"You mean his waterbed, cause when I'm finished, I will have it so soaked with cum, like I was a man having a wet dream."

♋

When we finally arrived at the mall, it was seven fifteen. Traffic was hectic as usual. It's just motherfuckers don't know how to drive. If there's an accident on the other side of the highway, people on this side wants to slow down and look--like damn tourists. I think it's just a bunch of nosey busters in the world.

"Nicolette, are you going to buy the whole store?"

"No, Dana, just half."

I laughed and was feeling deep down that I wouldn't mind having my own store. After I purchased about three shirts, a couple of pant suits, a skirt and a pair of shoes, we left Macy's and headed for the ice cream parlor. I noticed two guys. One was somewhat dark-skinned with a short hair cut and a mustache. The other was a tall, slim, bright-skinned, red-haired, dreadlocks, Bob Marley lookalike. They were heading our way and I know they noticed us. I wasn't in the mood to be bothered by some no-life busters trying to look like they somebody wearing Hilfiger and Kani. And the only decent looking one was the short one, and he was only 5'5'. I know cause I'm five six and three quarters, and I don't date anybody shorter than me. As a matter of fact, I would rather have someone taller than six feet, cause I wear heels and with my heels on, I'm five feet eight, or taller, and I still want somebody I can look up to.

"Here comes your husband, Dana."

"I know you ain't trying to front on me."

They stopped right in front of us.

"Hey, shorty, what's up?" the short one asked, and he had the nerve to be in front of my face.

"I wish it was your height," I told him.

"What is that suppose to mean? "

"It means...I wish you were taller, cause I don't date short men."

"Oh, I can't satisfy you or somethin'. I'm not cute enough? I'm.."

"Let me cut you off right there. I'm not interested. How 'bout that?"

I grabbed Dana.

"Let's go, girl. We don't have time for them."

"Fuck you, bitch!" the short one yelled at me as we walked off.

"Why is it that every time I don't want to talk to a nigga, I gotta be a bitch?"

Dana looked at me with no expression.

"Maybe because you are sometimes," she finally remarked.

"Just because I don't want to talk to anybody makes me out to be a bitch? What if I'm just not interested?"

"Well...Nic, you don't have to be rude. There's a way to be honest...and not rude. Plus, whenever we are out you always blow guys off. What about me? You're so busy trying to knock off what you don't like, and you always saying 'I'm ready to go', 'there's no one here I like, or 'I don't like this click'. And you're never patient with me, or consider that sometimes I may want to get *my* mack on for a change. It's always what Nic wants. Don't you think that I may be interested? Like a minute ago, I thought the other guy was rather eccentric looking--but noooooo, you messed up any chance for me to get to know him because of your selfish, self-centered attitude that's developed into your full-blown personality!"

For some reason or another, Dana really was getting to me. Feelings of hurt and anger started rushing through my head, so I blurted out,

"You really think his friend was interested in you. Dana, you're FAT and the only thing that he would have been interested in is your wet, sloppy, wrinkled coochie. How dare you criticize me. You're just jealous because you never have the chance to turn guys away like I do. Yeah, the only way any man, even LaRon, would be interested in you, is if you attempted to make an appointment with Jenny Craig, and drink Slim Fast every day, while popping Ginseng to give you the energy to do it all."

I felt my heart beating fast, like an African elephant was pounding against my chest. Then, anxiety and tension was starting to arise. Dana's eyes filled with tears, but somehow she remained calm, like she always does when conflict, stress, or pressure springs up. Her head dropped to her chest, and there was a brief moment of silence. A silence like I've never felt between us before. Suddenly, her head lifted slowly and there was no sign of a tear. It was as if they dried up, evaporated, or disappeared abruptly. All of a sudden, I saw her mouth open.

"You're right, Nic," she uttered without sounding resentful or angry, "I want to go home now. For some reason, I lost my appetite for ice cream."

She laughed with sarcasm, "I don't need it anyway. I'll meet you at the car."

Dana walked off cool, calm and collected, as usual. I stood there not knowing what to do. Should I go after her?...yell her name out and pray that she'll respond?...or do both. Instead, I chose to let her go in peace. Why did I say that to her? I didn't mean it. I was just mad at her for telling me the truth about me. Maybe--no...I think I am selfish and self-centered at times. That's probably the reason I can't keep a relationship or have real friends. No, get over it Nic, it's not you. You just told her what she needed to do to get a man. That's all. I don't have a man or friends outside of Dana because there are no real men or friends. But Dana was right about one thing--I can be honest, but not so rude. So, I am going to apologize to Dana but not for being honest, but rather the way I said it.

♋

As I was walking toward my car I saw a sign on the side of the building which stated:

Malik Akbar
featured at the
Soul Coffee Cafe
Wednesday at 6:00 p.m.

Poetry readings, book signing, and pieces
of Malik's original works will be read
and put on display for a limited time only

    I stood there with surprise. I've always been in love with Malik's works. I have all of his books of poetry, fiction and nonfiction works. I've got to attend tomorrow, I better get there early because I know that it is going to be packed with brothas and sistas waiting to get in to meet him, get an autograph, and listen to his poems. Man, he recites them with sooo much feeling you can really empathize with what he is talking about.
    "I know you going," Dana sneeked up from behind me. "You always talking about your dream of being like Malik. I've read some of your poetry, and I think you have the potential of being his counterpart."
    "You really think so," I responded forgetting what had just happened inside of the mall.
    "Yes, I do. You have so much talent if you would just believe in yourself."
    I smiled. She always makes my day and for some reason I never can do the same for her. If I were her, I would still be holding a grudge about what happened between us in the mall. She has so many characteristics that I desire to have in myself. She has such a way of forgiving, and so much sensitivity.
    We rode back to her car in silence. I guess we both have a lot on our minds. I know I do. Neither one of us said

"bye"...we just went our separate ways. But I've got to be there tomorrow to see Malik, no matter what happens.

CHAPTER 3
Eatin' Out
♋

    I dropped by del Sol's on the way home and picked up a fresh Mexican pan pizza with extra jalepenos. It smelled so good I couldn't even wait till I got it home--so I ate three pieces on the way home.
    I'll just have a couple of slices tonight, and tomorrow I'll eat the rest at lunch when I'll have plenty of time to burn it off. Aw! I forgot about the gym...and my sponsor...you know, this reporting is getting a little old.

No! I'm not going to think that way--if I want to be thin, I've got to be willing to do whatever it takes to get there, even if it means calling Mother Knows Best every minute.

Man, look at this place, I really need to clean up in here before someone calls the sanitation department. Mama'nem coming over this weekend and I definitely don't wanta hear it. I'm a grown woman and you'd think they would leave me alone by now, but no such luck. I think it must be more fun to pick on me than Ed and Pinky--they don't give a damn. They just ignore Mama's judgmental, Ms. Righteous, know-it-all attitude, but me, oh no...I have to get mad and cry EVERYTIME. Maybe this weekend will be different since it's Father's Day.

Uuummh! This pizza is slammin'. Ain't nothing like del Sol's to end a perfectly scum day.

Ring!

Riiiinng!

"Hey Nicolette...smack, smack...what's up, girl."

"Dana..listen..I..uh..I wanted you to know that I didn't mean any harm by what I said earlier. You're right sometimes I do have a really terrible way of expressing myself, but I meant well."

"Girl, I didn't even give it another thought." (smack)

"What are you eating at this hour?"

"Oh...I...uh...picked up some...uuh..fresh fruit for my lunch tomorrow, and I was just..uh tasting these grapes. They're sweet as ever..I love the summertime..."

"Well, you should still watch eating this late at night because that's how the weight sneaks up on you."

Thanks Miss Fine--what the hell do you know about weight gain.

"It's a little late to be telling ME that..."

"Still girl there is no reason to add to what you already need to loose. Don't you want LaRon to look at you again like that time you told me about? Maybe it wasn't just your imagination? Maybe he did see something special in your eyes? I mean, any man who brought *me* breakfast *and* dinner for over a year, I would definitely give him some serious consideration. And speaking of consideration, guess who was on my voice mail.."

Here we go.

"..Rodrick. I told you he is a keeper. I mean he called from the Taber Country Club--I checked the I.D. Do you know what that means?.."

"No. But I'm sure it has something to do with money."

"Yes, girl, like yachts and six figure diamond rings..he's got to be getting paid to afford the membership, or come from the right family which is just as good."

"Just how long you plannin' to *keep* him?"

"Well, I'm not trying to get married or anything. But I guess he'd be nice to have around to escort me to nice functions..you know the kind where you don't want to be embarrassed by some brother with an earring or a royal blue sport coat when he should be in a tux.."

Like LaRon.

"..Plus, he has the tools *and* skills in the bedroom. To be honest, that's the only reason I gave him the time of day. He just looked like a man with the means, and who could miss his dick in those gym clothes. But everybody just stepped off once he started to pursue me..they knew they didn't stand a chance. Girl, did I tell you about the.."

"Roses," I butted in cause I couldn't help but listen to her bragging about them the other day, "Yes, I saw them. They were the bomb."

I couldn't miss that big rose bush since you sacheted into my office looking like a peacock.

"No, I was gonna say birthday party that he is giving for one of his frat brothers at Club Cierra. He hates clubs, but since his friend doesn't get to go out very often, he is having it there on Friday, and we're invited."

"We."

"Yes, we. He said I could bring a friend. So I know you are in there."

"I guess so."

"What do you mean 'I guess so'. Like you got a hot date planned for Friday night."

"Yea, I got a date with yo' daddy."

"Alright..watch yourself."

"Girl, I'm just joking. I gotta get to bed."

"Okay, see you tomorrow."

"Goodnight."

Okay. Just one more piece..then I'll stop.

That was sweet of Nic to call me. She know she was wrong. Why can't she just come out and say she is sorry. You know, I really think she has a hard time expressing herself. Shoot I probably wouldn't know how to express myself either if my momma died when I was two. That must have been really tragic for her, and she talks about it as if it doesn't even bother her. As crazy as my momma is, I wouldn't trade her for a million bucks, well maybe a million slices of del Sol's.

Alright, Miss Piggie. Just one more piece and then go to bed.

CHAPTER 4
* Sixty-Nine
♋

Dear Diary,

Today was a great day! I met up with this sista from Sudan at the Vegetarian Health Food Store, who has only been in the United States three months. She admired the attire that I wore for the Black Arts Festival, and asked if I could make the same one for her entire family of eight. I gave her my card, and she told me that she would give me a call next week sometime. Hey, maybe I should dress more Afrocentric for the next festival. I need to write her name down in my planner. Oh, I also got to meet some of my most respected and cherished authors of all time at the festival, like Alice Walker, Na'im Akbar, Iyanla Vanzant and Connie Briscoe. And I ran into my good friend, too, author, Michael Baisden, and he is really blowing up.. I was hoping R.Kelly was going to somehow, in some way swing through...ha, ha wishful thinking. If I had to be with any man it would be with him. I love a dark, baldheaded man. But there goes my luck. Both of our schedules are so busy, but he'll feel my vibe, and he will be searching, soon, for this sassy, educated, sexy, beautiful, got-it-going-on soul sista here! Ha!Ha!Ha! Yeah, right, Afrikka, in yo' damn dreams. Carry on, carry on. I have to go now, diary. You'll be hearing from me later. Now I dread having to listen to my voice mail. But, oh, well, people love me and I love myself.

Afrikka,
On a lovely late, late June 11th night

Okay, should I take a shower first, or listen to my voice mail? Hell, I've been in the sun all day and I probably smell like three billy goats doing cart wheels in the air, sweating hard. But who cares. It's only me. If I can't stand my own funk, I need to be put to sleep. Let me check and see what fans have been trying to get in contact with me all day.

I went into the second bedroom which I have turned into my office, and turned on my computer. Then, I pressed the access code to get my messages. A male voice told me I have five new messages, and asked if I would like to listen to them. I pressed yes, and the voice said, *"First voice message:"*

'Afrikka...where are you?...you probably out talking to Hillary Clinton and giving her tips on starting her own line of clothing, with your help of course. Hell, you need to go into cosmetics now, cause that sista need some help. I'm sorry, I shouldn't have said that about the wife of the man who runs this country, but you know that's the truth, and somebody has to tell it! Anyway, I just wanted to chat. See you at work tomorrow. Oh, this is Sydney, just in case you couldn't catch my voice.'

    How could I not catch your punk ass voice? You only sound like a watered down version of RuPaul. *"Do you want to save or discard this message?"* the voice interrupted my thought, and I pressed discard. I'm so glad I only have to put up with him for three hours a day...and only once a week cause he is straight-up hyper and crazy as Hell. But, I have to admit, he is such a good friend. He'd give you his last dollar, and we have some interesting conversations, too. I'm just not in a talking mood right now.

    "Second voice message:" 'Yes, this is Weston William Smith calling from the Institute. I just noticed the substitute in your place today and was just informed that you were out representing yourself at the Black Arts Festival. Even though you run your own business and may not need us, financially, your presence at our prestigious institution is necessary. The next time you want to take off, please inform me first. We would not want your students to miss out on any pertinent information taught by you. They only ask for your services three hours a day, and once a week at that, so try not to disappoint them next time. Thank you for your precious time.'

    Who this mothasucka thank he is. 'This is Weston William Smith'. Does he really have so say his whole name-- like he somebody. He's only the dean. You'd think he own the school the way he walks around all high and mighty--I guess that's what happens when you give some people a little power. He makes me so sick sucking up to the board, and making things much harder than they have to be. And the way he wears his pants so high above his waist that they might as well be on his back. I'm surprised he hasn't gotten blisters from having his pants wrapped so tight around his penis. Hell, he may not have a dick because I have never seen a print. Never. How he get away with wearing those seventies rejects at a major fashion institution I don't know. They need to fire him for being such a disgrace to the fashion industry.

    I quickly discarded his message and moved on to the "*third voice message*:" 'Afrikka, I have several new clients who are interested in some pieces from you. Most are interested in the designs that you haven't officially displayed yet. Preferably those fresh articles you were working on the other day. Guess who called with some inquiries...your two most adored females, Nikki Giovanni and Susan Taylor. I know..I know, I'm still trying to get you hooked up with Maya. It takes patience, baby, but don't worry, I will make it happen for you. Oh, and guess what, we are finally breaking into the record industry by getting some singers...(Lord, I hope he say R. Kelly)...an old friend of yours, Erykah Badu. You know she is lovin' your designs. You should get much business from her. And this will be a good way of getting back in touch with her since you haven't talked to her since she blew up. And guess who else, yo' man...(R. Kelly?)...don't let me excite you, it's not R. Kelly, but it's Maxwell. In fact, he will be in town soon, and I already have an appointment for him to meet with you to discuss some business propositions. But, I'll discuss the details with you the next time we get together.'

    That was Edward Hasselhoft, but I call him Ed. He's my public relations coordinator/manager/friend/in-need-of-a-male perspective counselor/someone whose always there when I need someone to talk to. I could go on and on about him. And he hooks a nigga up wit tha business. Maybe because I pay him so well. But he does know his stuff and knows how to take care of business. And yeah, I take care of him, too.

"*Fourth voice message,*" the computer blared out: 'Baby, this is Rod. I know you are busy and all, but I just wanted to call and hear that sexy voice of yours. I miss you. I haven't seen you in a couple of days, and I won't even try to mess up yo' already scheduled time, so I'm going to plan a date. Meet me at Club Cierra on Friday. I know you'll be there because it involves people and guess who's going to be the guest local talent this week--Simone. She'll sing a couple of her eccentric soulful songs. I thought that maybe you would like to hear her a least one time, cause I'm telling you the girl is baddd. But, if you don't come to hear her--be there at least to see me. Bye, sexual chocolate.'

Damn, I think I just came in my pants. That was Rod. I met him about two months ago at a record store. As I was reading Wyclef Jean's newly released CD, there he was, staring directly into my eyes as I lifted my head.

I thought to myself, 'this could possibly be the one'. He's single, too, with no kids, tall, dark, and handsome, but most importantly--he's a well established entrepreneur, owning his own software corporation. Now, here's a man who has a stable career *and* fine, and still I can't seem to make time for him. What in the hell is wrong with me. But I always believe, if it's meant to be...it will be...no matter what you do.

"*Fifth voice message:*" 'Hey, girl. This is Sha-Sha. I know you the social queen an' all, so I was just callin' to tell ya that Malik Akbar will be in town tomorrow night at 6 o'clock at the Soul Coffee Cafe to do a bit of poetry recitin' and book signin'. Thought ya might wanna know 'cause I know you like to get yo' networking on, girl. I'll holla at ya.'

That was Sha-Sha, a soul, ghetto former student of mine who keeps me in touch with all of the social happenings in the city. She has high ambitions of being an international fashion designer. Look out, hoochie mamas, Sha-Sha will be coming your way-way.

I can't believe it, only five messages. I need to do a bit more networking...Ring!

And why in the hell is my phone ringing at eleven o'clock at night. Let me look at my caller ID cause I don't really feel like talking to anybody right now. Lord, I should have known. I immediately picked up the phone.

"Mama, do you know what time it is...I'm sorry, but you know I've been busy all day. I'll try and stop by tomorrow...I know, I know, I haven't seen you in two weeks...mama, that's not a long time...okay, it may be since we live in the same city, but you know my schedule...no, mama, I haven't been to visit Daddy either, not since the last time I saw you. Yes, his wife is doing fine, like you are so concerned. It's been twenty years and you are not completely over him yet. Where's your man? ...tell him I said hello. Do you need some money? ... I'm not trying to insult you. You took care of me when I was young, I'm just trying to return the favor ...Rod?...he's doing okay...we are just friends and nothing else...it takes time, mama...Mama, I gotta go, I'll see you real soon. I'm just tired right now....I love you, too."

I'm her only child, and I told her that she should have had some more after me. Now, she's rushing me to get married so she can play with her grandchildren. She was upset when Daddy got married about eight years ago. I have two step-brothers. My stepmother is pretty chill. She's nice to me whenever I go over to visit them. She is always making sure I'm satisfied, content and happy. But anyway...

Finally, I'm going to take me a hot, bubble bath. I'm beginning to smell myself now. But not quite bad enough to put myself to sleep. I imagine Rod undressing me. His fine ass is already undressed--Buck Naked! He is taking off my black, bell-bottomed, Afrocentricly-designed jumpsuit designed by none other than 'Styles from Afrikka'. As he unties the knot from around my neck, I put my arms around his muscular, six-pack physique and kiss his tender chest in a rhythmic motion. By then, he has my jumpsuit untied, and it drops slowly to the ground as if we were in slow motion. We are both standing there naked like an African King and Queen on a hot summer day. He puts his arms around my waist and I feel myself melting like ice on the equator and...his penis--rising on my stomach like an inflated balloon. He lays me down and starts licking between my legs. I imagine his tongue becomes an instant massage against my heated, wet vagina with movements like waves going up the Nile River. Then, he entered me like a rigid mountain rushing into an open sky and ...boy, was I on cloud nine. Suddenly...

What am I doing? He would not make love to me smelling like a construction worker. What was my ass thinking? I wouldn't make love to him if the roles were reversed, even if his dick was hanging to his knee. As a matter of fact, I'd probably run from that shit anyway. I haven't had a Dexter Saint Jock, yet. And I haven't attempted sex with Rod yet, but if his dick came to his knee, I'd take off running like Forest Gump--and he won't see me no mo. It's been about eight months since I last had sex and I ain't about to get sprung behind some dick. But, man, my body's calling.

CHAPTER 5
Entering the Backdo'
♋

Oh, my Lord, I'm going to be late. If it wasn't for that Weston "Worrisome" Smith holding me up at the Fashion Design Institute for some last minute meeting that he labeled mandatory on the memo--I could have been at the Soul Coffee Cafe by now. And, can you believe it, the meeting wasn't all that important. Here I am teaching only three hours a day, less than part-time now, and he wants to talk about policy, procedures, benefits, workers' compensation, budget, etc. Of course, I was not interested in all of that crap because any rule written can be changed at the drop of a hat, and plus, they gon' do what they want to any way.

Then I got home about five o'clock and guess what--my folks have called a thousand times. They probably called leaving messages asking why I haven't been by to see them. Really, it's not that I don't want to, I sincerely don't have time. But, Lord knows, I can make time. And my mom is probably the one who called over to Daddy's house trying to speak to him on the sly (like she always does) with a fake concern about my whereabouts. Then Daddy always calls me in a panic. Forget it, I'm not checking my voice mail till I come back from the Cafe.

Ring!!!!

Damn, should I answer that phone?

Riiing!!!!

I don't have time to run over and look at the ID box while I'm changing clothes.

Riiiiiiiing!!!!

Oh, I gotta answer it. Ed left a message at work that he would come by and pick me up to go to the Soul Coffee Cafe.

" ...Daddy...no, Daddy , I'm fine...Yeah...I'm sure mama did call you like she always does...I'm sorry, I've been really busy with my business and I haven't had the time....Daddy...of course you're still my favorite Father, partially because you're the only Father I have, unless you and mom ain't told me something I should know...You know I'm joking, and stop taking me so serious...How is Tijuana and little Dedrick and Colby?...good...I miss them too...and tell them I got a present for them that I bought yesterday at the Black Arts Festival ...well...I gotta finish getting dressed, Daddy...I'm running behind schedule...going to see Malik Akbar at the....yes, I'll make sure I get you an autograph. I know him personally...oh, my gosh, somebody's at my door...I gotta go Daddy...I'll see you ...tomorrow..yeah...tomorrow...'cause I don't have nothing planned Thursday night...not until Friday ...and do me a favor. Call mom and tell her I'll be over tomorrow, too...Daddy, I don't know who's house I'll stop by first...Bye, I gotta get the door..."

    I didn't mean to slam the phone down in his face, but he will talk you to death if you let him. He'll get over it after he see me tomorrow.

    "Ed, I should have known you would be ringing my doorbell, keeping me right on schedule, as usual."

    "Afrikka, get your purse and let's go, how are we going to look stepping in there late with front row seats that Malik himself sent to your box this morning," Ed calmly stated.

    "He did? Well, how was I suppose to know? You're the only one who checks my mail."

    "I sent you a message at work, and told you I would be coming by to pick you up, and that Malik sent up the best seats in the house."

    "Oh, I got the message, but I didn't read all of it. I'm sorry, it's just Weston called a mandatory meeting at the last moment and the message somehow slipped out of my hand."

    "If I didn't love you as much as I do I would say that you are trying to run a game on me. But since I know you...let's just get out of here."

    I grabbed my purse and as I was trying to touch my makeup up, Ed pulled me from in front of the mirror, and dragged me from out of my house locking the door behind me 'cause he knows I've left my door unlocked on a number of occasions. Boy, if everybody knew where I lived, "Styles from Afrikka" would have been out of business long time ago. Thank God for putting someone like Ed in my life.

As I am sitting in the passenger side of Ed's black Lexus Sports Coupe enjoying the sights and sounds of the city, I glance over at Ed and notice that he looks kind of cute in his Armani suit. He needs a girlfriend because he has pretty brown skin and he's fine. I would probably talk to him if he wasn't my PR man. And even though he has the bomb personality, I just don't think he is my type of guy.

See, I've been knowing Ed for about five years now, every since I met him at the National Black MBA Conference. He was filled with so much energy, and I was too, and that's when we decided to start our own business. He has a background in business management and relations, and my background is in fashion--and we've been inseparable every since. Both of us are extremely ambitious.

As we pulled up to get his car valeted, I see this young lady, maybe in her early to mid-twenties, standing outside of the side door looking in. She was sorta cute and I must say, her outfit is the bomb.

"Why is she standing in front of the side door?" I asked Ed.

"Maybe she looking for a friend."

"Let's go ask her."

"Okay with me."

"Hey, honey, is something wrong?"

She kind of twitched a little and jumped back.

"I'm sorry," I reassured her, "I didn't mean to scare you."

"You didn't," she responded, "it's just I got off work late. I'm a therapist intern and my last client didn't leave until five thirty, and I had to fight the traffic to get over here...you know how that is...and I got here too late, and they are not letting anyone else in...he's only my favorite author....I'm sorry...you may think I'm looking at you funny, but your face is so familiar."

"I'm Afrikka..."

"Oh, my Gosh!...from 'Styles from Afrikka'. I own a few pieces from your clothing line. You make some great stuff."

"Why, thank you. And this is Ed--PR Coordinator, or right-hand man, as I would call him."

"It's a pleasure meeting you...ah, ah...". Ed raised his hand to shake hers.

"Nicolette, I'm sorry," she shook his back, "most people call me Nic for short." Gazing at Ed interestingly with her big green eyes.

"Well, I like Nicolette," I told her. "I hate it when people try to shorten your name. It's like cutting off your total self, and besides, most successful people use their 'whole' name."

"I never thought about it that way," she whispered glancing into the air and blinking those long eyelashes showing her obviously professional charm skills.

"Anyways, what is that you're holding in your hand?"

"Oh, I write poetry...occasionally, and I thought that if I got to meet Malik Akbar that, perhaps, he would take a look at some of my work, and tell me if I got potential, or not."

"Well," I put my propositioning voice on, "if we let you go in and sit on the front row, with us, and get the opportunity to meet Malik, you have to, at least, read one of your poems to the audience."

Ed smiled at me. He knew I was up to something. And Nicolette's eyes got bigger than anyone that I have ever seen before.

"Okay," she almost passed out, "but just one poem."

"Just one poem," Ed added.

♋

Finally, we entered the cafe with no hassles. I was hoping no one would notice me, but as I walked passed them all toward the front, I was hearing voices saying 'that's Afrikka....she's here...hello, Afrikka'...and, of course, sistas can't let another sista go without having to put somebody down. I hear them blurting out 'why she late?'. Lord, if we could just stop playahating.

Malik just completed his first reciting, and of course, it was a moving piece. He smiled at me from the podium as he completed and I slyly walked up beside him. I whispered something in his ear. Nicolette and Ed looked at me like I was crazy. I walked silently back to my seat. Malik made a few comments about his newly released book then he stated:

"Now, I'd like to add a lil' somin' somin' to the program. We have a young poet in the house, who is a good friend of my dearest friend, Afrikka." Malik extended his hand and the spotlight came to me. I stood up as everybody applauded at my presence. "Let's show some love for our special guest, an up and coming poet." Nicolette looked at me like she didn't know what was going on, and Ed looked at me like he knew what was going on. Malik continued, "She will recite to you her latest piece which I know you will enjoy. Nicolette--do yo' thang, girl!"

Nicolette paused for a second, looked at me, then walked confidently toward Malik like a debutante. When he kissed her hand, I felt her melting on the inside.

"Hello, my name is Nic...I mean, Nicolette." she said proudly. "Today I will recite a piece entitled <u>lovin' black</u>." She began:

*I love black men,
the blacker the berry
the sweeter my cherry
Black cars,
that travel very far
and disguise me in the dark
Black clothes,
sophisticated and classy
...no man can walk pass me
Black hair,
whether kinky or smooth
short or long is cool
Black-a-moor,
there was no man before
black belt,
black mail,
black hole,
black head,
Why get blue balls? when you can have black balls?...Because...
Once you go black...there is no turning back...ain't that a fact?*

You should have seen the look on Malik's face. He was overwhelmed, and so was I. Sistas and brothas got up from out of their seats saying "you go girl...that was the click...it's the bomb...etc". Ed looked at me and smiled. I didn't know what to say. I mean, I didn't know tha sista had it in her. Her half white, prissy looking ass got reeeal black up there. She stood on stage with amazement as well.

Soon after, she finally got to meet Malik personally, and he ranted and raved about her all night telling the audience, "A sistah got much talent and look good, too. Ain't nothing wrong with that." I almost got a little jealous over all the attention she was getting. But for some reason, I was happy for her. After all, she has a lot of talent and I may need her to boost my sales. Listen to me, sounding greedy an all. Let me stop. She sounds like she would make a good friend. As closing time was ending, she ran over to me.

"Afrikka, I really appreciate this. Thanks for everything. Malik gave me his card, can you believe it?"

"Yes, I can, and you were great. Listen, here is my card, give me a call sometime. As a matter of fact, Friday night I got a table reserved at Club Cierra to see Simone live in concert. Would you like to come?"

"Oh, my gosh, Afrikka, I would love to...oh, can my girlfriend, Dana, come, too, you would love her? Plus, my boyfriend is having a birthday party there anyway."

"Of course," I smiled. "I'll see you all there. I'll put your name and Dana's on the guest list so you should have no problem getting in. Have a safe trip home and I'll see yo' wannabe-Nikki Gionanni self then."

We both laughed, then she blurted out, "Remember, I'm my own person--Nicolette, baby."

She slowly did a pivot turn and walked out the door.

♋

As Ed was driving me home, for some reason I was thinking about Nicolette. She's only a few years younger that me, and she has a lot of potential. I wonder why she's getting a career in psychology with all of that creative talent she got stocked up. But, that's not for me to worry about. Maybe she's happy doing what she is doing. Maybe....maybe God let us meet for a reason. Who knows? Ed kissed me on the cheek good night, like he always does. I told him that I had a great time with him, as usual, ran in my townhouse and into my bed. Damn, I forgot to make a journal entry. Oh, well. I'll make up for it tomorrow. I'm sure I'll have a lot to say after I visit my wonderful, loving parents.

CHAPTER 6
Master-Baiter
♋

"Hey Daddy. I really miss you. I'll be glad when you get back...so many exciting things are happening that I want to tell you about. Like tonight I met this cool fashion designer-- Afrikka, oh I didn't get her last name, I'm sorry. But, anyway, she introduced me to Malik--and daddy you know he's my favorite poet in the whole world. Well he is just the greatest-- next to you, that is...." The automated voice interrupted, "You have 30 seconds to complete this message." "And, well I'll tell you more when you get a chance to call back. And don't forget to leave the flight information when you call if I'm not in. Roselda sends her love and..." Your time is up. To send your message press one; to re-record press two.

    I hate machines, and I hate talking to him this way, but since he's been working on this murder case, the only time I get to see him is on the news. I don't know why they don't just put that man behind bars where he belongs. Any person who could lock his own mother and father in a cellar with no food or water and just walk away, needs to be put away for life. I don't care what they did to him. I'd give my left arm just to have my mother back, the nerve of some people. If she were here I'll bet she would be able to help me figure out these coo-coo men, since she obviously had great taste in men herself. I wonder if she would like Rodrick? Surely, she would. I mean he's a lot like daddy: a self-made man from humble beginnings who gives back to the community, handsome, romantic, intelligent, well-read and educated, strong, decisive...God! he really is a great catch. I'll bet *she* would be proud of my accomplishments...She might even help me to convince Daddy that I'm a good writer and that I deserve a chance. I know she would understand how hard it is to find a man that would live up to Daddy's standards for me. I can't believe he can be this way considering the hard time he had getting mother's hand in marriage. Why they practically eloped! God! I wish she were here. Why did you take her away from me God??!! I feel so alone, so inadequate, so incomplete! I could feel the tears streaming, I ran to the phone and dialed as quick as I could. It didn't hardly even ring and his voice came across--smooth and strong as ever: "Helllloo." I could hardly catch my breath from holding back the tears that were causing that tingling feeling in my nose like my sinuses were about to explode.

"Hi." I mustered.
"Nicolette. You Okay baby?" I already felt better.
"Yea, I just needed to hear your voice."
"Is everything alright?" Rodrick said in the most compassionate voice I'd ever heard.
"Uhh, sure...I was just havin' a moment."
"Is your dad still away?"
"Yes, he won't be back til' Saturday night."
"Would you like some company? Maybe a little hot tea and a massage will help--plus, you know I've got great listening ears."
"Well, I really don't feel like talking, but I don't think I could ever turn down a good massage."
"Hey, I'll be right over, and you have my car phone number so if you need me you can call me on my cellular until I get there, okay?"
"Rodrick, you are so considerate. Thank you so much."
"Hey, just treating you the way I hope you would treat me if I needed you for anything."
"If you ever need anything, just ask."
"I'll see you in a minute."
"Alright. Bye-bye."
I hadn't even bothered to look at the clock. It was almost 11:30. Rodrick is so sweet to even consider coming over at this time of night. I hope he never asks me to do the same--I may just have to renig on my promise to return the favor. I looked around and thanked God that Roselda had gotten a hold to this place today. She only cleans my place once a week. It used to be her living quarters until I got old enough to want it. I put up a really big fuss and my dad said no way was he going to put Rosie (that's what he calls her) out since she been living here since I was real small. But she overheard us and knew how much it would mean to me, and

she insisted that I needed my own place. She's always been like a mom to me, in fact, on Mother's day and Christmas and her birthday I always get her something that says "from your daughter". She doesn't have any children of her own, but she has lots of nieces and nephews, and she seems to get a real kick out of having her own sort of adopted daughter to tell her family members about. I've overheard her on the phone telling one of her siblings about me graduating or about my job, and she tries to speak too fast so that I won't be able to figure out what she is saying like when I was a kid. But now I can understand every word.

Buzzzz.

Gosh that was quick. I grabbed my purse and added some lip gloss for that Donna Summer kiss-me-boy pucker.

I looked over at the flickering scented candle and decided against the perfume in my makeup bag. I straightened my clothes and opened the...

"Roselda!?!" I said with great surprise.

"I'm sorry to startle you, mija."

In Spanish that means my daughter literally, but we might say sweetheart. I like it when she says that so gently like right now.

"I saw your light was on, and I wanted to give you dis note from your fahder. I wasn't sure if I would see you on tomorrow since I leave early for weekend."

"Oh, that's okay, Roselda. Thanks for the note." I said rushing her off.

"Good night. And have a good weekend."

"Y tu."

"Gracias."

I shut the door as she turned and walked down the stone pathway by the pool that led back into the house. I usually stood watch until I saw the light inside the kitchen go out, but tonight I was too preoccupied with thoughts of Rodrick rounding the corner to take care of me. I really am lucky..although I've really never been in love, except for with Israel and that was just puppy love, I've always been fortunate to pick the right kind of men that would never hurt me. I don't understand how some women can pick up slime at Tiffany's. It is as if they are looking to be used, but my motto is use or get used.

Eleven forty-five. Rodrick lives at least twenty minutes away..even as fast as he drives. When he drove us to the lake in my vette, I thought my hair was going to pull out of my head. He said that by the time he pulled over and let me put the top up that we would be there. Besides he said he likes my hair a little tousled.. 'messed up' he called it. He thinks it makes me look more exotic.

I may have just enough time for a quick shower. I pinned up my hair. Then, I slipped out of the matching silk shell and wrap skirt I'd picked up at the sale, and just as I was about to step into the shower I heard the buzzer. I grabbed my white linen robe and moved towards the door. I could see Rodrick's smooth skin reflecting the moonlight through the textured glass in the door. As I opened the door, he picked me up and gave me a giant kiss, his tongue extended deep into my mouth making little circles around mine while ever-so-delicately sucking it. I felt a wave..no, a flood of pleasure overtaking my body from my toes all the way to the little blond curls that danced around the edges of my hairline.

"Hi," he said in that mellow voice he'd used that night we'd made love so many times that I couldn't even move.

"Hi," I cooed, returning to the earth. I can just barely see the reflection of the full moon shining in the pool over his shoulder.

"May I come in?" Rodrick grinned.

"Absolutely not." I teased, forgetting that the world or my problems exist.

I stepped aside to let him through the door, and he disappeared for just a second. Then he returned and stepped through the door with a bottle of wine and a peculiar looking basket. He handed me the wine and said, "I thought this might help you to relax. It's one of my favorites--I hope you like it."

It was a Chardonnay--my favorite.

"This is my favorite! How did you know?" I said as I headed for the kitchen.

"Oh, it just reminded me of you: classy and smooth with a bit of a wild streak."

I returned from the kitchen with the two chilled glasses I always kept in the freezer, just in case. I stood over him and handed him the glass.

"Gosh Rodrick, if you know one more thing about me without me telling you, I'm gonna...."

Rodrick grabbed me, hugging me around my thighs and letting his head rest on my flat tummy. I could've sworn his chin brushed against my hot spot, but the way I'm feeling right now that could have been the wind. As I placed my wine on the table next to the sofa, I felt his hands loosening the belt on my robe. I hope he doesn't think I planned this. Oh, forget what he thinks, I want him NOW.

The robe lay crumpled on the floor as Rodrick admired my body. I gave a silent thank you to Russell, my trainer extraordinaire.

"I was just about to take a quick shower," I told him.

I didn't have to say another word. Rodrick swooped me up and into the steamy hot bathroom.

"I forgot to..."

"SSShhhhhh." Rodrick whispered firmly, letting me know that he was taking over.

I love a man who knows what to do. I get so tired of trying to educate these men. In two more seconds I knew for sure it was me who was in for a schooling.

♋

By the time I got to work, Dana was there. I tried to sneak in without being noticed, but just as I was passing Dana's office, she was coming out of it.

"Look at this! I can't believe Ms. Perfection is late," Dana smiled as if she knew something happened.

"Yea, yea, yea. Rub it in while you can cause you know you'll be late a hundred times before I will again."

"Okay, who was it?"

"Wha...What are you talking about?"

"The nigger..I mean man."

"You know I hate that word."

"Okay, whatever, quit stalling and give me the dirt. And don't be trying to skip stuff..I want every juicy detail."

"Okay, it was LaRon."

"Quit trippin'..you wouldn't know LaRon if he walked up here right now and bit you on your butt."

"Yea, but I'll bet I would bite his ass back...I don't play that Mike Tyson stuff."

"Girl, you crazy. Look, the longer you stall the longer it's going take us to get our work done and get the hell out of here today. And you know I ain't trying to stay late on no Thursday."

"Okay, I'll tell you, but you gotta promise not to say a word to a soul in this office. It's like the People's Court around here the way people get in your business."

"Do I ever say anything? Shit, it is my job to keep a lid on people's private lives, and Lord knows sometimes it's hard, reeeeal hard."

"Well, I'm not your client, and I'm not even a full-fledged employee yet so you know how it is, you just can't be too careful with your reputation."

"You been listening to your dad too much. Now gimme da juice."

"Rodrick came over last night."

"You mean 'last night Rodrick came'."

"Yea, that too. We took a hot shower together and he washed my *every*thing. He kept on teasing me by hugging me real tight and he even picked me up one time and I thought he was just gonna slip it right in, but he didn't. Then he washed my hair."

"Washed your hair!!"

"Yea, girl. Now *that* shit felt good. Then he dried me off and he wouldn't even let me lift a finger."

"Umph umph umph!"

"He carried me up to the bedroom, turned down the covers and placed me in the bed. Then he turned out the lights, and disappeared for a few minutes. I wanted to scream out 'come back here, I'm not finished with you yet', but I realized that I wasn't in control. In a few minutes he returned with the basket he'd brought with him and pulled out a bottle. He turned me over on my stomach and poured something that felt so warm and so good that I felt myself purring like a fat Persian cat with a new ball of yarn."

"Girl, I know you were hot."

"I'm just glad my bed's not flammable. He massaged me all over on both sides twice. First, with something that smelled like rubbing alcohol spiked with perfume, and then with some kind of oil. I felt so relaxed that I couldn't move. Then, he got into bed and kissed me goodnight."

"That's it??"

"Yes, I wanted to revolt, but I just couldn't move. Man, I was so relaxed, I've never felt so limp and carefree."

"That's all good, but you mean to tell me that he did all that and didn't get none."

"Well, not exactly. When I woke up this morning I went down on him and we made love three times. Then he went home and I came to work. Now are you satisfied.?"

"I know you are, but what am I?"

"Ha ha ha. Well we'd better get to work....Oh yeah! I almost forgot to tell you who I met last night!"

"Who?"

"Afrikka...you know from Styles..."

"from Afrikka!"

"Yes, the one and only. Not only did I meet her, she invited me to sit with her and this guy who works for her--Ed, he's really cute and he looks awfully familiar. I would have said something, but I didn't want him to think I was just trying to mack on him. I'm sure he gets plenty of that."

"That's great, Nic!"

"But that's not all..let me finish!...They invited us to come sit with them for this singer Simone's show on Friday night at Club Cierra."

"I thought you were going there for some birthday party."

"*WE.. are* going for the party, but this is even better because we won't have to pay *and* we get to sit in the front with Afrikka. And you know all the athletes and people with big money will be down front with us. Girl, this is just what I needed."

"Yea...well I don't have a thing I can wear."

"Don't you start with that again. I'll help you put together a little som'in-som'in. Remember, it's not always whatcha got, but how you put it together."

"Dana, is Nicolette down there with you?" Vicky interrupted.

"She's right here." Dana said enthusiastically in a professional tone.

"You have a call, dear, on line two. It's your dad."

"Thanks. I'll take it at my desk."

She was gone before I could get the words out of my mouth good.

"Man, that girl must have a little hidden video camera under that desk somewhere..she knows everything that goes on around here..don't even try to hide anything from her. See ya later Dana. And...uh..."

I put my index finger to my mouth signaling to Dana to keep quiet as if someone were listening to our every word.

"This is Nicolette. How may I help you?" I said mustering up my VIP voice.

"Hello, Nicci..." Daddy said in that syrupy way that let me know I wasn't about to like what he was going to say. He always used that voice when I was little to make me feel better when he wasn't there for a recital or something. He really tried to give me the best of both worlds: all the material things I could ever hope for and that happy family life. It was just hard on him without my mom.

"Hi Dad." I said hum-drumly acknowledging his nonverbal language.

"How is the job?"

"Fine Daddy," he was stalling.

"Did you get my note?"

"What note?"

"Oh, Roselda was supposed to give you a note from me. I guess she hadn't gotten around to it just yet. The note was just to let you know that I won't be coming like I thought I would for Sunday."

"What!!?? Why not??!!" I heard myself sounding like a mother hen.

"Well, Nicolette, I told you I would try, but it just didn't work out honey. This case is just draining every little bit of my energy. I'm just not up to traveling there for just one day. I'm sorry, but maybe we can celebrate Father's Day when I get back. I've got to get back now--we are on a fifteen minute break."

I listened half-heartedly since I know this speech all too well. I tried to be sympathetic since he does work so hard for us to be able have the things we want. "Okay, Daddy, I love you."

"I love you too, sweetheart. Keep up the hard work..it always pays off. Bye now."

"Bye-Bye."

I almost wish there was a woman in his life. At least then I'd have a *right* to be jealous.

CHAPTER 7
It's On When the Club Close
♋

Here we are. Finally making it to the club. And it took Ed and I twenty minutes just to get from the door to our table. It's too many people in here. I haven't been to Club Cierra since it first opened, which was only four months ago, but, man, it's triple the number of people in here than it was on opening night. I have on my long black dress that I made especially to fit these hips of mine. And I made it to where my busts look kinda of big 'cause I don't have no titties to fill up nobody's dress in a store. If I didn't make my own clothes and had no choice but to buy them in a store, I would be assed-out 'cause it seems like they all made for white folks.

"Why are there so many people in here tonight?" I leaned over to ask Ed because if I didn't, trust me, he would not hear me.

"Afrikka...because Simone is singing tonight."

"What's that got to do with anything?"

"It's obvious that you haven't heard her sing, yet. She sings in most of the clubs in town."

"Oh, so you a club-hopper now?"

"No, Afrikka. I like the way she sings and I'm sure you too will after tonight."

"Well, maybe I can meet her and, perhaps, see if I can hook you two up with a date."

Ed didn't respond. He just laughed. Is he serious? I hope not. I can never play match-maker with him. He's too good of a friend and I wouldn't know how to act he if got hurt by the person I hooked him up with and came crying on my shoulder. Besides, it'll probably mess up our friendship anyway.

"Speaking of a date...where is Rod? I can't wait to finally meet this guy you've been dying for me to meet."

"Who knows. I thought we would have noticed each other by now."

I started looking around, checking out the scene, looking for prospects with potential then Ed starts tapping on my shoulder.

"Afrikka, I see Nicolette heading our way."

"Oh, yeah," I told him still peeping around, noticing some cuties here and there.

"I guess she got her girlfriend...and I guess that's her man on her arm."

By the time Ed got those words out of his mouth, I heard Nicolette's voice just over my shoulder.

"Afrikka, this is my friend, Dana and my boyfriend, Rodrick."

I can't believe what the hell I'm seeing. This mothafucka standing here like I don't notice his mothafuckin' ass. He got her calling him Rodrick and me calling him Rod. He not even acknowledging my presence. He know who I am. Hell, I just saw him less than a week ago and he got the nerve to call me the other night leaving all of that soft, mushy shit on my voice mail telling me to meet his ass here tonight because he misses me. Yeah, he misses me all right--and Nicolette's bright ass, too.

Look at his no good self. Then he finally smiles at me. What the hell you smiling at me for. Oh, naw 'cuz. I can't even front him and I won't any way 'cause he is not my man. You know what--he must be fuckin' Nicolette because men, see, they will try to hold on to tha pussy once they get it or until they get sick of it, or till they get some other fresh coochie. That's why he ain't speaking to me. And he know that I'm not the type to clown. I can't believe I got myself all wet the other night fantasizing about him making love to me after that message he left. But, I'm going to play his game and be a lady about it, too. But, I've got to have a plan.

"It's a pleasure meeting you," I shook Dana's hand, then gently grabbed Rod's hand and softly squeezed it, too, "And this is my friend, Ed."

Dana sat down beside me, then Nicolette, then Rod. I think he intentionally got close to the end just in case something popped off.

"Afrikka," Ed leaned over as they were getting situated, "Tell me that he is not your Rod. "

"Yes..he...is--was...my Rod," I whispered back to him smiling at the same time." But I'm not going to trip. Let's enjoy ourselves. You know that I don't have any luck with men...so let's just pretend that he is just somebody we...I just met who is also--unimportant."

Ed just smiled back and he kissed me on the cheek. He's never done that before unless he's dropping me off from somewhere, but never in public. For some reason at this moment it made me feel, uh...'wanted'. I can't believe what I'm saying about Ed's behavior. As a matter of fact, it sent chills up and down my back because I haven't been touched or held in months.

"Nic told me so much about you," Dana said to me interrupting my train of thought, "I feel like I know you already."

"Well, thank you," I smiled. "Now you've got to tell me about Nicolette so I'll know what I'm getting my hands into."

Everyone laughed except for Rod. He just smirked like he was too nervous to laugh with the rest of us. And he has a reason to be nervous too because any minute now he may think I might explode.

"So, Nicolette--how long have you been dating....um, I'm sorry, what's your name again?" I looked at Rod playing dumb. He had a look on his face like he just shitted in his pants.

"Rodrick," he coughed like he had a frog stuck in his throat, "but my friends call me Rod."

Yeah. I'm sure they do. So there's my answer. I call him Rod, therefore I am just his friend. And he emphasized that part like he was giving me a hint or something. Don't worry Rod, I won't blow your cover.

"Oh, we've been dating a couple of months now," Nicolette grabbed his arm.

"Sounds like you guys may be getting serious," I inquired.

At that moment, Ed hit me from under the table. He knows me real well and he knew where I was going. But I guess I won't go there.

"Oh, no," I cut Nicolette off. "You don't have to answer that. I'm just being nosey."

Nicolette looked at me like she didn't want to answer that anyway. I could tell by her body language. She put on that prissy, 'none-of-yo business' look with those slanted green eyes that soon became crossed with my question as her eyebrows raised. And Rod looked at me like I was psycho.

"Naw," Dana whispered in my ear. "Nic,... only likes tha Dic."

I put that 'okay...really' look on my face. Thanks Dana. I like you already. You told me just what I wanted to hear. And she validated what I said before--he is hittin' it. Well, I don't believe in that three strikes and you're out stuff. As far as Rod is concerned, he made it to bat, but he will never get a hit from me. He's out already. History.

"Hey, I see a homey of mine," he looked at Nicolette as he was getting up.

"I'll be back in a second."

Rod took off like he was Speedy Gonzales not even giving Nicolette time to respond. She didn't even look like she was worried anyway. He walked over to some fine, dark brown brotha with a sweet suit on. Rod pointed to our table, and everyone, except Ed who was staring at the drink menu, looked in his direction.

"Oh, my God," Dana screamed in our ears. "He knows LaRon, Nic, he's talking to LaRon, Nic."

"Dang," I looked strangely at her. "What has he done to you?"

"Nothing...," she said hyperventilating, "it's what I want him to do to me."

"Afrikka," Nicolette calmly stared into my eyes while grabbing Dana's hand to calm her down. "See, Dana has had a crush on that guy since high school. His name is LaRon. It's been over a year now and just because she is overweight, she thinks that he won't feel the same way about her. All Dana needs is a little confidence to go with her personality. I tell her that all of the time. She can take him to the moon if she had a boost of self-esteem to go with her pretty face."

Nicolette was talking about Dana as if she wasn't at the table. This must happen often because Dana didn't respond to her comments. I mean, it is true that Dana is overweight but she has a gorgeous face. She does seem a little shy but I wouldn't say that she lacks confidence. But then again, I don't know her. However, Nicolette appears to be accurate in regard to her personality because so far I'm picking up good vibes from her.

As both Rod and LaRon look toward our table, suddenly, LaRon had this look on his face like he didn't want to be bothered. Rod was hitting him like he was saying 'come on, man, just for a minute'.

"He doesn't want to come," Dana exhaled like she was picking signs of that up, too.

"Oh, yeah," Nicolette smiled as she pointed. "Is that why they are both heading toward our way."

"Oh, my God," Dana panicked. "How do I look?"

"You look fine," I reassured her.

"Is my make-up okay?" she asked Nicolette.

"It's okay," Nicolette blew her off.

Man, the way Nicolette blurted that out, Dana has a reason to be insecure. She doesn't even seem concerned that Dana's concerned about her looks. She could at least tell her she looks cute too.

"And I meant to tell you that color looks good on you," I smiled toward Dana to perhaps decrease her anxiety level. Nicolette just looked away.

"Hey," Rod stepped up and LaRon kind of looked around." LaRon tells me that he knows you, Dana, already, and I already told him about Nic, so I guess he doesn't need an introduction. We're old college roommates. Isn't it a small world?"

"It sure is," I replied staring directly into Rod's eyes. He immediately looked away." LaRon, I'm Afrikka this is my friend, Ed. "

"Nice meeting you," Ed finally said something. "Won't you join us. Simone should be coming on any minute now."

"Sure," LaRon said slowly but like he really didn't want to be bothered.

He came around, pulled up a chair and sat between Dana and me. He didn't say a word to Dana other than 'hey'. After that he stared straight ahead and Dana stared straight at him. Suddenly, the music stopped.

"I guess your girl's about to come on," I whispered toward Ed's way.

He just smiled back at me. Sure enough DJ Daryl introduced Simone. She walked on stage like a goddess in her cherry red, long skimpy gown. I must admit, she is bad. She appears to have that Dorothy Dandridge attitude of when she played in 'Carmen Jones'--flirty, confident, go-getter or better, come-and-get-me-now look.

LaRon finally started talking to Dana after Simone sang her first song. And at first it appeared that he really didn't want to talk to her, but by the middle of the performance he was all in her mouth. I guess he is starting to see what is really beneath Dana's skin. And Nicolette, on the sly, scoping the club out for I guess mo' potentials and Rod had to balance his eyes between me and Nicolette. He couldn't decide who he should look at. When I wasn't looking at him, I felt him looking at me and when I caught him he shifted his eyes onto Nicolette and, of course, she didn't catch what was going on. Ed, well, he had his eyes closed moving his head to that sulky, soft, sensual voice of Simone as she was releasing from her inner self. I must admit, her music is moving me. It's obvious that she is feeling every word she is saying. Looking at her from the outside, one would say that she looks like a whore, acts like a bitch and dresses like a slut. I may have judged her too quickly. People tend to do that and I fall in those traps sometimes without knowing. But Simone...is singing from her heart, a spirit that I can not describe and if I did you may not understand.

As she concluded her last song I watched her as she glided off of the stage. The audience stood and applauded but I...sat in my seat with an amazed, overwhelmed look on my face. At that moment, I felt a connection between her and I, in an almost spiritual sense.

"Are you okay?" Ed looked down at me with concern.

"Ah...ah...yeah," I stumbled my words out of my mouth. I rose from the table and joined the crowd with applause. " Excuse me," I looked at everyone as I walked off. "I'm going to the ladies room," I told Ed.

On my way there, for some reason I felt tense and uptight, like I've been shot or punched. It's a feeling I've never experienced before. Why am I feeling this way now? As I focused on my thoughts, I felt someone staring at me from around the corner of the stage. It was Simone.

"Are you okay?" she asked me. But not like she was concerned but rather in a 'what the hell are you doing' way. Did I look that obvious that I wasn't acting quite normal at this point in time? Are these feelings real or just a figment of my imagination?

"Oh,...why yes," I finally answered back. "That's very sweet of you to inquire about my health."

"Believe me," she popped off. "I wasn't inquiring about your health. I just didn't want you passing out in front of my dressing room before I was able to go inside."

At that moment, everything I felt before became somehow diminished. Is it a calling for me that led me right in front of her dressing room without even knowing that it was here? Somehow, I became myself again. "I'm sorry," I smiled. "I was really wanting to say that your music is very different. I mean, you sing with so much soul, and passion, and..."

"Thanks," she cut me off while putting her hand on the door knob.

For some reason, something told me to stop her from opening the door. So, guess what I did--I grabbed her arm.

"I'm Afrikka..."

"I know who the hell you are--that uppedy so-called designer, and if you don't get your hands off me I'll own your label," she warned me.

"Look, Simone," I stood up to her. "I'm giving you my card and I want you to call me when you want me to design a look for you that no one else will ever share with you in common."

"Look, Af-Ri-Kka," she turned around and faced me. "Can't you see that I've got my own look?" And she pointed from her head to toe. "And I needs no help, especially from you. We're in two different worlds."

"Yeah," I laughed at her. "But I think we share the same world beneath all of this madness."

For a moment, I think she actually thought about what I said. I expected her to respond. Consequently, she snatched the card out of my hand, which at first I thought was a good sign until she tore it up piece by piece in front of my face and dropped those pieces and my ego to the ground with it. But me, I kept my composure.

"You did a great job tonight," I smiled, turned around and walked off. I looked back and I knew she would be still looking at me. And she was, then she slowly turned around and went inside of her room.

As I was turning back around, I bumped into my husband. At least, he's what I want, physically, in a husband-- tall, brown-skinned and fine.

"Excuse, me," I softly said looking into those hazel eyes.

"No, excuse me," he leaned over...and he has an islander accent, Jamaican perhaps. "I did that on purpose. I've been checking you out every since you stepped in this club. Pardon me, my name is Jamal."

He didn't have to say anything else. It was like love at first sight. We found a secluded place in the club where we could sit and talk. I found myself disclosing more information about myself than I have with anyone else. And it's not like we was on a date or something. I just met him. And he, too, disclosed information to me about his family (he was born and raised on the Virgin Islands and only been in the States two years), what he does (he just completed his medical residency and will start practicing soon), and his hobbies, places he would like to travel, and his view about relationships. We both discussed our views about meeting people in the club and we both felt that somehow, between the two of us, that this time, our vibes were real and not just gamey. By the time I looked at my watch, an hour and a half had passed. I forgot about my friends. I've never felt so connected with anyone else the way I do with Jamal at this moment.

"So, this is where you sneeked off too," Ed crept around the corner.

"Oh, Ed," I jumped. "I'm so sorry. I just got carried away with Jamal....Jamal this is my friend, and business partner, Ed," I introduced them both.

Jamal just stuck out his hand and Ed shook it back.

"Where is everyone?" I asked Ed.

"Oh, they all left. Don't worry, they didn't mind because they both left with their dates--Nic with Rod and Dana with LaRon."

"They didn't seem mad at me did they?"

"No, Afrikka. Don't worry about it. I'm sure Nicolette will understand, but I really think they didn't care. They seemed too preoccupied."

"Well, how 'bout you. Did you find a honey...or two?"

"I won't find my soul mate in here..that's for sure," Ed said looking around, while Jamal and I just stared at each other and smiled.

"Well, Jamal," I held his hand. "We've got to go. I want to get out before everybody starts crowding out of here. Call me in the morning. Maybe we can do lunch."

"Maybe..." he added. "...we could do lunch and dinner." He gazed into my eyes, and if I would have stared into his any longer I would have been hypnotized. "It's a pleasure meeting you, Ed. "

"Same to you," Ed told him back.

On the way home, I thought so much about Jamal. Man, he's fine, educated, comes from a stable, close-knit family--and he's single. Lord, is this a sign? Please let me know. And if he's not the one, let me know soon, 'cause I don't have the time to waste on another so-called romantic episode.

I just prayed on it, and now I'm going to sleep on it.

CHAPTER 8
A Fire in the Hole
♋

Saturday already, this week has gone by so fast. Well, God must still love me even after me dissing him this week with my selfish attitude. Sometimes I can't believe he takes me back after all the stuff I say and do, but the bible does say 'he throws our sins into the sea of forgetfulness' when we ask him to. Not only did God forgive me, He answered my prayers even though I didn't even consciously pray that LaRon would be there. We had such a great time talking once he loosened up. It was just like old times--when we were together and kickin' it. He used to tell me how fine I was when I lost the weight and it made me feel so good. Whenever we went out people were always staring at us and noticing how gorgeous he is, and I loved all that attention. And even though we have always been just friends, there is this special kind of passion between us that I've never had with any other man. I used to think that that feeling must be love, but I know if it were love we would be together even though I gained all the weight back. But God, when I'm with him I feel like there is a point to all this madness. Maybe there is still a chance for us to be together, I just need to get myself together. I promise I'm going to get into more ministries at church, but it is so hard because they're so demanding or at least I feel that way. Like the women's ministry, they act like you don't have no life out side of them. We have a meeting this morning at eleven. We are planning a trip to the women's shelter and I'm heading up the committee. I didn't even sign-up. Sister Jean said she just knew I would be the perfect one to get everyone mobilized. I'll bet if she could see my lazy ass sittin' up here now, she wouldn't say that. I can't even get myself moving. Lately I've felt like a big wad of ... oh I don't know, mud or something useless. I need to get back into the Word, that's the only thing that ever gets me out of these slumps. ......A slump--that's what it is a slump. I just can't let it overtake me. I'm gonna start on my diet and start exercising everyday on Monday, or maybe I should start on Tuesday or Wednesday since I'll have all this bad food in the house after tomorrow. I'm going to stop cursing and starting reading the Bible everyday, starting tomorrow.

June 15 @ 9: 52 am

I thought Sister Jean would never stop praying. I'll bet even God got sick of us praying today. I hurried to the grocery store and hurried through the isles picking out everything on the menu, plus a few nick-nacks for the kids. The lines were all the way back into the food isles--I should've known better than to go to the only store in the hood on a day like today. Suddenly I begin to feel eyes on me and I look out the corner of my eye and notice an older gentleman supposedly reading the magazines. His eyes are on my feet, which I always get compliments on, and he works his way up to my eyes after slowly roaming over my thighs, hips, and breast. I just look away since I ain't interested in the father-type even if he is kinda good-lookin'. But he's still staring I can feel it.

"How are you doing today?"

I looked around to see if someone else was standing there. By the time I turned back around, he was right in my face. I know I must have looked like I was about to go off because he backed up a step and said, "You know those are some *bad* shoes and you have the perfect feet for them. I love a woman with great taste."

He grinned to show his perfectly aligned teeth, and I was half-heartedly smiling when I saw his big gold chain with a gun on it that looked big enough to shoot with. Now it's bad enough these young negroes wear all this gold and gangsta paraphernalia, but his old ass ought to know better. How he gon' step his old, decrepit ass to me? He probably got a wife at home anyway. That just goes to show a nigger ain't shit.

"Thanks." I said sharply enough to signify the end of the conversation.

I added a head-whip-around on him, and pushed my cart up so that I was out of his range since his lane was proceeding much slower than mine, thank God.

I finally got to the front of the line and when the salesclerk said hello, I couldn't even speak I was so mad. Why do I have to catch all the rejects and married men? It ain't fair. I've got to lose this weight, my ass is just too fat to meet the kind of men I like, and I'm gonna get braids and grow my hair out too, like Nicolette's. I've got to do something, cause even if I never get married, I would like to go out on a decent date once in a while.

The stock boy was waiting for me to lead him to my car when I heard someone calling me.

"Dana...Dana? Is that you?"

Oh no! Darlene, the rub-it-in queen.

"Hey Darlie," I responded, which is what we called her in school. We had gone through elementary, high school and college together and I still couldn't stand her. It's not that she's not nice, it's just that she has this way of bragging about how 'incredibly wonderful' her life is and always has been, that will drive you absolutely batty (boy, I'm beginning to sound like my mother).

"Girl, I love those shoes--you always had great taste in shoes. Have you met my husband, Don?"

Sure, where is the midget? Just then I noticed him standing slightly behind her with his little ass--who needs a man who can't pick you up.

"Yes, I met him at the homecoming game last year," I told her.

"Oh, that's right. Well, this is our little boy, Justin, and our little girl Earth."

Now what kinda name is that for a little girl.

"Well, I guess that makes you Mother Earth." I giggled. She didn't.

"You know we've started having class meetings for the reunion."

"Yea, Markita called to see if I wanted to be on the committee and I went to a couple of meetings, but I've been so busy lately that I haven't had a chance to go again."

"Oh, well, we're supposed to be getting people's addresses when we see them, so we don't have to hunt down as many people. You should try to come to the meetings, so far Keydra Gamble, Toni Robertson, who looks incredibly wonderful, Simon Peldry..." LaRon flashed into my mind as she talked on and on about the reunion plans in between bragging about her vacation in Spain and her new Lexus recreational vehicle.

She must have noticed my absenteeism because she started to move towards the door, but did not stop talking for one minute. I followed suit pushing my own basket by now, since my po'bag boy just gave up on her, while remembering how LaRon had brushed me off last night after Rodrick used him to devert me while he buttered up Nic. I don't know what it is, but there is something about this guy, Rod, that ain't right. He's just a bit too smooth or something. As soon as LaRon was away from me, some hoochie-mama in a ho-tight dress jumped on his ass like he was white on rice. And you know you ghetto when you clip your pager on your spagetti strap. And he so silly, he don't even know all they want is his money and sex. Or maybe he does know, but he's just happy to be getting attention from a woman since his mother treated him like crap when he was growing up....

My thought was interrupted by Darlene's hen-pecked husband's weak hand shake. "It was nice to have seen you again."

We were at the sidewalk and nearly in the street now. I saw my car, and I said good-bye and made a dash for it. Good exercise I thought. Darlene yelled across the parking lot, "Call me sometime," and that's when I noticed that dirty ol' man looking at me again.

"Okay!" I yelled back, knowing good and well that I wasn't.

I got to the car and put the groceries in as quickly as I could hoping ol'boy would not come this way. But, I already know my luck ain't that good. As I try to squeeze into the small space left between me and the car next to me, he walks up smiling again, and hands me a card. I looked at it because I don't know what else to do. It says his name and his business is....

"Fire extinguishers...I help people to protect themselves and their assets by placing fire extinguishers in their homes. Are you looking to earn some extra income?"

Oh hell, it's bad enough I can't get a man, but not the multi-level people. They worse than the Jehovah's Witnesses, and I guess I must look like a sucka cause I been approached by everybody from Amway to Nutricize-Your-Life.

"Uh.. no, thanks... I'm not interested."

"Well just in case you change your mind, take a couple of these," he stuffed several cards into my hand, "and pass them on to friends."

"Okay. Have a nice day." I added to *end* the conversation.

"You, too, and if you ever want to use that number for personal reasons, feel free to," he threw in and watched me while I squeezed into my car in the little space I had to do it. I hate people who do that shit! One of these days I'm gonna key up somebody's ride where I bet they won't do that to nobody else. And why is this nigger still watching me, ain't he got some fire to put out or something. He wouldn't be smiling so hard if I ran over his ass.

♋

As soon as I got home I called Nic and told her about that fool at the grocery store: "Girl, you wouldn't have believed his wrinkled-up ass."

"I'm just surprised he didn't have any gold teeth, or did he?"

"They was probably in the back of his mouth."

Nicolette agreed. Then I asked her when she was going to pick up her dad.

"Oh, he's not coming." I could hear her voice sullen.

"He's not! What happened?"

"Well, he really wanted to, but just couldn't get away from his case."

"That's too bad, I know you must be disappointed."

"Not really, this happens all the time."

"Well, you know I'm cooking dinner for my family after church and you're welcome to join us."

"Thanks, but I doubt it. Rodrick and I are going out again tonight. So I'll probably just rest up tomorrow."

"You'll probably need to with all the steam that's going on between you two."

"Yea, well I'm about to go work out."

"On a Saturday afternoon?"

"Dana you ought to know that fat does not discriminate. You gotta work out all the time if you want to stay fit."

"You're right..I just mean you are so committed."

"I've got to be--no offense, but I can't stand fat. I freak out when I gain one pound. Maybe I'm anorexic."

"Girl, that's not a joke. That is a very horrible way to live."

"Yea, well I gotta go before I'm late cause my trainer makes me run extra laps."
"Okay. Bye."
"Bye."
Dana hung up so quick I barely got a chance to say bye. I'd better get going. I popped on my sunshades and whizzed over to the country club's new athletic center. I signed in and jumped on the stairmaster to get warmed up. I spotted Russell helping someone finishing up their routine on the leg extender machine. I got tired just watching the lady attempt to squeeze those last few reps out; I can't wait til I'm finished. Just then, some skinny white girl came and got on the stairmaster next to mine with her towel and headset. She looked awfully muscular to be so skinny. I'll bet she doesn't have one ounce of fat on her. Then, my competitive drive kicked in, and I forgot that I was only supposed to be warming up. She was zoomin' on the stairmaster and jammin' at the same time. She was also doing some kind of arm movement like she was using the fly machine at the same time. I pumped up my stepper to a higher speed, I'm not about to let this lil' skinny white woman beat me.

♋

"Man, am I pooped!" I said out loud as if somebody cared. I looked at the clock and it was a little after midnight. This is the first time I'm cooking dinner for the whole family all by myself without mama's nosey input. I spent the whole day shopping for the perfect meal. I want everything to be just right. That's why I've tasted everything at least twenty times and now I'm swole from eating all this stuff. I probably won't even be hungry on tomorrow.

Just one more hour before the roast is done. I flipped on the t.v. to make the time go faster. You know ain't nothing on at night, but infomercials, psychic hotlines, and.... hummm, "now that shit looks good." Some guy was fuckin' this lady doggy style, while her big titties swung voraciously back and forth. She was oooh-ing and aaah-ing and telling him to do it harder. He grabbed her tits and pumped her harder. I closed my eyes and pretended it was me making the noises that filled the room. "Oh yes!" she screamed out. I opened my eyes to see he had picked her up and was giving it to her while standing up with her legs wrapped tightly around his waist. Oooo, that looks sooo good. As if on automatic pilot, I laid over on the couch and began to stroke myself to the rhythm of his bucks. "God..yes!" she called out. Scripture flowed into my mind. Your body is your temple... "Fuck me like that!" He'd laid her on the couch now continuing to thrust in and out of her without missing a stroke. Her hips were matching his thrusts such that he was putting at least nine inches all the way inside of her. As her back began to arch, my back remembered the familiar arch too. "Ummm," I purred nearing ecstasy. "Are you coming?" he said. I rolled onto my stomach. "Oh! Oh!" she cried out, "Don't stop!" Oh no please don't stop. It feels so good. "Are you coming, baby?" he asked again. She grabbed his butt and helped him to pump us into orgasm. "YEESSSSS! Oh Yes! Yes! Oooohh! It feels sooo good!" she screamed as I writhed on the couch squeezing every bit of the tension out of my body as I shuddered.

Then I lay there limp. I cut the t.v. off, I'd seen enough. I must've dozed off because I was dreaming I was at work and a fire broke out and Mr. Wrong was extinguishing it. When I woke up and heard the buzzer on the oven, I jumped up and ran into the kitchen. Too late. The roast looked like a

pork chop, it had been cooking so long. I'll just have to get another one and do it in the morning, which means I have to get up early in the morning.
Damn.

♋

*Today was a nightmare. I woke up late. I didn't go to church so I could have time to re-cook the roast. Everybody got here early or rather on time while I was expecting them to be on C.P. time. There weren't enough seats and the food wasn't ready when I thought it would be. Mama brought enough food to have just made the darn dinner herself. And everybody ate up her stuff first. Nic came by right when my daddy was having a burping contest with one of my brothers. I can't believe they can be so nasty, and what's worse is I used to actually think that it was cute when I was a kid. My nieces and nephews got into my perfumes and wasted over half of my Pleasures. I ran out of drinks and had to go out to the store. My hair was a mess, and I was all swollen and miserable from eating all night and all day. And the worst thing of all was that my sister is going to make my parents grandparents again, and everybody kept asking me when am I going to get married and have some babies and then my cousin dropped the bomb with "I thought she **was** pregnant."*

I ran to the bathroom and was about to start sobbing hysterically when I looked at myself in the mirror and I just felt sick. I begin to throw up right there in the sink. It was just awful, but relieving. The peculiar thing is that I felt much better after I puked and I went back out to face the family, but it was too late to save the party; everybody was packing up and leaving.

June 16 @ 10:13pm

CHAPTER 9
In and Out
♋

Dear Diary,

Today is Father's Day, and it was, I must say, an enjoyable day. Before I went to Dad's house I stopped by to see Mom for a few minutes. Man, Mama was down and out because she broke up with her man. In a way, I don't feel sorry for her because she finally figured out how sorry his lazy ass is without me even telling her. I'm glad that she is starting to think for herself because she used to ask me for advice. And when my advice didn't work out she would blame me for the outcomes. So, I eventually stopped giving her advice, even when she continued to ask. Instead, I gave her my support and reassured her that everything will work out in the end. And, of course, it did. After our pep talk, Mama was confident that she made the right decision to end her relationship with Chris and now, she can finally exhale. At Dad's house, I was so happy I got the chance to play with Dedrick and Colby. Those two are growing up so fast and I'll be glad when they do, so people will no longer be thinking that my little brothers are my children just because they are twenty five years younger than me. Hell, I'm twenty-nine years old and I sure am old enough to have kids that age or older. It's sick to think that my Dad was still able to produce an embryo at 45 and now that he's 49, he wants another child. But my stepmom, she ain't having it. My Dad really enjoyed the CD walkman I bought him because he goes jogging two miles every morning and he would rather listen to pop, rhythm and blues, and even rap - instead of the screaming, squeaky sounds nature makes which bugs him to death. He almost cut my throat when he came to my house and I was playing my nature tapes while cleaning my house. I was shocked at myself that I stayed at their house nearly eight hours. After I left, on the way home I thought about Jamal. He is so beautiful--not in a physical sense but in an emotional, mental, and spiritual way. And, it never fails. It's happening to me again. I always meet the right man and...

Damn, who is that ringing my doorbell this time of night. It's almost nine o'clock. I can't even sit down and write in my diary peacefully without somebody ringing the doorbell or my phone. I'm going to pretend that I'm not home.

Ding!!!Dong!!!

Damn, it must be important because ain't no lights on in my house except for the lamp on my nightstand and I know whomever is at the door can not see that light all the way back here.

Ding!!!!!Dong!!!!

"I'm coming, I'm coming!" I yelled putting on my nightgown 'cause I normally sleep in my underwear--if even that. I looked through the peep hole.

"Dalton," I cracked the door open with the security chain still on the door." What do you want?"

"Did you get my message?" Dalton looked worried.

"Oh, yeah. How much money you need?"

"About a hundred bucks."

I slammed the door in his face. But not to be rude. Just to unlock the chain and let him in. He probably took it the wrong way.

"Damn, I thought you was trying to diss yo little brother."

"Now why would I do that," sarcasticly saying as I pointed him into my house. "Have a seat."

"Now, who is this girl you taking out tonight because she must be special that you are going to feed her a hundred dollars worth of meal?"

Dalton slowly walked to my sofa and sat down. He looked like he was up to something and was, somehow, afraid to tell me.

"Dalton," I tried to look into his eyes as I sat beside him and he, shyly, trying hard to avoid my eye contact. "Now we've been friends for too long now. You're like family. What is it?"

"Okay," he finally gave in, "You know that girl, Jennifer, I've been dating these past six months."

"Yeah, keep going."

"Well, you know we haven't had sex yet..."

"What? The man who has to have sex within the first two weeks or 'it's over' hasn't had sex with this girl in six months. Are you okay?"

"Afrikka...Jennifer is special to me. I mean, it's totally different this time. We have this connection like I've never experienced with no other woman in my life. She's become my counselor, my mentor, my partner, my confidant--my best friend. And you, of all people, should know."

"Well, to tell you the truth, you have been spending a lot of time with her but I just assumed that sex was keeping you around."

"No. Getting to know the 'real' Jennifer--not looking at her as just another sex toy--has kept me around. She always offered me a challenge and whenever I thought I was going to get it, she pulled away. But, it wasn't like she was teasing me. It was like she was saying 'good things come to those who wait'. Do you know what I mean?"

No, I don't know what you mean. I haven't dated anyone for over six months in what - five years. And that was with my ex-boyfriend of two years who turned out to be a DOGG. I found out he was fucking my close friend whom I've known all of my life, went to school with, and who I even considered being partners with. Boy, that would have been a big mistake.

So, actually I could not relate to what he was saying. I haven't began to have a relationship like what Dalton is going through since I broke up with that fool. And when I have met men who I thought could be Mr. Right, it has always been at the wrong time. Either they were married, already had a girlfriend, or they lived outside of the state, and, of course, distant relationships never work out with me. But I'll admit I'm beginning to think about Jamal.

"Afrikka, are you okay?"

"Yes," playing it off. "I'm just tired."

I thought about what he was saying and at the same time thinking about Jamal hoping that there was some chance I could have the same relationship with him. But, I'll be just pulling teeth.

"I'll go get the money," I was telling Dalton as I stood up. "Now, what is the money for?" I had forgotten to ask him. He smiled.

"I want to take Jennifer to the new, grand hotel they just built downtown."

"Man, the starting room prices are about a five hundred a night. Where's a hundred dollars going to take you?"

"Oh, the room is already paid for and the money will be just in case she wants to take a carriage around town. I left my wallet at work late Friday and by the time I noticed it yesterday the banks were already closed. Luckily, I had charged the room a few days ago on my credit card. I'll give it back to you tomorrow on my way home from work."

I went and got the money for Dalton and as I was heading back into the living room somebody was ringing my doorbell. Damn, obviously somebody must think I don't sleep at night.

"What's been up, Dalton." It was Ed and it was evident that Dalton opened the door.

"Nothing much, Ed," they both gave each other that nigga hug and hand shake black men always do.

"Ed, what are you doing here?" I stood there as I walked toward Dalton and gave him the money. "See you later, Dalton, have fun and I'm sure you'll tell me about it all tomorrow."

"Oh," Ed added. "You got a late night date."

Dalton just looked in the air like the word 'date' put him in a daze or something, turned around without saying a word and walked off toward his car.

"What's wrong with him," Ed looked at me strangely.

"*He's* in love," I said with a sigh.

"Is that a problem? " Ed questioned me as if he knew something was going on.

"Yeah, when the Mr. Right comes along and his timing is Mr. Wrong."

I walked and sat on my sofa like a spoiled little brat. Ed closed the door and sat in the chair in front of me and just stared at me without saying a word. He was just waiting for the right time. There was a moment of silence and then I think he felt it was long enough.

"What happened between you and Jamal?"

"How is it that every time something is wrong with me, you always know exactly what it is? Do you have my house bugged?"

"No, ...but it's so easy to figure you out. You informally dissed Rod last Friday night. So one problem has ceased. That same night you met another man--Jamal. When I spoke with you last night from my father's house you told me that he is...and I quote you, 'the right man for you'. You guys went out to lunch and also dinner yesterday like he promised. So what other man could you say who is Mr. Right at this moment. Unless, of course, you met someone this morning on the way to your father's house. And knowing you, you're a very attractive and sociable young woman, so anything can happen."

I sat there looking at Ed as if he was a reader and I was his book.

"Yes, it's Jamal."

"He's married?"

"No."

"He has a girlfriend ."

"No."

"He gay and wants you to make him some women's clothes to bring out his other side."

I just had to crack up and laugh because when Ed knows that I am down and out he wants to all of a sudden become Chris Tucker. As I was laughing at his remark, somehow I started feeling...sad and lonely and all of a sudden, I started crying uncontrollably. Ed noticed my change in emotion and ran over to my rescue. He put his arm around me and the more I tried to control and hold my tears back, the more out of control I got. I cried for at least two or three minutes, then I started to wind down. Ed just looked at me in a concerned way as I finally got those emotions I had built up all day out. I laid back on the sofa placing my feet across Ed's lap as he started massaging my feet. I thought I was in heaven then.

"Jamal called me this morning before I left to go to my father's house. I thought he was calling to tell me good-bye because he was going back to Virgin Islands to visit his father for a few days for Father's Day. He told me that I was everything that he desired in a woman. I won't bore you with the details. Then he dropped the bomb on me. His mother called him early this morning to tell him to pack all of his things up to come home for good because his father is suffering from a terminal disease. And since Jamal is the oldest child and the only son he feels obligated to take care of his family financially and emotionally. He wanted us to still keep in touch. But why start a relationship with no beginning - no history. It's too stressful. And with my schedule, I don't have time to just take off and go to Virgin Islands whenever I want. We talked about it and we both concluded that ending what we haven't started is for the best...."

"I'm sorry to hear that."

"Oh, don't be sorry. You know me, I'll get over it. I'm so used to meeting Mr. Rights and something always happens."

"Afrikka, how can you be so sure that the Mr. Rights you meet are Mr. Right when you haven't had a chance to get to know them, but for what--two, maybe three weeks at the most."

"But haven't you ever met someone and at the moment you knew that there was this indescribable connection between the both of you and for some reason, deep down, you knew that she was the one. Like it was love at first sight."

"As a matter of fact, yes I have."

"Well, what happened?"

"All of them turned out to be Misses Wrong."

"Why? What happened?"

"Well, looking at a woman when I first meet her--whom I think is Ms. Right from the outside--that attraction that I thought was, how should I describe it, emotional maybe mental,...ended up being physical and sexual. And most relationships, if you ever felt that way from the jump, never work out, see. Because that same, strong emotion that you feel when you first meet someone is all physical. And you have to ask yourself--now, is this emotion that I'm feeling at this very moment based on what I want in a partner or is it based on what I need in a partner. Because you can want a tall, dark, fine, got-it-going on brotha but is he what you need? And even if he appears to be what you want in a man--is he fulfilling your needs? Because, if he's not doing it within the first few days, trust me, your needs won't get done."

I sat there for a moment digesting what he just said. He was right, in some ways, because I have felt that same, strong emotion thinking they were Mr. Right with Terry, Myron, Carnelius, and then Rod--and of course, they all came out to be Mr. Wrongs. I had to be patient with Terry because he was still caught up with a divorce settlement with his live-in girlfriend and they were both fighting over who was going to get custody over their two kids; Myron was confused about his sexuality; Carnelius was married and was trying to convince me he wasn't. I could go on and on about his trick ass; and then there's Rod with his girlfriend and my new-found friend, Nicolette.

"You know Ed. I'm almost thirty. I'm an intelligent, beautiful, successful, strong, African Queen, but I just don't understand why I can't find a man. I mean, I can see if I was a Bitch--but I'm not, or a whore--but I'm not, or even a dike--as much as I like dick but rarely get it...I'm not. So what's my problem. I can see if I was on the manhunt for a man, searching here and there but they find me. My clock is ticking and I want to settle down, get married and have children. That's always been my dream--outside of the fashion industry. I'll be thirty next year, Ed, thirty. You know what that means? I've achieved all of my goals in life except in my personal, intimate life, and that is to get married before thirty and I can not see that happening by my next birthday. I will never find Mr. Right."

"You know what I think. I think you found your Mr. Right. And soon enough, you'll open your eyes and find that he has been there all along but you've just been too blind to see."

I sat there for a moment and thought about what he said. Maybe he is right. There are so many men in my life whom I consider as friends that I've known for years. Who can it possibly be?

"Well, it's getting late and I better go because we've got that big presentation to make in the morning," Ed announced.

"With who?" I sat up.

"That's the reason I dropped by. On my way home I saw your light on and I wanted to share with you this good news in person instead of over the phone," he said as he was walking toward the door.

"Well, what is it?"

"Brad, one of the buyers representing Mims, left a message on my voice mail inquiring about having a line of "Styles from Afrikka" in his department store. We talked over the phone and he and some of his colleagues want to meet with you and I to discuss a proposal at 10:00 tomorrow morning. Is that a problem?"

"Oh, nooooo. I don't have any problems anymore. Thanks to you. Come over early in the morning so that you can help me organize and put together my presentation."

"Don't I always help," he said kissing me on the cheek and walking out of the door. I walked into my room then I picked up my dairy and proceeded...

...it is always at the wrong time in " their " lives. Like Ed said, I may be looking for someone who is already here. Lord, please give me patience. I'm going to turn it over to you to send me the man I need and not the man I always desired to have. Well, I've got to go now. I've got to get my rest because

I've got a BIG day tomorrow. Who knows what's in store for me.

Afrikka,
On an eye-opening late, late Father's Day night

CHAPTER 10
Silent Cream
♋

Lord, Father God in Heaven, it's me again, Simone. Please forgive me for not coming to you sooner, Lord, but E.J. needed some stuff and I had to...well I needed the money. Anyway, I'm sorry for sinning again, Lord, and I hope you can find a way to forgive me. It's just that Earl ain't coming through as often as he used to and lil' Earl and me got needs that ain't being met. Lord, please try to understand, better yet, get me out of this mess. Help me to find a real man so lil' Earl and I don't have to put up with Earl's bullshit!--Oh God! I didn't mean to say that. Oh Lord! I'm just a mess and there's probably not much you can do with me, but he's just a baby. I just want him to grow up and not have to have the kinda life that I have, Lord. Somehow, I know you listening to me, Father God, and I know...I know you gon' bring us out. Amen.

    I got up off of my knees and stumbled to the chair. I was exhausted from fighting with Earl all night after he showed up for Father's Day all to' down at one o'clock in the morning. "I guess you think I should be grateful for these ragedy-assed flowers you probably stole." I replayed the scene from the night before in my head while I stared across the room at Earl's shifting body. I can't believe I once loved this man, the sight of him now disgusts me. He reminds me so much of my momma I just want to crack his head open. "No, please don't hit my momma!" E.J. screamed from his room when he saw us tussling last night. I swore I'd never let this happen to a child of mine and now here it is, like a nightmare, happening to us. When he wakes his ass up he getting out for good--this nigger will never set foot in this house again. I've worked too hard to get where I am and let some nigger come fuck it up. Hell No! I was really getting infuriated so I got up and went to the bathroom for a shower. I can see the sun barely peeking over the horizon out the window. It's going to be a beautiful day--as soon as he gets out, that is. The water is just right and I'm thinking over my day like I usually do before lil Earl wakes up and starts asking me a zillion questions. Just as I'm stepping out of the shower I hear a noise that let's me know my little storm is up. As I'm reaching for the towel the door swings open wide and fast near knocking a hole in the cheap ass wall. I check out the wall and stare at Earl big ass standing there buck naked, dick all hard. I know he don't think.. Just then Earl grabbed my ass so quick I didn't have time to cuss him out. He looked so possessed when he picked me up and put me on the counter. I started to scream and then I didn't want to scare little Earl again.

"Earl, don't do this shit. You need to get your ass out of here before I call the police. You stank." I fought and squirmed, but it was too late, Earl's penis easily entered my wet, rigid body.

I can't believe this is happening. As much as I love sex, this just ain't right. I feel so nasty.

♋

I finally got lil' Earl to settle down at the day care, and I jumped into my car and cruised to work as quickly as I could. Monday is usually full of new accounts which means I'll have a ton of paperwork. Brad was already in a meeting when I got there and had two more scheduled before ten o'clock this morning. That is one hard working man. If he wasn't married....

By the time I get settled at my desk he comes over and slaps me on the butt, flashing his Colgate smile. He really is fine for a white boy.

"Allright, Brad, you're going to start up those rumors again." I said trying to forget the last 24 hours.

"Well, Simone, as long as they're true. How about lunch today?"

"Uh, I've got some errands to run, sweetie. But here comes someone who'd love to give you a whirl anytime?"

It was the head buyer, Elyse: she's responsible for a large part of the inventory in our stores, plus the modules, artpieces, furniture, etc.

"Hi dear," she says to me since Brad had quickly jumped on the phone to avoid her.

They used to have a little somin-somin going on, until Brad kicked her to the curb. She still want him though, and showed me a note she wrote to him in a meeting one day offering to give him head at lunchtime. I tripped out.

Brad actually has a cute-ass wife. She's a swimwear model--5'11, long dark hair, olive complexion, exotic looking and built like a pencil with titties (I think that's why Brad quickly got hooked on the bootie--he LOVES some ass and he can truly hit it!) He took her right off the runway, and she still does a few things, but mostly spends her time volunteering with kids. She loves E.J.

Brad interrupted my thoughts, "Simone, I'm going to be running like a chicken with my head cut off today. I need you to sit in on this new line we're viewing at ten, if this meeting I'm heading to goes overtime. Okay?"

"Sure, Brad. I'm sure I'll pass for you okay."

"Nah, one look at this ass..."

"Damn, you horny today. Has Lizzie put you on the couch again?"

"Naw, can't a man just admire a woman." he said, sounding almost black.

"Not your ass. The last time you came to work like this, we ended up on the conference room table."

"Oh yeah!" he said obviously enjoying the memory.

"You better get moving before you miss both appointments while you stand here having a wet daydream."

"Okay. Don't forget the meeting for me."

"I ain't!"

I hated to see him whisk off to his appointment. He truly is one of my best friends. And I only have three people in this whole world that I consider my true friend. I have told him things about me that no one else knows. And he tells me everything. We make a hellified team and people around here can't stand it. He accepts me as myself, and we watch each other's back in this dog-eat-dog fashion world.

Our relationship has always been very candid. Before I even worked for him there was something in him that made me feel comfortable. When I was just a floor clerk, and he was an assistant like I am now, he was the only one of them who even spoke to me. The rest just stripped my cheap ho-tight clothes off and enjoyed the best goods they had ever had, and then pretended they didn't know my ghetto ass when they saw me on the floor. But, Brad was fun and gentle and treated me like a lady. That was before he got married and I would let him have it all the time. He brought me up, not just in the company, but helped me to know things like when to keep my big mouth shut, how to look professional and sexy at the same time, who to fuck and who not to fuck, and he's even helped me with my singing career. I love our relationship and although I love him very much I never want it to change from being just how it is right now. Commitment ruins shit.

♋

When I looked up it was almost 10. I had cleared the paperwork from Brad's morning client already, and I grabbed a pad and pencil to take notes on and headed to the conference room for the presentation. When we have a potential new account coming on board, at least two buyers and the head buyer had to participate and decide on the line. Brad had arranged this meeting himself, so I don't know what kind of line it is. And, I'm not about to ask Elyse, who is looking me up and down the way she does when Brad is not around. I think she's a dyke because I always get that vibe from her like I get from a man who is mentally doggie-stylin' me. I love that shit when it's a man, but it feels strange coming from a woman. Oh well, as long as she look and don't touch, we allright.

"Brad is going to be a little late, so I'm going to sit in and take notes for him." I told her.

"Yes, I caught him in the hallway before his appointment."

Caught is probably exactly what she did. She's like a damn tarantula with huge fake ass tits. And she so bad-built, like my girl Bette Midler, with a wide-ass torso on little, stubby legs. But at least Bette can sing, this woman knows her business, but can't get a date unless she black mails somebody.

While I'm waiting for the meeting to start I got up and got me a cup of water to help me stay alert in the meeting. On my way to get the water, I look down and see a huge red welt on my arm, and suddenly get nauseated from the thought of the smell of Earl funky ass all over me this morning. He make me sick. I'm putting his ass out of my place when I get home. I think sometimes I avoid going home because I never know when he's going to be there. I hate him. I hate him.. I hate him.. He makes me feel so nasty...so angry..... so scared.

When I get back, Elyse is helping some fine brother set up in the conference room. Hmmm...I wonder if this is a black line or if he just working with some white ass designer biting off of Afro-centric stuff like the rest.

Damn, now this brother got the Bulge if I ever seen it. He notices me staring and cracks a smile resembling Denzel. Elyse has obviously wasted no time in getting acquainted, cause now she pushing her big ass up on him asking if there is any other way she could be of assistance. Even though I could not hear what he was saying to her, I knew somehow that he wasn't the sellout type. He keeps working and I keep watching, but he is obviously zoned into his work.

The layout is tight, and I'm glad because I get so sick of sistahs and bros coming in here unprepared and unprofessional--misrepresenting my peeps. He has visuals, swatches, a video and a presentation outline that is the bomb. I must find out who does their graphic work for my demo.

I would go over and introduce myself, but I'm just not in the mood to be charming an' shit. He'll just have to wait to get that pleasure after the presentation. Knowing these fashion designers, the brother probably is gay. At least nine inches of love just wastin' away night after night in some tight asshole--humph, what a shame. Besides Brad says to be careful about getting too chummy-chummy with potential clients.

Everyone's here now and the presentation looks set, so what is Mr. Fine waiting on. If he need a little inspiration that can be arranged...

Ding! The elevator doors outside the conference room door pull open revealing the baddest cape I have ever seen. It's that sheer organza in red and beneath it you can see through the pantsuit in a red African print with bronze highlights and accessories to match. The sister strolls into the conference turning and flipping and demonstrating polished runway skills. Behind her is another woman wearing a bright green, double-knit, bell-bottom jumper with an attached hat. The two huge, oval cutouts in the back reveal most of her back, and there are oval cutouts in the bells to match--now this is me. I can hear rain and birds coming from somewhere. It is as if they are in the room, and I realize that the most wonderful nature sounds are playing in the background, when another beautiful model, this time white, parades in a floor-length, black velvet, one shoulder evening gown with a split in the back that revealed a delicate silver print resembling the robe of an African King. Her outfit is complimented with bold silver accessories including a huge silver cuff necklace, a matching bracelet, and barely-there silver hose under black dinner-style mules that create the perfect contrast to her sun-darkened, white skin. This is the bomb, I thought to myself, and looked around the room to see that I wasn't alone.

Then, Mr. Fine enunciated, "The RED. The BLACK. The GREEN. The African Queen."

The ladies continue to encircle the entire room looking like a flag waving in the wind.

"The mother of the earth. The mother of fashion. Introducing Styles... from Afrikka," he continued with the kind of confidence that really turns me on in a man.

Then, in walks...well I'll be damned, if it ain't Queen Neferteti herself. Shit! just my luck today. It was the bitch from the club Friday night. I turned my head partially hoping she wouldn't see me, and partially because her presentation is overtaking me already. She whirls around knowing that her shit is explosive.

"Thank you ladies," she says as the models twirled and left the room.

The music now changes to a jazzy instrumental. She really think she got it going on, I pouted. About that time Brad came in and sat down next to me, closing the door back after him. I started to get up and leave, but he motioned for me to stay. I stayed as long as I could, and when it was all over I had this terrible feeling in my stomach. Afrikka caught my eye as I excused myself and left the room. I couldn't get to the bathroom soon enough. Damn maintenance, this tissue could cut glass. I didn't really understand what I was feeling, I just knew I had to get out of there. I sat down on the couch to just take a moment, and as I looked across in the mirror at myself, I saw Africa. No, not Ms. Thing, but the Motherland, Africa. I saw myself naked running across the desert with a cloud of dust behind, and then, dancing....I could feel a rhythm in me that was crying to get out. I started to humm a tune that was coming out of my soul. I closed my eyes and the tune took on words:

Soul free
Soul free
My humble journey
To a place I've never been
Yet know so well.

So free
So free
My heart can be
With the rhythm
That is inside myself.

I'm free
You're free
Our souls
Have been united
All along.

I sensed someone's presence and opened my eyes allowing the rest of the tears that were stuck there to roll down my face. It was Afrikka. And this time, I saw her differently than I had before. When I looked into her eyes, I saw something that felt so familiar, so real, and I wanted to be there, too.

"Hi," she said.

She must know she's gotten the best of me.

"I don't make any decisions around here," I said, feeling vulnerable, "so if you lookin' for a hook-up..."

"No, thanks sistah, but I would suggest you wet that tissue if you don't want them to scratch up your face."

I looked up at the mirror. I looked terrible. My makeup was to' up, and my eyes were puffy and swollen enough to start office gossip. I'm definitely not going back to my desk til' I get myself together. I want her to leave me alone, yet something about her presence is so soothing.

She is fixing her makeup now.

"You're presentation was pretty good," I said trying not to sound too excited about it.

"I'm really glad you liked it," she said applying powder to her nose and snapping the compact closed.

Then, she leaned in to get closer to the mirror. She picked at her eyelashes, arranging each one neatly. "I'd love for you to make some suggestions, since you obviously know your stuff. Your buyer was just bragging on you out there. He says he couldn't make it without you. In fact, he said 'she basically runs the shows, I just stand back and watch her work.'"

I looked at her and kinda paused wanting to believe her. And when her honest eyes looked at me in the mirror, I felt almost stupid for not believing.

"I laughed to myself, and thought 'now you know he coulda left that *basically* out.'"

I had to laugh, too, cause she knows she is right.

"Yea, well I really love my job, and I've been blessed with a great boss."

"That's good to hear...there's enough of us sistahs complaining about our lives, it sure is good to hear someone say nice things." She was quiet for a few minutes and then she asked me, "What about your singing? You know you can blow!"

Why is she giving me all these compliments, when I was just sending her mental daggers during her presentation.

"I been singing since I could talk; singing in the church, at school, at the boys club, at weddings, anniversaries, parties, just everywhere. You know, it's just the only way I know how to truly express myself."

"I know what you mean."

It was quiet again, but with Afrikka in the room the quiet was more noisy than talking, if that makes any sense.

"Well, I'd better get back out there. Ed's probably finished wrapping up the business end of things. I hate dealing with the figures, and he's just great at talking to people and negotiating and all. We work well together, like you and Brad, and I must admit that he too does most of the work, which is great, because it frees me to be the moody, creative person I am."

"I think moodiness and creativity go hand in hand." I added.

She nodded in agreement. I wondered if she and Ed had *exactly* the kind of relationship that Brad and I have. She must have heard me thinking because she said,

"Oh by the way, don't tell Ed I told you this, but he is really a big, big fan of yours. In fact, he talked me into coming out to see you the other night. He has been trailing you all over town and he loves your show."

"I *am* flattered," I said, coming to myself. "Well, please do not hesitate to introduce us. You know I'm doing a little private party on Saturday...you know, professional athletes and their cutesy wives. Uh.. you could probably pick up a few clients. I could leave your names on my special guest list.. if you'd like to come."

"We'd love to. That's sounds great," she said on her way to the door.

I hopped off the sofa, suddenly feeling alive again. And headed back towards my desk for a quick touch up. I know she'll get the account, and maybe I'll get me a little somin' too.

CHAPTER 11
Four-Playing
♋

Dear Diary,

It's been two months since the four of us last went out together as a group. Everyone has really been caught up in their own lives. Dana has lost a tremendous amount of weight. About 25 pounds, at least. She has been exercising every morning and night and when she gets a chance, she will *leave work during lunch to go to the weightroom. I've even noticed that she is starting to forget mandatory meetings at work because I would call her house and she is always in a rush to get to work--late--or to a meeting that she has forgotten. Even Nicolette hardly even sees her anymore. Not even at work because Nicolette says that she is always in her office with the door shut and when she does have her door open, Dana pretends that she is too busy to talk to Nicolette-- not even for five minutes. In the meantime, Nicolette has been spending so much time with Rodrick. He has even given her the key to his apartment and she goes and comes as she pleases. Because her dad is on a new case, she hardly ever sees him anymore either. It must be hard on her and that's why she has been depending on Rodrick for her emotional, and sexual, support. Simone is the only one of us I see and talk to on a regular basis. I have been working with her on her confidence and her emotional security. And sure enough, Earl is recognizing a change for the better in her and his behavior is still changing for the worst. While she is out in the studios making demo tracks for this record deal she is trying to pursue, Earl stays up all day and night waiting for her to come home. Sometimes she would leave him in the middle of a fight and I would let her and E.J. stay at my house for a few days until he calms down. I'm glad he does not know where I live because I'm sure he would be beating my door down any minute now. And when I call her I make sure I press *67 so my number would not show up on their caller id. My life is still the same. Busy as ever...new accounts, new projects, special appearances, all with the help of Ed and his determination and hard work. One day, I will make it up to him with something very special. I haven't met anyone romantically, yet. But the postcards I get from Jamal makes* *me feel special. I've decided that I'm not going to date anyone for a while. I'm just going to let whatever happens happens.*

*Afrikka,
On a lonely, quiet Friday night*

Ring!!!
Who could be calling me? I forgot to cut off my ringers 'cause I just wanted to take a hot, bubble bath and watch a good movie on cable.
Riingg!!!
Let me look at my caller id. Oh, well, well, guess who...
"What's up, girl?...Nicolette...why are you crying? ...Okay...calm down and tell me everything..."
She went on and on, in between breaths to tell me how she left work early and wanted to surprise Rodrick by going to his house early to prepare an early dinner. Since she had the key, she could go in his apartment and fix it up cutsie before he got home. But she got the surprise instead. She caught Rod fucking her co-worker on the oriental rug she bought him last month for his birthday. (That sorry son of a bitch. I should have told her about that two timing bastard early but I didn't want to spoil the high hopes she had for him. Plus, she was falling in love with him and he had her just where he wanted her. He knew what he was doing. And I was beginning to believe that he was becoming legit.) She also told me that when she opened the door, they were right there in front of the door and he just looked up and kept on fucking her while saying 'Okay, Nic, you caught me, now let me buss this nut then we can talk out moving our relationship forward'. And she said that Raquel--that's her co-worker--she looked at

her and kept smiling and fucking too. (And she used to be in Nicolette's face everyday at work. That's why Rod used to take her to lunch every other day, cause on the opposite days, he would pick up Raquel and take her ho' ass to lunch. Man, men ain't shit.) Nicolette told me that she just turned around and left. Man, it took a real woman to do that. (If that was Simone catching her man, knowing the kind of person she is, she would have beat the shit out of both of them like they stole somethin'. Let me take that back--if Simone caught Earl fucking, she would have beat the bitch for not letting her catch them together earlier so that she really could have a reason to leave him.)

"Girl, everything will be okay,...yes..it's good that you found out now before you got too deeply involved with him...sure...I was just about to say that.....and I will call Dana and Simone to tell them to meet you at your house...I will be there as soon as I can with some food...oh...I forgot I'm the only vegetarian out of the bunch and, yes, I will make sure meat is included in our menu, darling. Now, give me the directions to your house.... "

After Nicolette gave me the directions to her house, I called Simone and you know she was game since she had taken a couple nights off from her normal gig at the club. She had no problem getting her sister, Candy, to babysit E.J. for the night. And, of course, she had no problem leaving Earl and not telling him where she was going. Dana, on the other hand, took some work. I had to convince her that Nicolette was truly emotionally upset and hurt and that this time, it wasn't one of those two minute phases that she used to have. Therefore, Dana assured me that she will be right over as soon as she completes her thirty minute work-out. I immediately threw my shoes on, ordered some Chinese food for pick up down the street and was out the door.

♋

By the time I got to Nicolette's house, Simone was just pulling up in the drive way. This is my first time coming to Nicolette's house and I think the first for Simone, too. For some reason or another, it seems Nicolette always avoided us coming to her house. Dana is the only person that visits her on occasion. All of us would usually meet at Dana's or my place, or somewhere else. Of course, we couldn't go to Simone's place because of Earl's clowning all of the time.

"Take a look at this crib," Simone looked around. "How come we never visited her place?"

"Who knows," I wondered.

As we were looking around her...palace...as I should call it...heading toward her front door...I think it was the front door, even though there were many doors, we heard some footsteps coming around the corner.

"Hi, guys," Nicolette whispered, "Come around this way."

"Trick Nic," Simone blurted out, "How come you never invited us to your mansion? I know you wasn't ashamed of this."

"No. I just didn't think it was all that important. Besides, you guys live closer to the happening spots, so what's the sense of coming way out here in the boon-docks?"

No. Nicolette didn't want us to think that she was bougie. She was just trying to be down so that we would like her for who she is, not what she has. She is not going to fool me.

"Nicolette, we was going to like your Princess of Bel Aire skinny ass anyway," I told her.

"Yeah, but I like you even more now," Simone added and I think she meant that to. "Can you show us around?"
"Of course," Nicolette smiled.
We started off in what Nicolette calls the Master House that consisted of six bedrooms, five full baths, one bath (which was in her father's room) that was probably the size of a third of my apartment alone, an indoor pool that extended outside, a gameroom, a racquetball room, a basketball court, an exercise room equipped with a sauna, a whirlpool, and a jacuzzi, a huge kitchen with an island (my favorite), two dining rooms, one living room, and a study.
The guest house, which is bigger than my apartment, was located to the right of the house. It has everything necessary for anyone to live in, and in fact, Nicolette does. It extends off from the walkway of the pool. It was two stories alone with her bedroom and study on the second floor and on the first floor consisted of a den, a living/dining room, a huge kitchen and two full baths, (one on each floor), and a guest bedroom downstairs.
"Nic, with all of this I don't think I would need a man. And you never have to go to your father's side--'cause you have everything that you need right in this quarter," Simone said barely getting those words out of her mouth.
As they walked and sat in the den I went into the kitchen and put the food on the counter. I think I would need someone, even if it's not a man, to share all of this wealth. I mean, no wonder Nicolette is so lonely. She lives so far out in the suburbs in no man's land, no black people around that I have seen, her father is hardly ever at home--no wonder she is so hungry for affection, attention. That sorta explains why she is promiscuous and moves in and out of relationships--always searching for that perfect mate. But who is she really searching for?

"You know, it was like I was having a nightmare or a bad side effect or something," Nicolette added.

"Oh, no, you weren't having no side effect because if you did you would have side-kicked his ass," Simone laughed.

"That's not funny," I looked at Simone grabbing a pillow to sit on the floor with, " she is going through a crisis."

"I can handle myself, Afrikka. Plus, I'm glad I found out. I'm sure that there is a perfect man out there waiting to sweep me off of my feet....Deep down I somehow knew Rodrick wasn't my soul mate anyway...but it didn't have to end so tragically."

"No tragically is if you would have chopped his dick off like Lorena Bobbit and make a hot dog out of his punk ass."

We all laughed.

"Simone, ...I'm glad it wasn't you who caught him 'cause you crazy. Poor Earl would have been up shit creek by now losing his penis like that," Nicolette said still laughing.

"Oh, no he wouldn't have," Simone got serious. "He would have been in the county hospital because as tiny as his dick is I would have amputated his leg trying to find and cut off that little shit. I must have been on drugs when I met that muthafucka. That's why I fuck every big dick muthafucka I meet 'cause I gets no satisfaction at home."

"You crazy, girl," I told Simone.

"No, not crazy--just psychotic," Nicolette commented about Simone's remark using her counseling skills.

"Speaking of psychotic, I think Dana has gone belitzed. I saw her running around the track last night before my first show and after my last show, which was around one o'clock in the morning, she was still out there."

"So that's why she was late this morning," Nicolette thought about it.

"Guys, I'm not trying to be funny but Dana acts like she may be on drugs or something," Simone looked at us with concern.

"No. I've known and worked with Dana for too long not to have picked up on something like that. Believe me, I had a lot of friends in high school and college who were addicts, and I know the signs--that's sorta why I went into counseling. Dana's behavior doesn't have anything to do with drugs...I don't think..."

Ding-Dong!!!

"We talked her up," I told them.

Ding-Dong!!!

Nicolette ran to the door to let Dana in. She was smaller than last time and her skin seems a little paler like she's anemic or something.

"Simone," I whispered in her ear, "Let's not front Dana, okay? I'm sure that whatever she's going through that she may talk to us about it tonight."

Simone just shook her head.

"Dana, you look good," I told her.

"What kind of diet are you on," Nicolette added.

"Girl...," Simone burst out. I'm afraid of what she is about to say, "before long you gon' be catching more men than me."

"Oh, I doubt that, Simone,"Dana said in a monotone voice. She grabbed a pillow and sat down with the rest of us.. "You not singing tonight."

"No, I'm giving myself a break the next few weeks. I've been in the studio trying to make demos to get a record contract."

"Oh, how come I didn't know about this?"

"Probably because your fat ass is never around anymore," Nicolette said in a very, negative way. Everyone got quiet and we all looked at Nicolette then at Dana waiting on her to respond.

"Well...ah.." I tried to think of something to say, "Are you guys hungry yet 'cause I brought Chinese."

Everyone looked at me.

"Not yet."

"I just ate."

"I don't eat after 6:00."

"Okay," I tried to change the subject again, "Let's play an old childhood game that will bring back memories of us being kids all over again. Like, ah...um..."

"Spin the bottle," Simone yelled out.

"The only reason you want to play that game is to get drunk," Nicolette added.

"Yeah...you think you slick," I told her.

"Nic, give that girl some of that Absolute you got stored up in your closet since 1985," Dana smiled.

I was surprised Dana said something after what just happened a few minutes ago. For a second there, I thought Dana was about to go off on her. One day, Nicolette's going to push her too far. Nicolette came back with a gallon of vodka that hadn't been opened.

"I was saving this for the good 'ol times," she sat down and Dana came back with three glasses.

"Okay, who's not drinking," Simone wondered, " 'cause you only have three glasses in your hand."

"I'm not," Dana told us. We were all looking at her waiting for some type of reason because Dana didn't usually have a problem with getting her drink on. Maybe she's afraid it will interfere too much with her diet.

"I'm not drinking either," I looked at them. "You guys know that you have never seen me with alcohol in my hand."

"Oh, I forgot," Simone remarked. "You're the square one out of the group....well, Nic, it's just me and you kid."

Simone grabbed a glass from Dana's hand, and Nicolette popped the top and each of them poured a full glass of vodka. Dana ran and grabbed some orange juice out of the refrigerator because they was not about to mix it and I guess Dana didn't want to see them too drunk. I played DJ for a minute while Dana and I watched those two play quarters. Man, they were drinking like two old men. Dana and I were meditating over the words of Luther Vandross, Nina Simone, and Donny Hathaway. After about fifteen minutes of listening to music and laughing at those two drunks, I started to get bored.

"Hey guys," I made a suggestion, "Remember ' Truth or Dare '?"

"Yeah,"

"Oh, I love that game."

"Secrets, secrets, secrets."

"Let's play it," I told them.

"Okay," Nicolette said. "As long as I get to ask the first question."

"Well," Simone concluded. "As long as everyone agrees to play the game fairly and not punk out. Because if you punk out, I'm kicking ass."

All of us laughed.

"Deal," Nicolette stuck her hand in the middle of the circle.

"Deal," I was next.

"Deal," Simone came.

There was a brief pause as we looked at Dana waiting on the last set of hands to complete the pile.

"...Deal," she finally agreed.

Nicolette started off first, then Simone, then Dana, and I was last to ask the questions. After a while Dana and I were the only ones asking truths or dares. Nicolette and Simone were drunk so Dana and I were making up some funny daring things that they had to do if they didn't answer their truths. It was funny watching them smell each others feet, to making prank calls to Pizza Hut saying that they were Dominoes and wanted to buy them out, to imitating their favorite actor, singer, dancer, or comedian. Nicolette did the best imitation of Whoopi Goldberg that I have ever seen and Simone became Diana Ross within ten seconds. It was amazing because Dana and I got the best of those two. They were drinking so much that they had forgotten to ask Dana and me questions. We were too threw. They both talked with a slurred speech.

"Wait a minute!" Simone yelled out with her drunk ass. "Ya'll niggas thank ya'll slick trying to get out of playin' and making us do stupid shit and tell our most intimate, deepest, darkest secrets."

"Yeah, Simone, just 'cause we've been drinking--a little--they wants to take advantage of us." Nicolette added, " We gon' ask ya'll truth or dare and you have to do what we tell you to do without no questions. You got to just do it...okay?"

I laughed because they were so drunk and so serious. Neither one of them could barely talk clear enough for us to understand what they were saying. But Dana understood.

"Okay," Dana agreed. "But if Afrikka and I do or tell everything that we are suppose to, we get to truth or dare you guys one last time."

"Now, that's a pretty good deal," I put my two cents in.
"Okay."
"Sure, why not."
Nicolette spoke first. "Dana...truth or dare?"
"Ummm...uhh...Dare."

"I dare you to call LaRon and tell him how fine he is."

All of us laughed and smiled 'Yeah...that's a good one...you can do it'.

Dana paused and with confidence she picked up the phone.

"..Yes..LaRon..this is Dana...the thought of you just crossed my mind...I know what time it is...so, ...no, I don't want to come over...you a bad boy...I just wanted to tell you how fine you are...and you...looked good at the mall the other day...in those Levi's that fitted yo' ass so tight ... and...well, it made your ass look juicy enough to eat...yeah...thanks...so I look good enough for you now...but wait till I lose twenty five more pounds, then I'll have you wrapped around my finger...uh, huh...tomorrow?..nothing...what time?...at the Soul Coffee Cafe...see you then..I'll let you get back to sleep..."

She hung up the phone and had this glow on her face.

"Don't tell me you got a date tomorrow!" Nicolette stated as she was hanging up the other phone. You know she had to listen in to make sure Dana really called LaRon.

"Of course I do!" Dana cheesed.

"You go, girl," I told her. "See where a little confidence and aggressiveness will take you."

"I should have done that a long time ago," Dana said.

"You 'bout to get whipped after he hit it one good time tomorrow night,"

Simone had to get in. "I see it coming now."

"You right," Dana added. "I'm cummin' right now as I speak."

"Nasty ass," Simone moved away from her. "It's my turn, Afrikka...truth or dare?"

"Truth." Lord, why did Simone have to ask me a question?

"Afrikka, have you ever slept with any of your friends' boyfriends, ever in your life--or wanted to."
Whew!!!
"No and......No!" I teased them. "You thought you got me, huh, Simone."
"You mean, A-Freak-Ka ain't never thought about sexing neither one of our mens, ever."
"No, nigga. Af-Rik-Ka, isn't like you," we all laughed.
"Okay, my turn. Nicolette--truth or dare?"
"Dare!" she yelled.
"Calm yo' drunk ass down," I told her. "Since you've been checking out Ed these last few months, call and set up a date with him."
"No problem," she said. I dialed Ed's number for her.
"Ed...this is Nic...yeah, I've just been drinking a little...whatever...listen...I want us to go out on a date...me?...you have?...when?..."
For some reason, I was beginning to feel a little jealous. I didn't know Ed would respond to her so well. Why am I feeling this way?
"...okay...yeah...Rodrick?...oh, *that's* over...I can't wait...yeah, tomorrow would be fine with me...Of course, I'll bring Afrikka along with us...so, just call me in the morning and let me know what time you want us to meet up there....bye."
"Oh, no, you not bringing me on your date like a third wheel," I told her.
"Afrikka, calm down," Nicolette told me. "No...he didn't accept my invitation..he wants me to meet his cousin, Robert, tomorrow and wants all four of us to go out for lunch or dinner."
"Cool," I exhaled.

"Good for you, Nic," Dana touched her shoulder, " it'll help you get over Rodrick fast, hopefully."

"Yeah," Simone threw in.

"Simone," Dana looked into Simone's eyes. "Truth or dare?"

"Aaaahhhh...truth," she calmly said.

"Have you ever had sex with someone without your consent?"

Everyone looked at Simone waiting on her response. Simone's eyes got huge like she wasn't expecting that kind of question from Dana.

"Oh, yeah," Simone laughed, "sure, I have...lots of times...no big deal."

"Really," all of us wondered.

"With who?" I asked her.

She did not answer but laughed hysterically while the rest of us kept asking 'with who?...tell us...come on..' that went on and on for about a minute and Simone wasn't giving in. Suddenly, and unexpectedly, Simone broke out crying full of tears.

"Simone, are you okay?" Dana asked.

"She's drunk!" Nicolette laughed.

We all sat there, on the floor, observing Simone like she was an experiment to be tested. I think Dana's question really hit a nerve that she did not want to be pinched.

"Guys, quiet," I told them. "I think she is serious....Simone talk to us."

Dana added, "Simone...trust me...you will feel better if you talk about it."

Nicolette got serious, "We feel your pain, Simone...even me...now please, we're your friends...we'll always be here for you."

"Earl," she finally spoke out, "he...he...rapes me...make me do things with him that I don't want to be done," she mumbled.

Simone started telling us how she met Earl right after high school and at first, their relationship was the bomb. They moved in together. She didn't have to work. He bought her anything she wanted and, basically, took care of her until...E.J. was born...that's when the trouble began. She told us that she thinks that he didn't really want a baby and that he blamed her for getting pregnant saying that she set him up. He then started coming in at all times of the night then eventually, didn't come home at all. He stayed gone for at least two years, until E.J was about three. When he came back in her life that's when she started a career singing in night clubs to support E.J., pay bills, and put food on the table. She told us that the only reason she let him come back into their lives was because E.J. needed a father. I think it was also because she was still in love with him. She told us that soon after that he started becoming possessive and jealous of the attention that she was getting from the night club acts and he would sometimes beat her up so bad after a show if she so much as speak to a guy more than two minutes. That's when he came up with that two-minute rule because he told her that if any man talks to a woman longer than two minutes that he has strong interest in her or that he wants to fuck her. About a year ago, she told us that's when he started making her have sex with him in odd places--like in an alley, on an open field, in a public bathroom, or on top of buildings. She told us that he wanted her to perform mascinistic and sadistic sex acts. She even admitted that he made her have sex with another woman in front of him, then beat the shit out of her later saying that she looked like she was enjoying the sex better with that woman than with him. So, he never tried that anymore. She told us that he beats her whenever she rejects or declines his propositions. She told us that this type of behavior, unwanted sex acts, has been going on for the past year and that she can't take it anymore and wants out for the sake of E.J. and her up-and-coming career.

All of us sat there as we listened not knowing what to say. I didn't know what to feel or how to feel at this moment. It was dead silence now. I could not relate. I have never in my life had an experience like this before. But I do feel something. Maybe concerned about her mental--and physical health? Scared for her life? Worried? Uptight? Disgusted? She has had a horrible life. I don't understand how she can be able to hold all of that pain and suffering in. She should be on the verge of exploding by now. How could he? That bastard deserves to go to Hell. Lord, I pray for his soul. Simone must be filled with so much guilt and self-hatred...and shame. How could she hold it all in and hide it from us, from her audience, from herself.

"I'm feeling you, Simone," Dana started counseling her with tears in her eyes. "Your escape to this has been releasing your frustrations in the songs that you sing. That's why they feel so real to me, to us, to your fans. You have been hiding all of this, wrapped around lyrics in ballads that you spill through your guts. But, you can no longer hide and escape into this fantasy anymore. It won't work forever unless you do something about it now."

Nicolette grabbed Simone's hand, "She's right. You can not stay in an abusive relationship like that. I got an idea...stay with me. You know I have more that enough room. Plus, I need some company out here. You guys could stay in our guest house. And E.J. will have more room to play than he needs..he'll love it..and you will to. You can sing as loud as you want. I would love to have you here until you get on your feet or you can stay as long as you want."

Simone smiled. We all smiled after her.

"Yes," I added, "stay here tonight with us, then get up early in the morning and go home and pack up all of your stuff, pick up E.J., and leave without clueing Earl on shit."

"Yeah, and I'll give you a key before you leave in the morning," Nicolette added.

"Awe, guys," Simone grabbed us while still crying. "What would I do without ya'll? I should have met you guys a long time ago."

"But you met us at this time in your life for a reason," I told her.

"God has finally answered my prayers...I'll take you up on your offer, Nic, but I'll warn you now...E.J. is very hyper, so when he gets on your nerves, just smack him one good time and he'll understand what that means," Simone warned her.

"No,..I'll just beat the shit out of his ass," Nicolette joked.

We sat there as the tears turned into laughs because, I guess, we were all happy, now, that this issue is resolved. I am confident that Simone will leave Earl. I really think that she is fed up with him.

"Okay!" Nicolette broke out, "My buzz is gone and I am hungry."

"You got that right," Simone said whipping her tears away.

"I'll heat the food up," Dana ran into the kitchen.

We sat there and talked as Dana, I guess, heated up the food. But, damn, it doesn't take nobody ten minutes to heat up the sun. I suddenly realized the time.

"Damn, Dana," I yelled in the kitchen, "It don't take a two year old that long to heat up food."

As soon as I said that Dana came rushing through the door with a tray of food and sat it on the table. All of us gathered around it picking up a fork here, a plate there, except for Dana. She grabbed her purse.

"Guys," she said walking to the door, "it's been real. I've got to go 'cause I've got an early appointment with my trainer, and if I stay here I would have to get up too early in the morning to make it there on time."

Everybody looked around surprised.

"Well, okay," Nicolette spoke out first, "drive safely. It's been real."

"And Simone," Dana looked into her eyes, "we'll see you tomorrow, right?"

"I don't know if I'll see you tomorrow...I thought you had a hot date with LaRon," Simone made her remember.

Dana just smiled and closed the door behind herself.

We all sat down to eat.

"Guys," Simone questioned. "I know there was more food than this."

We all looked at each other for a brief moment as we all at the same time yelled out-- "DANA!"

CHAPTER 12
Face Down
♋

    After working out at the gym for nearly two hours, then, running the four miles home and doing the stairmaster for twenty minutes, I felt like a million bucks. Nicolette is right, it feels sooo good to be in control of my body. I have a couple of hours before LaRon is due to come by so I guess I'll get cleaned up and get ready for tonight.

It was just a joke to call him and ask him out, and although men have been coming on to me like crazy, I still can't believe that LaRon actually *wants* to go out with me. I migrated toward the kitchen as I begin to daydream for the one millionth time what LaRon would look like naked--I mean I knew from the pin-ups what was there, but it just wasn't the same as the real thing. Not that I'm going to give him any tonight. I just want to tease him a little..

What am I going to wear? I looked inside the refrigerator. Am I trying to achieve sexy or innocent? Ummm. Pickles--not fattening. Maybe I'll make some tuna fish to eat now so I won't be so hungry tonight and pig out in front of LaRon. Momma says to be careful to eat like a bird around men so they don't think I'm greedy or something. Maybe he'll think my weight was a gland-thing or something. While the eggs are boiling for the tuna, I grab a box of Crunch 'n Munch to tide me over til the eggs are done.

God I can't believe all this is happening to me. It is like a dream come true...but what if I screw it up. What if I say something stupid.. I'd better call Afrikka for a little encouragement--she's good for that. I finished off the box of Crunch n' Munch and headed for the phone after tipping the box over my mouth to get the last of the crumbs. The phone rang twice and then the message service answered, so I hung up and called her on her cell phone.

"Hey Dana," she answered after obviously looking at the caller I.D.

"Hey Afrikka, I..uh need your fashion expertise over here girl. I'm really getting nervous about me and LaRon going out tonight." I turned off the eggs and poured cool water over them to loosen the shell while I was talking.

"Hold on a minute girl, 'OOOoo these people cannot drive'" I heard her say in the background.

I grabbed the Lays potato chips from the cabinet to eat with the tuna sandwich. I shoveled about ten into my mouth chewing quickly so I would be prepared to talk by the time Afrikka came back to the phone. I finished cutting up the eggs and placed them in a flowery old margarine bowl with the tuna.

"Okay, girl...I'm sorry. What's up!"

Damn! I knew she was gonna come back when my mouth was full of chips. I swallowed them almost whole, and said, "Afrikka, do you think I should go for sexy or simple and classy?"

"Well, it depends on what you're trying to achieve on the date...Do you want him to sit up and take notice or do you want him to see you as his 'girl'?"

"No, definitely not his 'girl' anymore. We been there and done that. We've actually been friends for years..since high school. I was there for him through some really tough times like when he dropped out of college because he just knew he was gon' get drafted, and then didn't. And when his girl and all his friends dissed him because he wasn't the Man no more..."

"Dana, girl, you *are* a damn good friend, and I'll bet he knows all that quite well. Now, the question is, are you ready to move your friendship into a new level?"

"That's just it. I'm not so sure of what I want. Before it was easy because I always knew where I stood. But now I don't know what to expect." I squished a piece of the fresh bread I had in my hand into a little ball and ate it. Then, I started to mix the Hellman's into the tunafish.

"Well, that sounds like a great place to start to me!"

"What do you mean?"

"I mean just go in with no expectations, be your wonderful self, and let the rest just happen. That way, you win no matter what happens because you didn't have any expectations in the first place. Cool?"

By now I had a mouth full of the tuna I was tasting to make sure I'd put enough mayo in it. ...humhnn ...something's missing. "I guess so, Afrikka."

"What is there to guess about? It is as easy as just putting on the first thing that comes to mind, and you know you look fantastic in anything since you've worked so hard on your figure. Plus, I've always thought you are one of the most beautiful women I've ever met...and you know I'm around models all the time so that's quite a compliment. Girl, you got it going on, and there is nothing to worry about. Just have fun, okay?"

"Okay." I murmured half-heartedly, feeling even more uneasy for some reason. "Pickles!" I thought aloud.

"Huh??"

"Oh, that's what is missing in this tuna that I'm making for a snack so I won't be too hungry tonight."

"Oh. Well, I'm home now. Do you want me to call you back when I get inside?"

"Nah." I said, looking into the fridge for the pickles, and spotting what was left of the bag of apple fritters I bought last night on my way home from hanging out with the girls. I just can't help myself, I've got to have at least one. Half-way through the first one, I was already thinking how good the second one would be warmed up. I popped the bag into the microwave for a few seconds, and before I knew it I'd eaten three of the four fritters. Since there was only one left, I might as well eat it too, I reasoned as if the last fritter was going to be lonely in that bag all by itself. I turned around feeling a bit swollen already to face the tuna I'd been making, and realized

I hadn't finished it. I reached in the fridge again and this time quickly found the chopped pickles and plopped a huge spoonful into the bowl on the top of the tuna salad. I stirred it up and considered placing it into the refrigerator since I know that donutty sweets like the fritters I ate digest pretty quickly and my time for getting rid of it is running quite short. Oh, what the hell....I said to myself giving in to the temptation. Afterall, tuna fish sandwiches on fresh Mrs. Baird's bread with Lay's potato chips is the bomb. Besides, I don't know where LaRon's cheap ass will take me tonight. I polished off the whole bowl and headed for the bathroom.

    Ring!

    RRRiing!

    Damn...who is it? It was Nicolette according the I.D. box. It actually says unavailable, but it does show the number and I just happen to know it's Nic, and I don't have time for her right now. I've got the hurry before these damn fritters show up on my ass.

    I'm glad I've got a large bathroom. I spend a lot of time in here. I'm standing over the sink now, and my mind floats to Daddy playing with my nieces and nephews; they seem to have such a grand time together. Now I'm looking at myself in the mirror, noticing the latest contour in my face, then suddenly I envision LaRon's tight little waist leading to toned hips and his big round muscular ass and that reminds me it is time to get down to business. I really hate doing this, but it is the only way...the only way to have a decent life. Before I chicken out, as I do more and more often now that I'm getting closer to my ideal weight, I start reminding myself of how miserable I was fat. Which is worser--throwing up or being fat? I quickly decide that being fat is the worse thing in the world and as usual this thought catapults the first two fingers of my right hand into my mouth. It takes a minute or two of slow rhythmic poking to get my throat primed with the saliva that always comes up first. Then I step up onto the telephone book that I keep in the bathroom to further tilt my body and make it easier for the food to just slide out. I feel the familiar bubble in my throat and shifting in my stomach, and then a large amount of the tuna fish and potato chips comes up in the sink. I turn the sink on to quickly wash it down and continue plodding my fingers down my throat until I'm pretty sure I've gotten all that I can. I stand up getting that lightheaded feeling from being almost upside down for about twenty minutes. My stomach is nice and flat and I admire it in the mirror--the fruits of my labor.

"Now that wasn't so bad," I say aloud. "And look it only took fifteen minutes. Now I'd better find something to wear so I won't be naked tonight. Huh, LaRon ain't ready for all this just yet."

I've been thinking all week about wearing that smooth white jumpsuit with the back out, but I'm not so sure about my arms--nothing looks worse that a woman with her flabby arms out. It makes me want to cringe to see a sistah with cellulite in her arms in a sleeveless outfit. I just want to walk up and say, "Excuse me but when people say they love dimples, they don't mean the ones in your arm."

I guess I'll just have to try it on and see. It has a high neck capped with a short mock turtle neck. It has no sleeves, and it's cut so just a enough of the shoulders can stick out and reveal all those down deltoid reps. It has two hooks behind the neck that hold the top up and that's it. The rest is skin tight except the bells at the bottom. When I saw it in the store I just had to have it...that was months ago, when I wouldn't even have thought about putting my big toe in an outfit like this. I slip into the bottom part which has a tight, thick elastic high waist. It takes quite a bit of squeezing to get the band over my big ol'butt. Finally, though, the band slides over the butt and onto my small waist which is one of my best features. I want to look in the mirror, but I won't let myself cause I want to get the whole picture. I put my arm into the holes where the sleeves would normally be, and pull the top on hooking the hooks behind the neck.

When I go to the mirror, I can't believe my eyes, IT IS THE BOMB! It looks just like I thought it would on my tiny waist and big ass hips! LaRon is going to drop his teeth. Better yet his.... Umph umph umph... I am so fine in this that *I* would fuck me (if I wasn't tired of doing that already!) I keep turning and flipping in the mirror, looking at everything from the curvature in my ass to the muscles in my biceps. I just can't believe it's me! It fits even better than I thought it would. But I still could stand to loose about ten more. I decide to get out of it and try on some other things while I decide whether or not I want to wear this. Just as I have pulled the jumpsuit down half way over my hips, the phone rings. Oh God! It's LaRon.

What do I do? How should I sound? I decide to go for that sultry Anita Baker sound.

"Hello," I say cool and calmly as if I do it that way everyday.

"Hi, Dana. This is...."

"LaRon." I say almost loosing my cool.

"Yea. Well, I was wondering about tonight. Other than meeting at the Soul, we didn't really set any specific plans when we talked last night, so I was wondering if we could just get a movie and kick it at your place. I'm really tired from playing in the Hoop-It-Up tournament all day today."

"Is it that time of year again already?"

"Yep. The finals are next weekend, with teams from all over the nation."

"Oh, I know...I used to volunteer with the children at my church every year when I first got out of school, but I've just been too busy to get involved these last couple of years."

"You're probably the HNIC at your company by now?"

"What's that?"

"Head Nigger In Charge, Dana. You must be loosing touch with the peeps."

"I guess so. Slang is taking on a whole new flava it seems, and I just can't keep up."

The conversation was abnormally good and long between us at the mall when I saw LaRon, and I thought it was just a coincidence. But now it seems like we may really be clicking.

"Well, I know you must be tired so if you want we can just reschedule," I heard myself say, partially trying to be considerate and partially scared to death because things are going so smoothly between us.

"No, Dana, I really do want to hang out with you, I just don't want to be around a whole bunch of people. You know what I mean?"

"Yea....I definitely know that feeling."

"So...uh, let me take care of a little somin' somin', and then I'll call you back when I'm on my way. Cool?"

I looked at the time and it was almost seven o'clock. I wanted to ask him how long or about what time he thought it would be, but I didn't want to discourage him. Besides maybe I'll have time to hit the treadmill for a few minutes so I agreed.

"Okay, I'll talk to you then, sexy." Whoa, that was really bold Dana.

Their was a pause before his next words...I must have shocked him too.

"Ah-ight then, peace out."
"Bye," I said and hung up the phone before I said something else stupid.

I checked my voice mail to find this message from Nic:
"Hey Dana, girl this is Nicolette, and I was just calling to see if you were getting all gee-d up for your fantasy date with macdaddy LaRon. Anyway, Rodrick keeps calling ...asshole motherfucka...I guess he think I'm supposed to just say whatever and keep seeing his sorry ass...well, he can think again...he'll never..." Nic trailed on realizing she was sharing her feelings, and worse, she was sharing them with a machine. "Girl, I ain't never giving in to no man like this again." She laughed,..."got me talking to machines and shit. Have fun tonight, and remember my motto, Use or get Used."

I feel sorry for Nicolette, she's just looking for a replacement for the emotional sharing she didn't get from her dad. What's ironic is that she is just like him. I laid back on my bed and listened to messages from some of my other homies and my mama who's always calling to remind me to do something, as if I'm twelve years old. One message was from my soror callin to remind me of an upcoming event they need me for.

Just then, I heard a knock at the door. Who in the world could that be? I grabbed a robe out of my closet and rushed to the door, yelling "Who is it?" on my way.

"It's me...Nicolette." I heard a faint voice saying. I unlocked the door, and there she was looking somewhat strange.

"Nic??" I said sounding like I didn't recognize her.

She read my expression and just started explaining, "Dana," she said near tears in a voice resembling a wounded dear, "I don't wanna go." The dam broke and a flood of tears came down Nicolette's flawless cheeks.

After calming her down, she told me that she really loved Rodrick, and hoped that he would be the one, but as soon as she started really wanting him, he stopped wanting her. She had been on her way to Sweet Georgia Brown, a new restaurant in the hood to meet Afrikka, Ed, and Ed's cousin when she started to think about Rod and got all upset, so she dropped by my place to get a pep talk. I assured her that she wasn't the first one this had happened to and she assured me that it was going to be the last time for her.

"The thing I really feel stupid about is that I still want him after what he did," she said and burst into tears again.

"Nicolette, you have so much going for you...there are guys practically lined up just to get to say hi to you. You will feel sad for a while, but I promise you it will end and you will get on with your life. Going out tonight with this new guy is just the thing you need to get your mind off of Rodrick."

"How do you know Dana!" she screamed at me. "When was the last time you had a boyfriend? You don't even give out your phone number, but you're always giving advice..."

"You're right," I yelled back at her, "yes, you're one hundred percent right I don't give out my number to just any ol' body because I don't have time to waste just jumping from one bed to the next...I have better things to do with my time, like spending time with some children who might die any day, or taking old people to the park to see the children play. See, Nicolette, your real problem has absolutely nothing to do with men," her eyes looked like she was shocked, but at the same time expecting what I was about to say next, "your real problem is that you are a spoiled brat who cares only about your wants, needs and feelings. You are too afraid that someone is going to find you out for who you really are and that's why you don't really like to get close to people, especially men."

I wanted to stop there, but I had gone too far and something in me knew she needed to hear all this. So I went on despite the wild stare and huge tears welling in her eyes.

"Listen, Nic. It ain't easy for me neither, you just have to keep going and stop looking for something on the outside of you that ain't on the inside. If you want someone to really love you, you got to have love in you. You can't just treat people like garbage and expect them to treat you like a queen. If you want to be treated like a queen, you got to be one. You hearing me?"

She sat there in a daze and shook her head up and down like a zombie. In a way I felt sorry for her, but in some strange way I didn't. I mean one day the dog always gets bit, and with Nicolette she didn't really care about this man anyway, she was just interested in what he had to offer.

It was quiet for a long time and I wasn't sure what to say, so I went over and sat next to her and handed her the box of tissues.

"We all go through painful times, Nicolette, and you're not immune. I'm sorry if I've hurt you..."

Nicolette jumped up off the couch like one of the springs had let loose on her. "I'm allright, and you're right, Dana. I do go around treating people like shit and expecting to be treated like royalty. But that's because I am royalty...I am special..." I'm not sure who she trying to convince--herself or me. Nic went on, "And you're just jealous!"

"Jealous?!?"

"Yea jealous!"

"Of what you and your big ol' house with no family in it!" I had more to say, but realized I'd gone too far already. Nicolette looked at me with daggers in her eyes and stormed out of my apartment calling me a bitch as she slammed the door.

♋

  The hell with her Jenny Craig loving ass, I thought to myself. I sniffed my last bit of snot, and decided to put Dana's righteous ass and Rod fonky ass behind me for the night. I'll never talk to either of them again, in fact, I'm gonna block Dana off my phone, too. That'll show them! My hair swung over my shoulder as I got into the vette and to' ass as Simone would say. Something *told* me I should've gone by her place instead.
  I drove until I got to the restaurant which wasn't very far. I didn't have much time before we were due to meet, but I had to fix my face and my attitude or there was no way I was going in there. I really wanted to just go home. Maybe, I could call Afrikka on her cell phone and tell her to make a good excuse for me. Just then, Ed, Afrikka and Ed's cousin drove into the parking space next to me and honked. Oh shit! I must look like crap. I can't let them see me. I halfway waved to them and ducked down like I was looking for something. When I came up, Afrikka was standing right by the door of my car, and Ed and his cousin was standing behind her looking scrumpscious. Both of their crotches were at my eye level and I wasn't too bad off to notice that it must run in the family. I cracked the door just a bit, knowing they couldn't see me that well behind the factory tint I had.
  "Hey!"Afrikka said in a very bubbly voice, "you gon' leave me out here all alone with these two vivacious men."
  "I..uh..dropped my lipstick under the seat..and..uh..why don't you guys go ahead and get our table, and I'll be right

there," I said coming to myself. I gave Afrikka the I-need-a-minute eye, and she nodded.

"Sure, take your time..you know how the wait is here."

She's sooo good. I'm glad she didn't try to introduce us now or anything. I dropped a couple of drops of ClearEyes in each eye, and let it roll around while I relaxed and took a deep breath. Visions of me fucking LaRon with Dana looking on in terror came to my mind and I shook them out knowing that any thought of what just happened might put me over the edge. I put on some lipstick and decided not to reapply all the makeup I had previously put on, just powder and a little mascara. There. Ain't no use in getting all made up--either...he'll like me or he won't. I'm tired of getting all boofed up for these un-grateful negroes. I'm just going to be my damn self, and if they don't like it..fuck'm.

When I got inside, the place was very nice and elegant, it's a shame it is all the way down here in the hood where they can't charge very much...po' ass welfare recipients down here will run you out of business.

The maitre' D was a friend of mine from school. She looked real cute all dressed up.

"Hi, Deaqueenisha." What a ghetto name, I thought to myself. And she certainly lives up to it.

"Oh, hi, Nicolette. You came just in time..there are some real honeys in here tonight," she said all loud.

"Oh yea!"

"Look at those two over there by the bar..they just came in..damn they fine!"

"Uh.. one of them is my date," I said proudly staking my claim.

"Oooo, girl. I need to hang out with *you*. You be pullin'm. But, I thought you had a boyfriend. The last time I saw you out you was wrapped on some tight brotha that looked to have you sprung."

"That didn't work out," she must have noticed the change in my attitude cause she quickly escorted me to the bar and rushed off, but not without first showing off her big tatooed titties. I saw both guys lookin'.

"Ya'll gon' and look," Afrikka said revealing her true southern roots, "cause that's the only set of breasts you'll see tonight."

"There's nothing wrong with a little cleavage *Afrikka.*" I said to break the ice and to show a bit of my risque side since I'm dressed pretty conservatively tonight in a soft yellow knit tunic with matching pants.

"I couldn't agree more. But like I always say, there's a time and a place for everything...and this ain't it," said Afrikka.

Now, I'd never heard her talk that way about anyone. Ed looked somewhat surprised too.

"Uh, Nicolette. I'd like to introduce you to my cousin Robert Shoderaux," Ed interrupted. "Robert this is Nicolette, the beautiful poet that I told you about..."

I reached out to shake Robert's hand, and somehow it turned into a hug.

"I feel as if I already know you. I mean, all the way over Ed and Afrikka kept going on and on about your poetry. And, truthfully, I wished they would just shut up and let me see for myself, because you know how these things usually go. But, well, ...they didn't even scratch the surface...you are not only talented, but also excruciatingly beautiful. And I can sense that you're an incredibly passionate woman, aren't you?"

From that point on, the night just got better and better. And Afrikka and Ed just seemed to soak into the woodwork.

Robert had just gotten his MBA, and was about to start working here for one of the largest law firms in the country. He was down for the weekend getting his new place set up.

Whenever he talked I just felt so comfortable, like his words were just swallowing me up. There was something so comfortable, so familiar about him--and no matter how hard I tried to think about what I was doing with him, I just had to feel my way through.

After dinner and a little dancing, Afrikka and Ed were tired and wanted to go home, so we went to the lake and they went home after mother Afrikka gave me a lecture about not staying out too late or getting in over my head too soon.

I felt so inspired. It was like Robert was the vibe. I was running off words like Maya, and Robert just sat there listening intently and encouraging me. I can't believe it because I usually can't write around anyone, but with Robert it seemed I could write for hours.

By the time we got back to Robert's new place it was about four o'clock and I was so tired, and mentally drained. Robert asked if I'd like to stay, and usually I would have jumped at the opportunity, but I didn't want to get too close, too soon this time. So he called me on my car phone and talked to me the full twenty minutes that it took to get home.

When I hit the bed, as tired as I was I just couldn't sleep. I got up to get some tea, and the phone rang. It must be Afrikka callin' to check and see if I made it home okay.

"Hello," I said, sounding still very much awake.

"Hello, miss night owl. And where have we been?" Rodrick's smooth voice said.

"Rodrick, what the.... what do you want.?" I had to calm myself down.

"To see you."

"No you don't. You want to get cursed out."

"Aw..come on Nickity Nic." He always said that when he was trying to get his way.

"Look, Rod. It's over and I don't ever, ever, ever-ever-ever, want to see your face or talk to you again."

"But I love you, baby."

"Tell that to your bitch!" I yelled and hung up the phone before he could say another word.

About two minutes later the phone rang again. I grabbed it quick, "Look Rod, don't let me have to get my dad in this."

"Hey...hey...hey, I know it's late but I was just making sure you got in and settled down okay." Robert said.

"Oh Robert," I said doing my best to hold back the tears, "I was just talking to my X, and he gets me so...pissed off. Forgive me for being so harsh, but he gets me so worked up. Why the nerve of him asking me where I've been as if it is any of his business." I wanted to go on, but I didn't want to burden Robert with all of this.

"Hey...it's okay to be upset, and if anybody understands I do. The reason I chose to live here instead of staying in Philly is that my X purposely got pregnant by some hardhead after we broke up so she could go around spreading lies about me."

"Are you *sure* it's not your baby?"

"Oh yeah! My momma don't play that; she would kick my butt. We had a paternity test done, but I just knew it wasn't mine from jump. I mean I'd love to have a son like him, but I'm not going to lie. At first, I felt sorry for her and would spend time with him and everything since she said she didn't know who the father was if it wasn't me. But she kept on telling everybody in town that I was the father and even tells the baby I'm his daddy. I just thought it best if I get away for a while."

The phone clicked, and I just knew it had to be Rodrick this time and I was prepared to give him a piece of my mind when Robert asked, "Is that your phone?"

"Unnh-huh." I said sounding like a loaded gun.

"Don't get it!" Robert said quick, "I mean trust me, he's only going to keep calling if he knows it is upsetting you because, as I learned, with some people negative attention is better than no attention at all."

"Yea, you're probably right. More fuel on the fire."

"That's right. Why don't you turn your ringer off and get some rest."

"I would, but I couldn't sleep anyway. I got in the bed and just laid there...I was actually having a cup of tea before all this commotion started."

"Well, let's change the subject. I had a great time with you, and you may not believe this, but I couldn't sleep either. I had the best time I've had on a date in a looong time."

"Really?"

"Yea, usually I spend most of my time on a date trying to figure out what to say to impress her, or trying not to put my foot in my mouth. But with you I felt so relaxed."

"Yea...me too. You want to hear something funny."

"What?"

"I've never composed a poem in front of anyone, and there I was pouring my heart out in front of you."

"Man, I wish I had half the talent you have, I would be reciting and writing everywhere."

"Yea, well, it's really hard while I'm in school to focus on anything other than the books, you know?"

"Yea, I feel you. I was so sick of school that at one point near the end, I almost dropped out."

"I would if my dad..." I trailed off for some reason.

"If your dad, what?"

"If he would let me."

"*Let* you..Nicolette, you are a grown woman and quite a woman might I add. And, trust me no matter how many other things you try to do to take your mind off your dreams, it just won't work."

He went on to tell me about his mother's dream of him becoming an attorney, and how he'd even gone to law school to try to fulfill her dreams for him. But, he was so unhappy he nearly committed suicide. He'd actually been in therapy several years before he realized that he was living a lie, and that he had to start pursuing his dreams before he *really* went crazy.

We were on the phone way past daybreak talking about our dreams, our parents and our X's. Yes, I told him everything, even how I had slept with Rod on our first date, and how I had, out of habit, wanted to go to bed with him, but something just held me back.

"Do you believe in fate, Robert?"

"Yes, wholeheartedly," he replied.

Turns out Robert gave his life to Christ earlier this year, and is turning his life around. And when we finally hung up the phone, he was going to church. Needless to say, I was truly impressed. He said he'd call later. I went straight to sleep.

CHAPTER 13
Booty Call
♋

Riinngg!
Riinnngg!
"Hey Dana, this is Afrikka. You up?"
"Just barely. What time is it?'
"Oh it's about 10:45. ... sooo... how did it go?"
"10:45! Man, I must have slept right through the alarm clock."

"Well?"

"Well, what?"

"How was your date silly girl? It's not everynight you go out with the man of your dreams."

"Oh it was nice."

"What did you do? What did you end up wearing?"

"I wore that green sundress with the three spaghetti straps on the shoulders."

"Oh that's very flattering on you. Where did he take you?"

"Well, we didn't exactly go anywhere."

"You mean you stayed at your place?"

"Yea," I said revealing my disappointment.

"What, did you not want to stay at your place."

"Well, it's just that it wasn't exactly what I had in mind for a romantic evening."

"Being at home can be quite romantic, Dana."

"I guess I just had something else in mind...It felt like a booty call."

"Did you tell him that?"

"No...well he'd been playing in the Hoop It Up tournament all day and he was really tired....He didn't even get to my place til almost midnight.

"Oh. I thought you had planned to go to the Soul Coffee Cafe."

"We did, but he called and said he was sooo tired. I was trying to be compassionate."

"Well, did you have any fun?"

"Yea, he talked and talked about how he had whipped up on some guys in the tournament. Then, halfway through the movie I rented, he was knocked out on my couch. It was really late so I took off his shoes and put some cover on him.

As I was covering him up, he woke up and started kissing me, and we almost made love right there on the couch."

"Almost?"

"Yea, he gave me a massage and he just kept going on and on about how 'fine' I am, and how much I'd been working on my body which made me feel really good. But he just seemed to be so focused on getting the bootie, and you know I can't go out like that--I just couldn't do it."

"Well, that's okay, Dana. That doesn't mean it was a bad date."

"No, it's just that I had such high ex..."

"See, you should learn from this and work on just relaxing and going in without those expectations--they just set us up for failure cause no man is ever going to live up to our dreams and fantasies. In fact, that's what makes them dreams and fantasies--they're not real."

"I agree, but putting that concept into practice is another story."

"Girrrl...ain't that the truth. Something that really helps me when I go out is that I don't ever spend time thinking or fantasizing about the date beforehand. I force myself to think about other things all the way up to the date. Otherwise, I'll catch myself designing our wedding or writing out my new name just like in high school."

"You still do that, too!"

"I think all women do. We just don't tell anybody anymore."

"I guess you're right."

"You wanna know what really pisses me off?"

"What?"

"When you talk to married people about being single and they say 'take your time'. It's as if they've forgotten what's it's like to come home to a cold empty bed, or to cook a meal for two and no one else is there.

"Or to be left off of an invitation list because you don't have a spouse."

"Or to go everywhere by yourself, or worse have people setting you up with their pitiful nephew who still wears baggies."

"Or to wonder if you're ever going to have children."

"Or, how 'bout this one, to be asked 'how come you're single?' about a thousand times a week. It's enough to make you want to scream. And, I know they're trying to encourage you to enjoy being single, but there's got to be a better way to do it. I don't think all marriages are that bad, just the ones where the people involved got married for all the wrong reasons, and now they feel trapped so they say negative stuff about the marriage instead of doing their part to make the marriage better by working on their own problems."

"Afrikka, you are soo right. I didn't know you thought about being alone."

"Sure I do. And I get very lonely sometimes, too."

"You just have so much going for yourself, I can't even imagine why you're still single anyway. If I was a man, I'd jump at having a woman like you--creative, expressive, positive, beautiful and getting paid! Humph I don't know what's wrong with these damn men!"

"Me neither, girl, but I ain't gon' let'm worry me. You feel like shopping? Maybe we can all go to the mall later on."

"Maybe so...I don't have nobody's money though."

"Like I do. We can just hang and window-wish."

"I don't know. I've got some things to do today."

"What about later this afternoon about four-thirty. The mall closes at six, so that will automatically limit the time we can graze. Then, maybe we can catch a movie."

"I don't know, I might run into somebody from church."

"Hold on, Dana. That's my other line...Hey guy. What's up?"

It was Ed.

"We didn't get a chance to go over Monday's schedule, and it's a tight one so...."

"Boy, you work too hard. It's Sunday and we can go over that in the morning. I am trying to get the dirt on Nic and Robert. Have you heard anything?"

"Zero."

"Yea, well I've got Dana on the other line, and we're trying to cook up an afternoon shopping and movie hang out. You wanna come?"

"Uh....that sound like a "waiting to exhale" evening to me. Ya'll have a good time, but I don't think so. I've got some things to do anyway."

"Oooh, you must have a lil' somin' somin' going on over there."

"Nothing you wouldn't like, Miss Afrikka."

"Uh-oh, watch yo'self. Call me and give me the 4-1-1 if it's not too late."

"Okay, later."

"Bye."

"Dana...Dana..., you there?"

"Yep. That must have been a man."

"Just Ed."

"Oh yea! How did *your* date go?"

"Date?!? Girl, pleez. We felt like chaperones for Nic and Robert. They really hit it off and I don't even think they knew we were there after a while, so Ed and I just left them alone."

"Girl, Ed is fine *and* he really knows how to treat a lady"

"Yea, girl. He's ambitious and hardworking, too. You want me to hook ya'll up."

"I don't think I'm his type. I don't know why you two don't hook up."

"Well, for one he's a business associate, for two, he's one of the best friends I've got--and ain't nothing like romance to tear up a perfectly good friendship."

"It looks like you might be right."

"Dana, go easy on LaRon--you've been waiting on him all this time, so the least you can do is give him a chance."

"Now, there goes my phone. Can you hold?"

"Why don't you just call me and let me know if you wanna hang out this evening after you finish what you've got to do."

"Allright."

"Talk to you later. Bye-bye."

"Bye."

Dear Diary,

Today was a beautiful day; the sun was shining bright all day and not a cloud in the sky. Boy, I miss Jamal. I can't wait til he gets here. He should be here any minute now. After I read all of the postcards he has been sending me from the Virgin Islands for the third time today, I went to the mall and did some browsing and got some ideas. I saw Lovejones at the dollar movie again, and cried my eyes out. Love really can be a beautiful thing. The whole weekend was very pleasant and I didn't even do one ounce of work. Went out with Ed, Nic and Robert on Saturday and had a ball dancing with Ed. He really is a sweetie for putting up with all my ways. He is so in touch with his feminine side without losing the essence of his masculinity--I definitely have to add that to my list of desired qualities in a husband...let's see...I have to separate my needs from my wants. I want a man like Jamal who is fine, sexy, educated...

...Damn, who is this calling me at 12:30 in the morning. It better be good or else I'm hanging up quick.
"Hello...hello...Jamal?...Jamal!!! Now you know that you can't cover up that accent of yours...You must have felt me thinking about you...Yes, of course I want to see you, too. Where are you?...Around the corner!...out my window?!!!... Okay, I'm going to hang up."

I ran over to the window as fast as I could, knocking over my table lamp on the way. I can't believe that he is already here. He got here sooner than I thought; he said he'd be here in the morning. I raised my shades and noticed his perfectly defined physique under the streetlight next to the pay phone.

"Are you going to stand out there all night?" I asked him as I yelled down to him sounding sexy at the same time.

He smiled, put his hand to his mouth and blew a kiss right up my way. I stood there and imagined his lips moistening my cheek. Then, I did the same to him.

"I'm going down to the corner store to get a couple of snacks and then I'll be right over...so give me about ten minutes," he spoke in a sweet and sensual voice.

I nodded without saying a word. I stood there as I watched him walk down the street. Lord, are you answering my prayers? If so, you always do it at the right time.

Okay, I probably have about eight and a half minutes to clean my body and especially my coochie 'cause I'm going to get some tonight. Yes, I am. It's been long enough and now that I have a Dexter St.Jock in my life I'm going to take advantage of him.

I ran to my bathroom tearing my clothes off along the way. I looked at myself in the mirror noticing that I need to trim my pubic hairs and shave my legs.

I jumped out of the shower and looked at the clock to see how much time I had left. Damn, I'm good. I did that all in less than five minutes. After I brushed my teeth and lotioned my entire body from head to toe, I decided to throw my hair in a bun so that he could snatch it down as we make passionate love. As I was dabbing a little Amarige de Givenchy behind my ears and between my thighs, the doorbell rang. Damn...what can I throw on? I grabbed my black silk robe and ran my hot ass to the door like a dog in heat.

"Come in," I said as I stood behind the door.

"Are you hiding from someone?" Jamal asked as he stepped in.

"The neighbors...I wouldn't want them to think I called an escort service," I smiled into his eyes noticing he was hiding something behind his back.

I closed the door. And without moving his arms, he leaned over and gently placed his lips on top of mine. He allowed me to take control--and I did. I put my arms around the back of his head and motioned mine as I worked my tongue in his mouth. After a brief moment, he pulled away and stepped back. Why is this brotha teasing me in the middle of the night? From behind his back was a half dozen of roses in one hand and a small decorated box in the other.

"You are so sweet." I told him as he handed me the roses. "You didn't go to the corner store to get these."

"No," he said, "but I went to the store to get a nice bow for this box."

"What's in it?" I asked and I think I sounded a little bit too excited like a kid getting some candy.

He grabbed my hand and directed me to the living room. He sat me on the love seat and he got on his knees between my legs. He eased the roses from my arm and placed them on the table. He sat the decorative box on my lap.

"Open it," he told me.

I looked at him and picked up the box.

"What is the occassion?" I wondered.

"Missing you...wishing you were by my side on the beach on the Islands," he spoke with that accent to die for.

"But you don't know me," I told him, "we met one day, went out the next, and you were gone the day after."

"But it means something when you think about someone everyday when that person is not around. You read my postcards. I couldn't express my feelings any better. There's something about you, Afrikka, that keeps me from not going a day without thinking about you. Maybe...just maybe you are my soul mate," he said without moving.

I didn't know what to say. I think I feel the same way. For some reason I just couldn't say it back. I paused and looked into his eyes. I looked at the box and slowly unwrapped it. I hate opening a box wrapped so beautifully. As I unwrapped the box and noticed the Tiffany and Co. named imprinted on it, something was telling me that he is serious. I held in my hand the most immaculate diamond necklace that I have ever seen. This can't be real. What am I to do?

"It's beautiful," I whispered.

"Just like you," he told me.

I held the necklace in my hand, staring at it for some unknown reason.

"My father is getting worse..." he spoke, "...and I know this may be asking you too much...but I want you to move back with me. You can still have your business there. As a matter of fact, I found a building that I know you would love to work out of. Tomorrow, you can fly back with me and you can look at it to..."

"Tomorrow?" I asked. "You just got here..."

"Today," he interrupted, "...I know...and I'm sorry that this is such a short notice. I came in town to sign documents to get my residency transferred. But I want you to go back with me. I need you, Afrikka. We can make each other happy."

I looked into his eyes and somehow I knew he was telling the truth about what he was saying and feeling about me. It all sounds so good. Finally, a man I know who wants me unconditionally for the rest of my life. I stood up, grabbed his hands and took control like I did before.

He followed me to my bedroom and I sat him on my bed. I slowly took off of his shirt and gently kissed his neck from front to back. I put my hands around his shoulders and I got on my knees while biting his right nipple then his left. As I was heading toward his abdomen, he pulled me up and untied my robe and watched it fall to the ground. I stood there as he admired my oh-so-ready-to-do-it body. He immediately jumped up as I took his place on the bed. He was now in front of me.

He gently laid me down and caressed my breasts with his tongue up and down and around and around. Man, it's been a long time and now I'm with a man who got it going on inside and outside of bed. His four play is the bomb. Ooohhhhh!!! Ahhhhhh!!!! Don't stop...ever. This is feeling too good and I haven't even got the real thing yet.

He stood up in front of me and unbuttoned his jeans. I watched him unzip his pants wondering what's in store for me tonight. A pencil...no, a pickle,...no, hopefully, at least a cucumber. I closed my eyes hoping that this will be worth my while. I opened it after a few more seconds. Damn!!!! You Mandingo you!!! I can't believe what I am seeing. I didn't think God actually blessed men with dicks this big. Should I chicken out? Hell, no. I am going to win this war.

He rolled on top of me with that big ass dick dangling between my thighs. I could feel the wetness developing within the walls of my vagina. I hadn't felt this way in a long time. Then, out of nowhere I started getting that stupid feeling in my stomach that warns me not to do something. That feeling is usually right on target, but it has got to be wrong tonight.... oooohh! I have really missed Jamal...haven't I? And he does treat me like a queen. So what is up with me, now? I can't ignore my own feeling--as much as I really, really, really want to, I just don't feel that this is the right time for us to get involved sexually.

"Maybe we should talk first," I suggested.

"About what?" he asked as he licked behind my ear.

I didn't respond. I guess it's because he is starting to move his rhythmic tongue in a circular motion around my nipples. Man, this is feeling so good. I love the way a man caresses one of my breasts with the tip of his tongue and the other with the soft, gentle movements of his fingertips. And Jamal knows *exactly* what he is doing. And I must say he is doing it well.

But although my body is on Cloud 9, my mind is thinking about how much I don't know Jamal. I've only seen him twice in my whole life. It was like love at first sight when I met him in the club. I never really believed in love at first sight. To me, all that really is that you feel at that moment is lust at first sight. Just a deep emotional form of physical and sexual attraction. I wonder if that is what I'm feeling about Jamal right now. We've never spent any quality time together to get to know one another except for the evening before he left and several postcards that gave me that false sense of security like I wasn't lonely even though I was definitely alone.

"This doesn't feel right," I whispered in Jamal's ear.

"It doesn't feel *wrong*," he whispered back in my ear.

He bent down to get a condom out of his pocket. Oh, he just knew that he was coming over to get some. The nerve of him and his oversized ego. As he was sliding the rubber on that Mandingo penis of his, even though it was looking good enough to suck, I decided that it wasn't the right time.

"Maybe we should wait," I suggested again.

"On what?" he asked. "You know you want too, Afrikka," he said gently easing his way back onto the bed. "You brought me back here...in your bedroom. And afterall, I flew all the way from the islands with you on my mind."

For what?...I thought to myself because you knew you were gonna get some. Oh, I guess he think I owe him or something for the necklace and those damn roses. I don't feel like I owe him shit. Just as he bent over and had the tip of his dick on the opening of my vagina, I pulled back.

"Stop," I told him, "I just think we need to get to know each other first."

"What?" he asked. "And you wait till this moment to decide that?"

He jumped up and started putting on his clothes before I could get anything out. I didn't say a word as I was watching him fix himself up.

"What are you thinking?" I asked him.

"What do you think?" he looked into my eyes.

He started looking around the room as if he lost something. I watched this brotha move like he was a chicken that just got his head cut off.

"What are you looking for?" I asked him as I placed myself against the headboard in a fetal position.

"My keys!" he yelled.

"They're on the living room table," I told him.

"I'll see myself out," he said as he walked angrily out of my room.

I can't believe the man I thought was my soul mate is leaving me just because I won't give it up. Why is it that when a man buys you something he feels like you owe him some pussy? Well, let his mothafucka ass leave then. Fuck that, shit. I'm glad I found out how his ass was before I got deeply involved. I heard the door close. I'm surprised his no good ass didn't slam the door as mad as he was. Oh, well...let me pray and sleep on this.

"Afrikka," I heard a voice and realized Jamal was standing in my door. "I'm sorry. I don't think that we should part like this."

I looked at him. This was not the beast that stormed out of my room a few seconds ago. He walked over and sat in the ottoman next to my bed. I sat on the bed not knowing what to say. I just looked at him in a weird way.

"I know you think I'm crazy," he began, "it's just that I've been waiting to see you for so long now. And then when I touched you...I had to have you right then and there. You felt so good at that moment. And when you pulled away, it made me angry. I guess I was letting my...my..." He looked down at his zipper and I knew what he was referring to. "I was letting it control what I was thinking and feeling at that time. I apologize. You don't have to forgive me, but I want you to know that I still think the world of you. Sometimes, it's just hard for a man..."

He stopped but somehow I knew that he had more to say but he didn't know how to say it. His words were sincere and somehow I felt that those sincere words were coming straight from his heart. Things do get beyond our control sometimes, especially when it comes to sex. But since he came back, he's one of the few who realizes that his penis was controlling him at that moment instead of his mind controlling his penis. At least he recognized that the action he took was wrong.

"I may not justify what you did, " I was telling him in my not so nice voice, "but I guess I can understand why you did it. Besides, Jamal, you're right that I could have been...oh, I don't know, Jamal, I really thought I wanted to, and then I just got this feeling that it wasn't the best thing to do. You understand?"

"Yea, I get that feeling sometimes, too. ...uh, but not about sex." He smiled a sigh of relief. And I smiled back.

After we both got that out, we decided that our relationship was just going to be strickly platonic. Since he was going to be spending a great deal of time in the Virgin Islands, it wasn't fair to either one of us to start a commitment with each other. I decided that it was a good idea that we shouldn't even communicate unless he came to town to visit or for business. At first, he was reluctant to the idea. But then he accepted it because he said that keeping in touch would only bring back past feelings and cravings of seeing each other again and that it would only make our relationship stressful.

Since he leaves to go back home tomorrow, I offered that he stay at my house. He accepted. It was late and both of us knew deep down that we wanted to spend the remaining time he had left in the States together. So we sat up all night laughing at each other's corney jokes, watching movies on HBO, and just plain old enjoying each other's company. He is so much fun and I love listening to him talk just so I could hear his accent.

We finally fell asleep around 5:00. He had to get up at 9:00 the same morning to catch a cab back to the hotel to get his luggage in order to catch the flight out at noon. When he left that next morning, I offered to give him the necklace back.

"It's not like you called the engagement off and that you should feel obligated to give it back to me," he told me. "This is a gift from me...to you. We will see each other again."

At that moment he kissed me like I've never been kissed before. But I sensed that it would be my last kiss from him. I felt like I was never going to see him again. But if it is meant to be, it will be.

CHAPTER 14
I'm Coming Out
♋

"*GOD! Why am I laying in this bed, feeling like I've been run over by a truck. It feels like I've been sleeping forever. Maybe I have been. That's probably why I feel so beat up, huh? Father?...Lord, please don't let Earl come back and hit me again. I don't want to open my eyes because I'm afraid he will beat the shit...oh,...sorry God. Boy do I have a way with words. Please, Lord, give me the energy to wake up, pack and get the hell out of this house. At least for E.J.'s sake. I'm sure Nicolette's waiting on me to get to her house. I'm surprised E.J. is not in here waking me up. Lord, please let this be the last time I have to go through something like this. Help me find peace in myself. I thought I found it when I met Earl. After all of these years, I just knew he would be able to make me happy by now. Lord, he has been unsuccessful....and all he has given me is Hell....and you know that God--don't you? Sometimes I wish that you could talk to me directly. Father, if I could just walk away from this...life...that I'm living, I somehow, some way will do my best to change...*

"Doc," I heard my sister, Candy's voice say. "How's she doing now. I thought I saw her eyes move."

"Me, too," another familiar voice said.

"She's been through a great deal of trauma. Some movement accounts to reflex. But, of course, any kind of movement is a good sign. We hope she will be coming out of her coma very soon."

I think that was the doctor. I must be in a hospital. What am I doing in a hospital! I thought I was in my own bed. Lord, please help me. What is going on. How did I get here?

"I'll be back," I heard the doctor say. "In a few minutes, you guys will have to leave because visiting hours..."

"We know, Dr. Cobern...it's about that time."

Hey,...that's my homegirl, Temeka. What is she doing here. I haven't seen her in months. What am I doing here? Why come I can't wake up. Lord, please help me. I can't move. I'm talking but they can't hear me.

"Simone," my sister grabbed my hand and Temeka grabbed the other. "You gon' come out of this real soon. And when the police find Earl I hope he gets the same treatment you got--or worse. He had no right to do you like this. You should have left him a long time ago. But, that's okay now. E.J. is safe with me and..."

Candy, don't start crying. I'll be okay. I promise. This is the last time that bastard will ever lay a hand on me.

"She'll be okay," Temeka told her. "She's always been the strong one and you know this so why you trippin'."

"I know," Candy said. "But why did he have to beat her head with a bat, breakin' her arm and ankle for some stupid reason, I'm sure."

I know this mothafucka didn't bust my head with a bat. And he probably used the bat I bought for E.J. on his birthday for the Little Softball League. I'mo kick his ass once I get out of here. His dumb, stupid ass gonna regret this.

"How's she doing today?" I heard Afrikka's voice. I think she just walked through the door.

"Well, Doc says she should wake up any moment now," Candy told her.

"Yeah, it's been two days. The sooner she comes out of this coma the better her condition will be," Dana's voice came in.

"Where's Nic?" Temeka said with an attitude.

"Well, you know Nic," Dana whispered, "she doesn't like hospitals."

"Yeah, and she had some late clients anyway," Afrikka added.

"Okay, ladies, I'm sorry but visiting hours are over," a voice whispered walking through the door.

"Dr. Cobern," Candy said, "five more minutes please."

"I'm afraid not," the doctor said, "she needs plenty of rest."

"Damn, Doc," Temeka burst in, "why not?"

"Guys, he's right," Afrikka came to his aid. "The more rest she gets, the better her outcome will be."

"Misses Chicago Hope, M.D." Temeka told Afrikka. "She's been getting enough rest these last couple of days, don't you think?"

"C'mon, girls," Candy whispered, "let's be out."

When my sister, Temeka, Afrikka, and Dana left the room, I think the doctor started checking my heart rate, blood pressure and whatever else he was doing because I felt cold instruments, devices or whatever else he was using being connected to my head, chest and arms. As a matter of fact, I think I already have some shit hooked on me. What in the HELL is going on. Please, Lord, let me awaken soon!

♋

I think a couple of days have past and I remember my sister, Candy, coming by at least twice a day to visit me. I think she came during her lunch break and after work and stayed and talked to me about how close we used to be in the past. She told me that she was taking care of E.J. and that he was in school. She also told me that she didn't want to bring him here to see me in the condition that I am in now and that she wants E.J. to always remember how beautiful I am. She told me that he misses me very much and can't wait for me to return from my business trip. She was so happy to tell me how glad she was that I dropped him off at her house right before this happened. Boy, was I ever so grateful, too. I wouldn't want him to see me like this. I was then curious to know why E.J. never asked her to call me. Today, she told me that she read a letter to E.J., supposingly from me, telling him how much I miss him and can't wait to get back home to see him and apologizing for not calling him, telling him that they are in a very distant country and that her company cannot afford telephone calls back to the States. And, of course, she said that he believed every word she said.

    I had twelve brothers and sisters and Candy is forty years old, and she is also the oldest. My mom and dad had all of us back to back. Man, they was doing some fucking back then. I'm twenty-eight years old, so that means that my mom popped out a brotha or sista every year. Ain't that some shit? And where are they now? I never knew my pops. Candy said the last time she saw him that she was about thirteen years old, shortly after I was born. I remember her telling me that she never missed him because he was never home that much anyway--only to fuck mom, beat her, then he would leave a little stash in the bathroom, which one of my brothers would use to buy drugs, booze, or some other unnecessary bullshit that caused trouble. As a matter of fact, that's how my mom got hooked on heroine. My older brother, James, introduced her to it by lying to her and telling her that it would make her feel better, and make her not worry so much about pops and what he doing, how he doing it, and who he doing it with. Then, the ripple effect occurred--most of my other brothers and sisters got hooked on that shit, too. And one by one I witnessed six of them die, either on the streets or on the living room floor. Four died from an overdose of the stuff and the other two died trying to steal the stuff. Two more brothers got shot trying to rob a federal state bank. They actually hadn't ever been in no real trouble, it was their first offense and last offense--what a waste! All I have left is two sisters, Candy and Rita, and a brother, Shelton. Candy, for her being the oldest and seeing all that is to see, is the wisest person I know. She always took care of me and always, I mean always, remained the most stable person in our family. She has a good head on her shoulders and I don't know how she did it for all of these years. The Lord has truly blessed her with a stable, good paying job. And now she has just started thinking about marriage and a family of her own. She's been dating some man I've never met yet but I'm sure that it will soon take a change for the better. Rita ran off with some man when she was twenty and we only get postcards from her every now and then letting us know that she is still alive and doing well. She never told us why she just up and left. I guess she couldn't take the heat. And Shelton, well, he is the successor in our family, next to Candy. Another stable intelligent sibling who has a wife and family hundreds of miles away from this place. He was lucky...no fortunate enough to get a scholarship to an elite university, and went to medical school. And now he's a famous doctor denying his past to the public. In a way, his behavior may not seem justifiable, but I understand. He only calls Candy on special occasions and holidays. We have not seen him since he went off to school, and he has never asked us to visit, and we don't ask either.

  If it wasn't for Candy I would probably have ended up like one of my brothers or sisters, God bless their souls. For some reason, Candy took a liking to me. She always tells me that I remind her of the younger version of herself, but I'm not allowing that side to show. I always think about that because I worship Candy next to God, but I will never let her know that. My grandparents also helped raised me. I'm sure glad they ain't around to see me in this place now. My grandfather was a preacher, and my grandmother, a housewife and the church musician. If they were still alive they would have been over here so fast trying to perform an exorcism or something, but they both died a few years ago. I was real close to them, even after what my grandfather did to me when I was younger, because they helped take care of me. I still haven't forgotten about what Papa used to do to me..

I think about my mom sometimes, wondering where she is, how she's doing and if she's still living. Every now and then when I'd pass the bridge I would see her, get out the car, and give her a little money. It's funny, ya know, she don't even recognize her own daughter anymore. Her mind is gone now. I don't understand how she can eat out of garbage cans, pick up nasty ass leftovers off of the ground, and then wonder around wearing contaminated clothes. Candy and I tried repeatedly to take her off the streets but she would yell at us, calling us murderers, aliens, and all kind of crap. One time the police wanted to arrest us for trying to kidnap a homeless person. Can you believe that shit? They should want somebody to take people like my mom off the streets. It's not like we could hold her up for a ransom. Now, I have just accepted the fact that my mom has fallen in the category of being a statistic or a menace to society and ain't nothing nobody can do about it.

Afrikka has come by at least once a day and in her busy schedule she spends at least an hour or so just talking to me. A couple of times, Ed came along with her. They are so funny together.

And Dana comes by about once a day, too. I guess whenever she get a break between clients. She talks to me with so much depression in her voice it's sickening. She is making it hard on me.

Nic, has only been here one time 'cause she so busy with her 'internship', and some new guy, she doesn't have time.

Brad came by to say hey and bring something for me. Probably the company flowers. He mentioned having piles of paperwork in the place where his desk used to be. He said he misses my smile and good humor, and that ol' Elsie, I mean Elyse, was offering to help out, so I should hurry up and get better before he either loses his job or his wife.

Some of the guys in the band came one day--I couldn't tell who all was here, but I know they were from the club cause my room smelled like a brewery for quite some time. I think the smell got caught in my nose or something and I just couldn't get it off my mind.

Henry brought some fan mail and stuff, and it's funny how mushy people get when they think you can't hear'm, cause he read every one of those letters out loud to me, with so much feeling, even I wanted to cry. He said a lot of folks were asking about me and that I should hurry up and get better so we could throw a big bash and make a lot of money, since everybody's so anxious to see me. I will have to tease him when I get better--I didn't know he cared so much.

And out of all of my friends who I grew up with in the hood, Temeka's ghetto ass is the only homie who has come by to see me. And the way word spreads, I'm sure they know by now. Ain't that some shit. I just met Afrikka, Dana, and Nic almost a year ago, and they come see me but my so called 'friends for life' don't know a nigga when she down. I guess I know who my friends are now. I just can't wait til they run up in my face trying to get into one of my shows free or som'thin. Lord, I think I'm ready...

"Her eyes are moving," Afrikka said. "Get the doctor, Ed."

I was coming out of my Snow White nap when I felt the doctor hooking and disconnecting shit to my head, chest, and arms again. It seems like he is taking all of the time in the world to do what he has to do. But I guess I should feel grateful and all. A few hours had passed and my friends, and Candy allowed me to rest as if I didn't get enough already.

When I woke this last time Afrikka, Dana and Nic were sitting in my room. I sat up and they looked at me with amazement. For some reason I felt refreshed like I just took a long nap. Damn, I guess I did, huh.

"Well," I looked at all three of them, "ya'll just gon' sit there and look at me like I'm a mannequin or some other related shit...or we gonna talk."

Afrikka stared at me, Dana had her head down, and Nic, well, her mind was somewhere else. They kept their distance.

"How are you feeling?" Dana raised her head.

"Okay, I guess. I mean, I did get beat up, right? How am I suppose to feel?"

Afrikka stood up and walked toward me.

"Candy was in here earlier on her lunch break. I don't know if she told you everything that happened to you or if the doctor told you."

"No," I said lying. It took me a little while to remember, but I knew everything that went on. "Tell me, please."

Afrikka looked at Dana, Dana looked at Nic, and Nic just looked. Then suddenly, I heard a phone ringing and I know it wasn't mine.

"Oh," Nic burst out, "sorry for the interruption, Simone. But it's probably Robert calling me from work. I'll be right outside for a second." She smiled and ran out the room before anybody got a word or two out.

"Did she say Rodrick or Robert? " I asked.

Dana burst out, "Robert. The new guy Ed set her up with, you know, about a week ago at Nic's little 'getting over Rodrick' party," she told me.

"Damn, that girl moves fast," I said aloud.

There was silence again and Dana walked over to the window. Man, she has lost so much weight. I know I haven't been in here this long. She's almost Nic's size or maybe smaller.

"Dana," I said to her, "you lookin' real good, girl. I'd hate to be in the same place with you 'cause I won't get no play....but then again, I still look good," I looked around in the mirror, "even with this big ass bandage around my head and a broken arm and ankle."

"Simone!" Dana yelled to me as she turned around. "We're not here about me, Simone. We're here for you...and you....you act like you don't know or even care why or how you got here."

For a minute there, I thought Dana was someone else. She has never expressed herself like that before. Deep down I know why and how I got here, but for some reason, it really doesn't bother me as much as it bothers them... well, Dana, especially, I guess. Afrikka just sat there because she knows me now. I'm closer to her than anyone else, and if something is bothering me she would be the first person to point it out. Nic, I think, obviously has a negative vibe around me for some reason. It's like she wants to care and will go out her way to show it, but at the same time...I don't feel that she cares.

"Dana," I finally spoke out, "I kinda know why and how I got here. The last thing I remember was Earl... me and Earl were arguing over something I don't remember...and that's how it always is anyway...well...I called Henry at the club to tell him that I was gonna be a little late, and...I remember he grabbed E.J.'s bat and was threatening me with it if I walked out the door. It's like he knew, ya know, that at that moment...he knew that it was my last time ever seeing him again...ever."

I paused for a moment and for one of the very few times in my life, I allowed myself to...feel. Because of this I knew I could not hold back my tears. I put my head into my chest and started crying, not uncontrollably...but calmly and with much relief. I was feeling a flashback of not the physical pain, but the emotional pain that I have held for so long inside. Dana just stood at the window and looked at me with this sunkin' look on her face. Afrikka sat in the chair and I felt her eyes glaring at me. At that moment, Nic ran through the door with a huge smile on her face, then she felt a change in the tension of the room and she slowly looked around at everyone and then back at me and she walked over to me, put her hand on my back, and rubbed it, gently, up and down. At that moment, for the first time...I think that she felt my pain.

"Simone," Nic grabbed my hand, "Dr. Cobern just walked by and told me that you should be going home in a few days."

"I can't go home," I whispered to her.

"No...home with me. You and E.J." Nic added.

Afrikka stood up and grabbed the end of my bed. Then she spoke.

"Simone, I don't know if Candy told you earlier but...Earl is missing. No one has seen him since he...since...after he did this to you. The police are still looking for him because he's also wanted for delinquent traffic tickets...and uh...the police told Candy that he may have been the one who killed that man in that robbery on the southside a couple of weeks ago! They said something about the prints he left on the bat matching the ones on a gun that was found around the corner from the robbery."

"That's why a cop is standing outside of your door," Dana added.

"You mean he may be a murderer, too?" I asked but no one answered.

"Candy has been taking care of E.J." Nic smiled. "And Candy's a clever one, you know, she told E.J. that you were out of town on an emergency business trip and you can only write because the phone lines were down...and guess what?..Candy self-addressed letters to E.J. saying that they were from you and he actually believes it. He's been going to school and acting just fine. It's funny that he hasn't asked about his daddy yet."

I smiled. "That's my boy! He so smart, I don't have to say a word to him--he know his daddy ain't 'bout shit."

"So what now?" Nic broke out. "I mean a lady from the battered women's shelter stopped by a few times and asked us if you were going to press charges against Earl or just look over it like she say most women in your situation ends up doing anyway. "

There goes Nic back to her normal self, as if she clicked her true colors back on.

"What the hell you talkin' 'bout, Nic," I struck back. "You don't know me very well. This is the first and the last time Earl has ever beat the shit out of me like this and where you gettin' off puttin' me in the same category as those so-called other women you talkin' about."

"I don't think she meant it that way," Dana said taking up for Nic.

"I just don't understand how you could let Earl, or any man, touch you that way that Earl's been doing....that's all," Nic said as she walked off and sat in the chair Afrikka was sitting in earlier.

"Nicolette...I don't think..." Afrikka was saying as I interrupted.

"Naw, Afrikka. I got this. Let me tell you something, Nic, that I've been wantin' to get out for a while. How can a person, a girl like you talk whose been so damn sheltered all of her life, livin' in a big-ass, oversized crib far from any nigga in sight, know anything about relationships or about other people in general, when you don't have a relationship with the only person you grew up with in your life...yo daddy. You can't even talk to your daddy or tell him how you feel or think...so why do YO half-white ass let your daddy treat you the way he does, huh? You are no better that me...you may have one parent but physically and emotionally, he's never there. Therefore...we're somewhat the same except I grew up in the ghetto, in the real world, and not some fake-ass fantasy...and another thing--when I get out of here, I'm going to do something about my problem. I'm going to make sure Earl will never breathe fresh air again in his life...Now, what you gon' do about your problem?"

It was so quiet in here that you could hear people talking in the next room. I'm glad I got that out. I had to tell Nic about herself.

"What are you trying to say?" Afrikka asked me.

I was hot now. Nic made me click now.

"I'm saying. I'mo kill Earl...just wait till I find him...I ain't lying."

"Aw, come on," Dana spoke out. "You talking crazy. I know you are extremely angry about what he did to you, and you got every reason to be, but you don't want to spend the rest of your life in jail over him."

"Simone maybe we should let you rest before you get your blood pressure all up, 'cause I know you ain't thinking about what you're saying." Afrikka added. "Earl is not worth giving up your freedom and E.J. growing up without a mother."

Afrikka stood there at the end of my bed and stared at me as if she was reading my mind. Dana walked over to the window and stared outside like she was doing before. And Nic, sat in the chair, looking down at the scratch she made on her Joan and David's. No one said a word, not to me, not to each other. I believe all three of them want Earl dead just as much as I do. I think Nic wants him dead the most to ease the pain she feels toward her dad. After a few minutes no one said a word. I closed my eyes only to awaken a few hours later with no one present.

♋

The nurses came in and tried to nurse my muscles back to health. It felt like they were trying to kill me or put me back into a coma. They were not just moving my legs and arms up and down or back and forth--they were throwing and tossing my limbs as if they were disconnected from my body. Maybe they do this so much that they have lost their touch with reality and have forgotten that we are human, too.

I decided to get my lazy ass up and go for a morning stroll. As I looked out the window, I take into account how huge this hospital is. Maybe I can find a cute, rich doctor who can sweep me off of my feet. Then he can, fo' sure, nurse me back to health.

Where am I going? I think I am lost. Can you believe it? How can a person get lost in a hospital? But, I guess anything is possible. Surgery room? No, I don't think I want to go in there. Let me see what's behind door number two. Damn, no wonder so many doctors and nurses get addicted to drugs--all of this stuff locked behind a glass cabinet. I better get out of here before they ship me off to some drug rehab center way out the country somewhere.

Chapel. Humm...I've never been to an actual hospital chapel. I used to see this on TV, but I never knew it actually existed. Brad, when he came to drop off the company flowers yesterday, did tell me that I should visit the chapel. But my mind was somewhere else yesterday, I personally thought he was losing his mind. Let me see what's in here. Look at me. Wearing a hospital gown in God's house. But then again, I am in a hospital. And I'm sure God won't punish me for the way I dress...will he?

"Excuse me," an older lady told me when she bumped into me heading out the chapel door.

Her eyes were full of tears. Maybe her husband is dying of cancer...or maybe her son has just had a bad car accident... or maybe her daughter just had her granddaughter, and she's happy because this is her first grandchild...or sad that her daughter has brought a child into this unforgiving, ungrateful, violent, selfish, and crazy world. E.J. is the best thing that has ever happened to me, but I sometimes wonder what direction would I have chosen if it wasn't for E.J., or where would I be now and, even, who would I have become if I didn't have E.J. Then, I sometimes regret bringing a child into a world full of much pain and little pleasure. I want the best for E.J., and I don't want him to have to go through the hell, pain, and suffering that I experienced for nearly twenty-nine, long-ass years.

"Ma'am" I heard a man's voice around the corner, "are you okay?"

I looked back and saw a black man in a watered down priest uniform holding a small notepad and pen and I notice that he is talking to me.

"Yes," I answered, "why you asked?"

"Well," he walked toward me, "you're sitting there with your head down like you have lost your best friend."

I just rolled my eyes at him and turned back around because he don't know me, my problems, and what I have been through. What is he doing all up in my mix anyway. Oh, Lord,...Lord, please don't let him stop and talk to me. Lord...give me the strength to not cuss him out.

"Don't too many sistas come in here," he said.

And he has the nerve to sit beside me like I asked him to. I don't want to be bothered right now. Plus, I can't stand preachers, anyway.

"So, what's your name?" he asked.

I looked at him. Lord...give me the strength.

"....Simone, " thank you Lord 'cause you know I wanted to cuss him so bad.

"What physical ailment brings you to the hospital?" he asked.

Now he is getting a little bit too personal. I can't believe he is trying to flirt with me. They are all the same. Lord, why do the people who are supposed to represent you act a fool and end up becoming perverts and have the nerve to go around saying 'in Jesus name' all the time. How hypocritical can you get? Please, Lord...save me from this child molester.

"What's it to you?" I asked.

"I'm just being friendly and...," he responded, "...my job is to..."

"You don't have to explain yo' job," I cut him off, "ya'll are all the same."

"It seems as if you've had some negative past experiences with people who was called to the Lord's work," he suggested.

Let me re-evaluate myself. He may not even act like my grandfather. As a matter of fact, he isn't my grandfather. Let me stop trippin'. I smiled and tried to change the subject.

"I'm from around here," I told him, "...I never seen a black priest before."

"Well," he smiled with a mouth full of dentures because as old as he is, there is no way that his real teeth could have survived a century, "there is a first time for everything."

I smiled, "yeah, there is...so how long have you been a priest?"

"About thirty years now," he answered.

"Do you have any grandkids?" I asked him.

"I have three," he smiled, "I love all of my baby girls. But they're grown now."

Girls! ...and he's smiling.

"Did they ever live with you when they were children?"

"Well," he sighed, he's gotta be holding back something 'cause he's taking too long to answer, "the youngest used to spend her summers with me and my wife since we lived in the same city, but the other two lived two thousand miles away, so I was happy to see them any chance we could get."

"So what did the two, or three of you do in the summers?"

"Oh..." he laughed. "We used to go swimming, to the fair and circus, whichever one came that summer, to the zoo....and I used to carry Stacie to the lake...fishing with me every other weekend. We used to have so much fun...me and Stacie...at the lake...'cause she would always...."

"You used to take her to the lake...alone?" I cut him off, "...where was your wife, her grandmother?"

He probably took advantage of her...touching her in places she didn't want to be touched...places where she felt uncomfortable...nasty...dirty..

"Her grandmother didn't like the lake...she couldn't stand those nasty water mosquitoes," he paused because I think he caught on to my change in attitude, "...is something bothering you?"

Should I tell him? I've never talked to anyone about my grandfather before and I don't think I could tell a stranger. Well, maybe I can because I can spill my guts and never see him again.

"Well..." I paused, "...my grandfather used to do all of those things with me, but he used to...he started too..it wasn't my fault."

"What did he do? Simone," he whispered tenderly, "...whatever he did, it wasn't your fault...because you were a little girl and he was the adult, in charge."

"He used to touch me...," I blurted out sounding like a pouty two year old , ".....and...my grandmama never knew.....and...my grandmama... well, she would have never believed me anyway," I mumbled, "...he could do no wrong...plus, he was pastor of the largest church in the area...no one would have ever believed that he could have committed an act so vicious...so I kept my mouth shut like a good little girl."

"And you told not a soul of what he..."

"Not a soul," I told him, "I was too ashamed...too embarrassed and too hurt to tell anyone. I was only nine years old. He was my grandfather. A man I admired and loved all of my life. What was I supposed to do?"

"You did what you thought was best at that time," he said. "Is he still living?"

"No, thank God!" I got angry, "he died in his sleep when I was twenty-two and my grandmother died less than a year later from a broken heart."

"Are you still angry about what he did?" he asked.

"Yes....yes....I am," I told him, "and I don't want to be. I want to forgive him for his...his perverted behaviors...but I don't know how."

"In the past..." he paused, " ...how have you forgiven someone?"

I sat there and I thought about ways I have forgiven Earl, Brad for his stupid, prank tricks, Temeka, and just recently, Nic.

"Well..." I thought, "I've confronted the person and told them exactly how I feel, I've cussed people out, I've ignored them and just said 'Fuc...' I mean...I've just gotten over it, and sometimes I've even damned their souls to hell...I know that wasn't a good thing."

I turned and slowly looked at him waiting for his attack on me brought by that last statement I made. But, he just looked at me and smiled.

"Think of me as a friend instead of a priest, or a preacher right now," he told me," ...because I'm human and those same so-called resolution techniques you just said, I've tried them before, too...but they never brought about forgiveness."

"So you actually cursed someone out?" I asked, "...you don't have to answer that..."

I felt so stupid. He just smiled, again.

"Since your grandfather is no longer on earth...you say you want to forgive him for what he did to you, so how can you do it?"

"I've tried just to get over it," I told him because that's what I have been doing.

He looked at me and smiled...again.

"And you haven't gotten over it, have you?" he asked me.

"Well..." I thought, "...not really...I...I..."

"Because you're still angry about what he did to you..." I had to cut in. "Yes! yes!...I'm supposed to be!" I told him.

"But, he's no longer with us, Simone," he paused, "...you can't forgive anybody without finding some way to get rid of the anger you have toward that person...and I sense, still, that you have much anger toward him."

"Well what am I supposed to do?" I asked him knowing that he is right. I am still past angry about what that dog did to me. "I've been praying and praying and praying...asking God to grant me the strength, the courage to forgive him for what he did to me...but I think God is not listening. Why?"

"Oh, God is listening, Simone. Have faith in that..." he grabbed my hand and at that moment, I didn't feel like he was coming on to me...I felt that he felt my pain, sincerely...and his hand, somehow, attached to mine brought about a sense of comfort, of peace,"...and miracles don't happen over night. Say you want a job...are you going to pray and just wait on Uncle Sam to come knocking on your door? Say you want to become an actress...are you just going to pray and wait on God to bring John Singleton to your living room holding a script for you to memorize for his next movie? "

"How do you know John Singleton?" I asked.

"I did see Rosewood..." he added, "...but do you get my point?"

"Yes," I laughed thinking that he is too old to be trying to stay hip with 90's movies. He should be somewhere still watching Let's Do It Again.

"But my grandfather is dead...how am I..." I asked.

"Simone..." he cut me off, "...pray about it...pray for God to show you a way for you to get rid of any anger that you have toward your grandfather, because that's the only way you can find forgiveness, and peace...trust me!"

He slowly released my hand and placed it on my lap, stood up and walked toward the door.
"Where are you going?" I asked him.
"I'll pray for you too," he looked back, "God is with you."
"Hey, will I see you again?" I asked.
He turned around slowly and just...smiled.
"What's your name!" I screamed. "You never told me your name."
As he was closing the door behind him, I looked down and noticed that he left his small notepad and pen. I grabbed them and ran out the door only to find that he was nowhere in sight. This is strange. No trace of any priest. No less, a black man at all in this hall. I was too embarressed to ask anyone if they'd seen a black man in a priest uniform. Hell, he might not even work here. I better go back in the chapel 'cause I am looking crazy standing in the middle of the hall like I'm lost, again.
As I walk toward the altar and sit here, holding that stranger's pad and pen, I began to think about what he said. I *am* still angry. But, how...how can I release this...this hateful emotion that I have toward my grandfather. Hey... hey...he must have been an angel sent by the Lord, himself...I've got it. God has revealed himself through him.
"Oh, help me, Lord, to release this anger! You've shown me how destructive holding on to anger can be, now show me how to find peace! I wish I had that priest here...that angel. Thank you God for sending him. Thank you for showing up...for hearing my prayers...you have always come through for me, even if it takes getting me to the hospital, for me to listen. I understand, God....oh, yes, Lord...I will. I will talk to Papa just as if he were here....No...I'll write him a letter to say everything I need to say to release myself from this

pain, anger and shame that I have been carrying with me for almost twenty years. That's the only way I can have peace. That's why he came to me and left his pad and pen here. Thank you, Lord. Is there anything else I need to do?...and I will leave it in your hands. That's it, I'm gone write this letter...right now...in front of you, God, and I will leave it with you, God. This will symbolize the beginning of my long awaited freedom.

Dear Papa,

    Before you died, there was so much I wanted to tell you...so much I wanted to say...

CHAPTER 15
Sometimes You Feel Like a Nut

Oh, Lord, please don't let me run into Weston ' Worrisome ' because I am not in the mood for his bougie attitude today. And please don't let me see Sydney. He's such a great friend but I really don't have time to talk to him right now.

"Afrikka," I hope that's not Sydney calling my name. It is...whew...better him than Weston.

"Sydney," I kept walking as he was trying to catch up with me, "I've got to get to my class. I need a little bit of preparation for Textiles."

"I know Afrikka..." he kept bothering me, "...but I've got to talk to you."

"Can it wait?" I begged him.

"No..." he grabbed my arm, "you're the closest friend I have working here and I don't trust anybody about what I have to say."

I stopped...realizing the seriousness in his voice.

"Sydney..." I looked him in his eyes, "...is it that bad?"

He dropped his head into his chest and inhaled....then exhaled.

"Yes," he whispered.

"Okay..." I gave in, "...class doesn't start until another twenty minutes. Let me go set up my classroom, put a lesson on the board just in case our conversation runs over, and I'll meet you in the courtyard."

"Thank you," he mumbled.

I hurriedly walked to my class, laid the fabrics out on the showcase tables, labeled them, and wrote a lesson on the board all in less than seven minutes. I then grabbed my purse, my art pad and headed toward the courtyard.

"Miss Afrikka," Weston's voice caught me.

"Mr. Worrisome," I mumbled. I hope he didn't hear me.

I turned around and stopped dead in my place so he wouldn't see what direction I was heading toward.

"What are you doing after class today?" he asked.

I don't have time for another one of his boring meetings.

"Well," I tried to think of something to say, "...I ...a friend of mine just got out of the hospital so I have to rush to her house after class to make sure she has everything she needs....you know how that is."

Well, at least I wasn't lying, even though Simone has been out for a few days now. I think she is probably going back to work pretty soon.

"I was thinking that maybe you and I could go have dinner at this new restaurant that just opened down the street," he suggested.

Oh, no he didn't. I wouldn't go to a dog fight in the middle of nowhere with Weston William Smith. Not even if he had all the money in the world.

"No," I told him straight out, "What I do with my co-workers remains business that never turns personal."

"Oh, c'mon..." he laughed with his cheeks just shaking side to side. He just spoiled my appetite for any food, "...it's just dinner."

"Maybe we can have lunch in the lounge," I suggested, " 'cause my personal life begins the second I walk out of this building."

He looked at me up and down but mostly down.

"Well, I'll take a raincheck on that," he said walking off.

Oh, no he didn't. 'I'll take a raincheck' like I asked him to lunch. The nerve of him. His nasty, high-booty ass is not gonna get to me. Let me head toward the courtyard. There Sydney is - waiting patiently, sitting on the bench under the tree. Everytime he has to talk to me about something, it's always been about relational issues between him and his boyfriend. I think he just likes to talk about him so he comes up with these strange problems for me to help him solve like I know anything about relationships--moreless, a homosexual relationship.

"Sydney..." I sat down looking at him, "...what's wrong this time?"

He just looked at me.

"Okay," I said, "give me the scenario for me to analyze. And remember I charge by the hour," I joked trying to lighten the mood.

He sat there with his lips perched and looked at me like I already knew what was going on.

"Okay, Sydney, give me something?" I asked.

"I'll give you my scenario," he finally said something, "...a man falls in love with another man...they decide to move in with each other...things are going great until one of the men cheat on the other while he was away on a business trip...the other man forgave him after a while because it was just a one night stand...however, a year later the man he cheated on finds out that he is Hiv-Positive..."

Sydney stopped. I can't believe what I am hearing. This can't be true. I do remember him telling me that Don took a business trip about a year ago and that he had a promiscuous affair after getting drunk at a social ball and that they both worked things out after a number of confrontations, a separation and a period of no communication. I hope this scenario is different. Maybe he's just testing me to see how I would react to that situation. I don't know how to react if this were true. I've never met no one who has AIDS or has even been tested Hiv-Positive. After taking a class about a year ago, I do remember that people don't die just because they test positive, they die only if they develop full blown AIDS.

I grabbed Sydney's hand because that was the only thing I knew how to do. I don't have the words to express my sympathy. I really don't know what to say...how to feel...or what to think. This is all so new to me.

"So when did you find this out?" I finally got some words out.

"This morning...I called the clinic as soon as I got to work," he mumbled,

"I thought since I got tested a couple of weeks ago...that everything would be fine because I've never cheated on Don and he told me he hasn't since that last incident...so this morning I was positive that the results were going to be negative...and I don't think I can teach my nine o'clock class."

Sydney sat there while I held his hand and I was waiting for him to burst in tears because he is so emotional. But he just sat there, tearless, and just stared into the grass. No expression on his face. Just a sunkin', sad look.

"What are you going to do?" I asked.

"I don't know," he answered.

"Are you going to tell Don?" I asked.

"I don't know," he answered again.

We sat there. I don't think neither one of us knew what to say. Lord, knows I didn't.

"It's not the end of the world," I told him.

"Oh, knowing that you're going to die is not the end of the world!" he got loud and threw my hand, that was once so gently against his, on the hard bench.

"Ouch! That hurt... I'm sorry, I didn't mean...."

"Oh, Afrikka, I'm sorry..I just don't know how to feel..what to say or do." he said reaching for my hand and checking to see if it was okay. I was happy he finally showed some type of emotion. I was beginning to think that he wasn't human. He jumped off of the bench like his pants were on fire or something and threw himself against the tree and slowly allowed his body to fall to the ground. I turned around and looked at him, waiting until I thought it was safe for me to respond to his last statement.

"No, it's not the end of the world," I stared at him, "...and you wanna know why?"
This time I waited for him to respond.
"...yeah," he stared back at me.
"We all know that we are going to die someday...I know that I'm going to die someday...I don't know how but..." I started, "...but that doesn't mean that you have to stop living."
"That's easy for you to say," he told me. "Because, at least, you don't know how you're going to die."
"And you don't know, either, how you're going to die," I threw back at him.
"I'm going to die because I know that I'm going to get AIDS sometime, I may not know exactly when, and die."
"But you can't think that far ahead. You don't know if you're going to die from AIDS. You may die in a car accident next week, or from a drive by shooting in the hood tonight, or next year you could be walking downtown and get stabbed by some common thief and die in the streets. So what I'm trying to say is testing positive doesn't mean that your life is going to end tomorrow, next week, next year or even in ten years. I mean look at Magic Johnson--he was tested positive I don't know how many years ago, and look at him--he's still living, he's never developed full-blown AIDS, and you know what else he's doing...he's living his life as if he has forgotten what Hiv-Positive mean," I can't believe I said that.
Sydney sat there as if he was absorbing what I was actually saying.
"But what am I suppose to do now?..." he asked "...now that I know? How am I suppose to cope?"
He looked at me like I had all the answers. I'm no psychologist. I don't know anything about that issue. What can I say?

"Sydney...what do you think you should do?" I asked as I walked toward him and sat down beside him. "I can't make all of the decisions for you. But whatever you want me to do to help you ease this pain, I will always be here for you."

"I don't know where to start," he said. "Maybe God is punishing me for being gay--for commiting the ultimate sin on top of sin--as other people may see it."

"No," I put my other hand on top of his, "if you believed that God is punishing you for that, then why does he allow innocent babies and children to die. So don't think it's a personal vendetta toward you from God. I mean, I don't know why God allows things like that to happen to anybody...to you...to the most caring and innocent people on earth. But, we can't get mad at God, you know...I don't know...I'm confused too..."

He looked away as if he was searching for answers in the sky.

"Did the clinic you went to have any type of assistance programs or did they offer you any help, counseling...." I was wondering.

"Yeah," he said as I slowly grabbed his hand again, "I was so angry and upset after I heard the lady tell me my results, that I just hung up the phone. But I do remember that when I called the hotline waiting for the doctor to pick up so that I can give 'em my anonymous i.d. number, I was listening to the hold announcements and I do remember it advertising counseling sessions for gay men who tested positive but I didn't catch when or where....just forget about it...I deserved this...I should just accept the fact that I'm going to die..."

"Shut up," I told him, "you're not going to die."

We sat there looking into the sky. I looked at my watch and noticed that my class will start in a couple of minutes. I didn't want to leave Sydney. Not while he was like this. What if he's thinking suicide then I'll really feel bad if he up and kills himself. Right now he needs me. I would not dare leave anyone alone in a situation like this at this moment, especially not while he honestly feels that he has been given a death sentence.

"What is the name of the clinic you went to?" I asked.

"Northpark Central," I told me.

"Meet me at my car in ten minutes," I told him as I was getting up. He stood up right behind me.

"What? I've got to teach this class in less than a minute."

"Not today," I pushed him. "Meet me at my car and I'm gonna take care of everything."

I walked toward the office as he stood there in confusion. I went straight to the dean's office and requested two teacher assistants immediately to take Sydney's and my place for the day. Hell, those assistants get paid for doing nothing anyway. So it's about time they get put to work and make use of themselves. I called the clinic and asked if Sydney and I could come in for counseling. I told them the situation and they were so understanding and requested that we come in as soon as possible. I guess that's what they get paid for is to be understanding. But then again, most people who are in that type of profession are compassionate at heart anyway.

Finally, I'm at the car and Sydney is nowhere around. Damn, where did he run off to? I can't believe...

"Sydney," I yelled at him as he was sitting on the curve.

I decided to walk over to where he was sitting. He was sitting there as if his life is over already. I sat beside him on the curve and put my arm around his shoulder. I waited for him to speak.

"You know, Afrikka," he was slurring, "I can't believe that this is happening to me. I thought that I was always so careful. And I fell in love with the only man I trusted."

I sat there just listening. He needed a good ear right now.

"I remember a time when my father used to make me play football, and basketball and all of those manly sports because, I guess, at an early age I think he suspected I was gay," he spoke out, "...but before that, he used to beat me everytime I cried...everytime my feelings got hurt...I cried...and then he would beat me and I would cry a little more...I thought it was normal to cry....everytime I watched the Discovery channel and would witness animal slayings...I would cry...and I guess that's why I became a vegetarian...he used to be so strict...so overprotective of me making sure I didn't play with my little sister...and I grew up being curious about how girls played and what they played with, other than dolls....so I played by myself all of the time...I was so lonely..."

Listening to this...I can't believe what I am hearing. I should be grateful my family didn't treat me like that.

"It's funny," he laughed, "my mother, after I came out the closet and told her I was gay; I introduced her to Don....I remember she told me that Don is gonna be the death of me...and...mom is right...she was always right...and my father...pops stop speaking to me when he found out. Mama used to beg him to at least face the fact that his son was gay. But...being his only son...he couldn't live with that. So he thought that it is better to just pretend that he never had a son. So...when I go home to visit every Thanksgiving...my sister is there, my mom is there...and always...mom sets a plate for pops but...but when I'm there his chair is always empty. He locks himself in the room the entire weekend. I haven't seen my father in almost eight years. Mom takes a picture every year so I can remember what he looks like and she would have to sneak and mail it to me. Man...pops may throw a party when he finds out the good news--as he may describe it."

He stopped and I was waiting for him to tell me something else but he just sat there. I didn't want to just hop up and drag him to the car. I am moving at his pace...whenever he is ready.

"Where are we going?" he asked.

"I set an appointment up with a counselor, Jay Jones, at the clinic," I told him, "'cause I don't have any answers on what you need to do and you seem pretty uncertain about all this yourself. I love you, Sydney, and you don't have to go through this alone. After this first meeting with Jay, you will have the strength to tell Don because I know you're scared. It's okay to be scared. It's normal. And if Don loves you, which I know and you know he does, you two can work this through to live a normal, healthy life together."

I smiled to give him reassurance that everything is going to be okay. After a few minutes he stood up, grabbed my hand and pulled me up from the sidewalk.

"Let's do this," he whispered.

♋

At the clinic we didn't have to wait two minutes before his counselor, Jay Jones, introduced himself. He took us back to a small conference room where we sat behind a table as if we were having group session. Jay admitted that he too is gay and he contracted the virus through casual sex ten years ago. He is a living example that people can live a full, healthy life being HIV-Positive. And you should have seen the look on

Sydney's face--he thought Jay was a walking miracle. Jay spent about an hour educating us on the Who, What, Where, When, How, and Why's of Hiv and AIDS. This was so informative to me because it uncovered many myths about the virus and the disease that I once believed in the past. After that, Jay allowed us to ask questions and, of course, Sydney was amazed at the information he was receiving.

Afterwards, Jay walked us through the emotional reactions or themes that seem typical of most clients, especially homosexual clients. He told us that within a homosexual's emotional state, there is often a struggle with what they perceive as two strikes against them. The first strike is that they have to adjust to being gay, and second, they have to adjust to being gay and testing Hiv-Positive. Other issues and responses that may arise, he says, that he may face are denial, anger and rage, and guilt and shame. Jay discussed those issues in brief detail.

Soon, Jay discussed what infected people can do now. He told Sydney that keeping a positive attitude and well-being and a healthy lifestyle is the key to a longer life. He named some steps on what he did to remain so healthy because Sydney was so curious. He told us that first, he took charge of his illness, he avoided infecting others by wearing condoms if he did have sex with someone else who knew he was infected, he consulted a doctor for nutritional advice, he sought legal help for advice on his rights, support and future decisions....but the main thing that is keeping him so healthy, he thinks is that he accepted the fact that he is infected and he is doing more of the things he always wanted to do--travel, have a pet farm, and made additional minor lifestyle changes.

After the discussion, Jay highly recommended to Sydney that Don should come in to be tested because more than likely, he is the carrier. He also suggested that both of them should join a community support group that meets every Tuesday and Thursday nights at 7:00 here at the clinic that is open to gay men living with the AIDS virus.

Jay was so compassionate and I could sense that Syndey was more than comfortable around him. We left the clinic with more information than I expected. I even found out that the fastest growing segment of the population contracting the disease is African-American females--now that's scary!

We sat in the car of the fashion institute's parking lot for about fifteen minutes without saying a word to each other. I was so enlightened by what I experienced that I forgot that Sydney was in my car. I obtained enough information in three hours to become a public speaker for AIDS awareness and prevention it seems.

"What are you thinking?" I asked Sydney.

He turned around with this weird but concerned smile on his face. Maybe I shouldn't have asked the question.

"I trust you, Afrikka," he finally spoke, "I knew that when I told you that I was positive that you wouldn't run away...but...I didn't expect that you would go out of your way to do this for me."

I didn't know what to say, so I just smiled back.

"You know..." he paused, "...earlier I was thinking that I should just go home and kill Don...because he did this to me...I was just an innocent and helpless victim and how dare he do this to me!!!!!...."

Man, I'm glad it was my day to teach class because I would've hated to hear about Sydney on the five o'clock news.

" ...but..." he paused again, "but after hearing Jay today...it's made me realize that it's not Don's fault...he was just a victim too...we all are."

"Yes we are," I reassured him.

"I better go," he told me opening the car door, "I'm going home and tell my man the news he doesn't want to hear...but...he has to before it's too late."
"It'll be okay," I told him letting go of his hand, "remember what Jay said...it's not the end of the world...he's a living example."
"I love you, Afrikka," he leaned back over and hugged me, "I don't know what I would have done without you."
I sat there for a minute and thought how valuable life is, and how we may, sometimes, take it for granted. And it is the little things that we do for people that really count.

Dear Diary,

Today I was faced with a situation I knew little about. My friend, Sydney, was tested positive with the virus that causes AIDS. This was all so new to me but I think I handled the situation the best way I knew how...going to the source of people who knew the topic best--an AIDS counselor whose name is Jay and whose life has also been altered by this dreadful disease that has no cure. I learned more about the virus and the disease that I could have ever imagined. Even though my values, morals, and beliefs has always been that homosexuality is wrong...it is a sin...I still don't think that they were born gay. Maybe something happened in Sydney's childhood. I don't know what...but the cause is really unimportant since when we get right down to it, we are all sinners, and we need each other's love to rise above our situations to be the best we can be. I just hope and pray that Sydney finds peace in himself to deal with this condition that he can not change, but must accept...so that he can adjust to a new lifestyle. All I can do is give him a hug a day showing my support...my reassurance...

*Afrikka,
on an awakening day*

CHAPTER 16
Midnight Snack
♋

I can't sleep. I feel so nauseous and so edgy. So I'll just get up and exercise--no use wasting this energy.

I got up and got on my stair master. Climbing, climbing, climbing and going nowhere I thought to myself. My life is still fucked up...maybe this last ten pounds will get rid of this little pudge. The more I thought about it, the more I wanted to cry and the less I wanted to exercise. The fact is guys still don't even look at me. I must have a sign on me somewhere that says "off limits unless you old, married, or fucked up in the head". LaRon has even stopped returning my phone calls. I don't know why I even thought he might want to get with me...he can have any woman he wants...why would he want me.

    I still have this cellulite on the back of my butt. It seems so unfair I work and work and work and still I'm fat. I'm so fat and miserable...I'll always be miserable...I'm just not meant to be happy like other people. God....why? I couldn't hold back the tears any longer. Before long I was sobbing so hysterically that it hurt me in my chest. I went to the kitchen to get a glass of water, and decided to take a drive instead. I grabbed the keys before I even thought about it and headed out of the house at three o'clock in the morning.

    While I was driving all kinds of visions were going through my head. I saw myself lying in a casket all dressed in white. "That'll fix'm I thought." What a huge funeral I would have, all the people from the church, from the women's shelter and all the places I've volunteered. My sorors would perform the last rights ceremony, and my family would be weeping and waling, as if they are going to miss me. None of them will really miss me. They just want me for the work that I do...if I wasn't such a hard worker in the community, no one would be there...just like now. Nobody understands me...I thought beginning to sob heavily again.

    "I just want to be loved, and to have a family. That's all I want," I said aloud to God hoping he was listening. "Please, God," I begged, "Oh please, I'll do whatever you want me to do, just please let me have a husband, a life, a family."

    By now, I was crying so hard, I had to pull over on the side of the road because I couldn't see. I just sat there like a pathetic baby leaning on the steering wheel with my head down. I need to pray, I thought, but I don't even have the strength to pray the same prayer anymore.

"I'm sick of it!!!" I screamed out to God. I knew I needed to get a grip, so I tried to think of a nice quiet place to drive and just sit and think until I got myself together. School. There's a beautiful view at the campus where I can sit and just pray for a while. I used to go there when I was in school and you'd think I'd be past this point in my life, but it is just the same old problems, and issues.

On the way to the campus I stopped at Quick Mart and got some coffee. They had some donut pieces available for sampling and I shoved a few pieces in my mouth before I knew it. They were great, and I was kind of hungry so I looked around to see if anybody was looking and then I took several more samples and put them into a napkin for later-- afterall, they are free.

As I walked through the store looking for something, I'm not sure what, I nibbled on the samples. I remembered having a craving for white powdered donuts and milk the other day at work, but I couldn't find them at the little store in our building. So I'd had fruit instead with some TCBY yogurt, and I must've gotten two tons of yogurt cause it was five dollars and some change. Those damn Vietnamese people charge an arm, a leg and half a' stomach for they shit cause they know we trapped in that building until five o'clock

I finally found the row with the packaged donuts. There was a small pack of six donuts for $1.29 and the one dozen pack was only thirty cents more. Then I saw the 36 small donuts in a bag for only $2.49. These people must think I'm crazy!...that's only a dollar more. I'm glad I'm a good shopper. I rush over to the milk and grab the thin one quick. To the counter. And then to the refuge of my car. Ummmm.

One donut after another I comfort myself and before long I've eaten the whole bag. All thirty six, and I'm soooo sleepy.

Where am I going? Oh, home. I can't wait to get there. My eyes are barely open. I know I dozed off a couple of times. I'm really glad no one else is on the road this early. What time is it anyway? The sun is about to come up. It's almost six o'clock and I have to go to work. Maybe I should call in sick. No. My boss is getting suspicious, I can tell. She has been supervising me closely lately, telling me that I can talk to her if I have a problem or anything. She even asked me if I needed to take some time off, and she keeps catching me coming in late. I have to go in, but after I get a teensy nap.

I barely made it home and fell on the bed. I was sooo tired. I laid there thinking about how many calories I'd just consumed. I didn't want to think about it, but I couldn't help myself. It was as if something else was driving me--an internal auto-pilot. 'Get up,' it said, 'and get that damn food out of you before it settles on your ass.' Come on, Dana, you've worked too hard to turn back now. You are not a quitter. You can sleep when you're finished. Can't you feel your hips expanding? Don't you remember how proud you were when the size 10 dress was too big and you had to tell the saleslady *loudly* that you needed a smaller size? Or when momma told Rinky that she could wear some of your old clothes until she lost the weight from the baby?

I got up and headed for the bathroom. I looked in the mirror and turned on the water. I felt miserable, and this will help me to feel better I rationalized. And then I heard the magic words "Which is worse, being fat or doing this?" And then it was over before I knew it, and I was feeling very energetic. "I'll be on time to work today," I thought proud of myself.

♋

    I was only ten minutes late to work which is better than usual. As soon as I got to the office I made sure my boss saw me and then I snuck down the stairs to the deli and ordered the "Big Breakfast" which includes fluffy eggs (I like'm with cheese), pancakes, bacon, sausage, and hashbrowns. I also ordered a large orange juice.
    While waiting on the breakfast, I sat in the back corner of the restaurant in a booth with my back to the door. I thumbed through an old Mademoiselle magazine that I'd actually seen before. I looked at all those skinny models and thought about how easy they have it, they must never get hungry or have an extremely fast metabolism. My metabolism demetabolized a long time ago. I can get fat just looking at...at a cake like this Betty Crocker one on the page in front of me. I looked around the magazine to see if my order was up and it wasn't, so I continued on making sure to keep the mag up so that no one would recognize me. It's not that we don't have the freedom to do what we want here, it's just that I don't want to talk right now. I'm not really a morning person and there's a couple of people around here that I could just kill in the morning. Like that receptionist on ten, she should be fat as happy as she is. She must never take a breath.
    "Dana did you know that Winona Judd was at the radio station in the building today, and I got a chance to see her, and get her autograph, and she is so nice and not nearly as big as she looks on t.v., I think it's just that her mama is so tiny that it makes her look bigger than she is...." she rambled on and on earlier this week when I saw her. She's got to be a threat to the ozone layer as much oxygen as she uses up.

I finished the magazine and decided to walk over and see if my order was sitting on the counter. It was. I took it, and a bag of Cheetos and a Snicker for a snack later on, to the counter. God this place is expensive! I need to open up a snack bar. Nah...none of the food would ever make it to the shelf.

I'm really hungry by now, and I need to get back upstairs pretty quickly. On my way out the door, I ran into the security guard.

"Girl, you done lost some more weight. Now, I don't know what you trying to do, but you know us Black men like us a little meat. I may be old, but I can see, and you was fine just the way you was. You better eat some more. You been sick, baby?"

"No, Fred." I responded and wisked off.

"Girl, you better listen to me...you fine...you just fine..and pretty as a peach..." I heard his voice trailing off.

I hope he don't think I'm interested in him. He's always flirting, and it really embarrasses me, especially when Leroy, the maintenance man, and James, the computer service guy, are down there with him. They start gaulking and flirting with me all loud and one day I was so mad at them, I tripped trying to get into the elevator and tore my pantyhose. I was so pissed off. Men get on my nerves, they get to just say whatever and do whatever they want. We got to act like a lady and just smile and take it.

By now I was back in my office with the food. I'd nibbled on it the best I could while climbing the twelve flights of stairs. The familiar contractions in my leg reminded me briefly of the muscles I'd just used, and I felt good about walking the stairs.

"Oh, Dana, there you are," Nicolette said. "Your boss was just down here looking for you. It really seemed urgent so you'd better get over there."

"Thank you." I said impersonally and quickly went towards my office.

Nic and I haven't been that tight since I have somewhat of a life of my own. She's been seeing some guy, and I halfway got the scoop from Afrikka. I kinda feel bad about how it's been between us, I just really need my space right now and if that little tif gives it to me then so what.

When I got to the door of my office JoAnne, my boss, was coming out.

"Hi. I was just leaving you a note. I need to see you right away in my office."

"I'll be right there, just let me put this down." JoAnne looked down at the food I was carrying as if it disgusted her.

"Okay, but hurry over, because I have a client coming in about ten minutes."

Only ten minutes. I wonder what she wants to say this time. Maybe they want to give me a raise for staying late all the time.

I stuffed some eggs and nearly a whole pancake in my mouth and moved towards the door. I stood at the doorway to chew and swallow all that food since her office was right next door. I knew whatever she wanted was pretty important since she usually will just come in my office and tell me whatever she needs unless it is very important or confidential.

I peaked into her office and she was on the phone, so I went back to my desk and ate the two sausage links, and another pancake.

When I got back to JoAnne's office she was just hanging up the phone, and she looked a little upset.

"Is everything okay?"

"No, Dana. It isn't."

I got the sneaking suspicion her look had something to do with me, so I just swallowed and kept quiet. In a minute, Dr. Hemminger walked in and sat next to me. Oh shit.

"Dana," Joann started, "I've invited Dr. Hemminger to our meeting..." *Our* usually means *we* planned it, I thought.

"...so that the seriousness of this meeting could set in with you and also so that we could document a few things. I've spoken with you on several occasions concerning your tardiness and your performance. Is that correct?"

I nodded my head yes for the record. She'd mentioned something, but she didn't seem too concerned when she said it. This meeting reminded me how much I've always hated meetings. When I was a kid, we used to have these family meetings on Saturdays or Sundays when one of my parents was fed up with something. Usually it was my mom, mad at my dad because he wasn't helping out with disciplining us, and it was her way of getting everybody in the room at the same time. It was sheer torture. We went around the room supposedly telling how we felt about things going on in the house. Usually somebody ended up in tears--me. My sister and brother were smart enough to just sit there and be quiet, but oh, no, not big mouth. I always had to express my feelings and usually ended up heading off with someone which usually meant I lost. As I listened to JoAnne carry on about some kind of the complaints about my lateness and forgetfulness from clients, the memory of those old meetings burned in the pit of my stomach, reminding me of the breakfast getting cold in the next room.

"Now, Dana," thank God she about to rap up, "we hired you because of your skill for working with clients to quickly resolve issues, and you have not disappointed us as far as that is concerned. In fact, at one point your caseload was continually expanding and now I've had to pull back for your own safety and ours."

"There are obviously issues that you are dealing with that are impairing your performance and while you are very important to us, our ultimate concern has to be the client. You already know that one of the highest suicide rates is among female psychotherapists, and perhaps that's partially because of the weight of the work that we do, and partially because many of us go into this business to help others so as to avoid dealing with our own problems. But what kind of example does it set for our patients if we need help and will not seek it. It totally undermines all the trust we work to build in our clients that it is okay to seek professional help. I know that you, yourself have diligently worked in the African-American community to dispel some of the beliefs about psychotherapy." I wish she would just get to the point. She must have read my mind, or perhaps my eyes rolling around to the back of my sockets gave her a little clue. "...we want you to take your two weeks of vacation time to get some assistance. I took the liberty of looking over your employment record where you did not mention when asked that you had seen a therapist in college for..." she was looking at some sort of paper that looked vaguely familiar, "relationship issues and bulimia."

Until she said those words I had been looking away, but now I glared at her like she'd just stolen my children. How had she gotten that information? That was confidential. I can't believe it. I'll sue that damn university. I'll bet if I was some white dean's daughter who'd had an abortion, like Terra, my ex-roommate, that it would have been buried so deep that Cujo couldn't have dug it up.

Dr. Hemminger took over the condemnation, "We were able to get your records because you falsified the information on your employment records, which is grounds for termination at this company." I took a deep swallow. "However, we'd like to give you an opportunity to get everything straightened out, once and for all. So, I've arranged for you to enter St. Peter Hospital's inpatient program. As you probably know, it is the best program in the state for eating disorders, and you'll be out of the city so that your identity can be kept confidential."

JoAnne took over again, "This is a mandatory stay, Dana. If you won't comply, we unfortunately will be forced to terminate your employment. Do you understand all this?"

"Yes." I heard myself say, because I didn't know what else to do.

I felt like I couldn't breath. I knew the tears in my throat would tear down the wall that was keeping them in any moment now. I just wanted to be alone.

"You are scheduled to appear there on Monday. And you can have tomorrow off to take time to get prepared," Dr. Hemminger added.

I can't believe this, who do these people think they are. This is my life. I feel so out of control.

JoAnne looked at me very compassionately, and Dr. Hemminger stood up. "I trust you to do what is best for you, Dana, you are a very capable woman," he said and then exited.

I couldn't even look at JoAnne now. I looked down just in case the tears in my eyes fell, I would be the only one who knew it. I can't let these people break me down. JoAnne came over and sat in the chair next to me where Dr. H had been. She put her hand on mine, and said "You know Dana the reason I got into therapy years ago was because I was so inspired by my own therapist who helped me to find the strength to overcome my drinking problem. I've been sober for years and you can overcome this. You are very strong and industrious...now go and do for yourself what you have been doing for others all along."

She squeezed my hand, and for a moment, I felt a ray of hope. I continued to look down while the tears streamed over my eyelids and down my sullen face.

♋

I spent the rest of the day finishing up projects that had to be finished before I left. A couple of times Nicolette passed by and said hello. She must know. Nothing around here is secret. Hell, she probably knew before I did.

I worked right through lunch and into the evening, calling clients to let them know about the change in therapist, and to let them know that I would be back after I took a brief trip. I just let it sound like business. I really can't believe they know. I knew I shouldn't have gone to the campus counselor with James. James was my first lover. I met him shortly after I had lost over thirty pounds. It was the first time in my life I had been an average size and I flaunted my big hips and small waist every chance I got. James and I were always fighting and getting back together like it was commonplace. But this one time we had a big fight and I was sure he was going to hit me, and then I knew we needed some help. So I made a deal with him that if we were to get back together, we would have to see a counselor. He went with me to sign us up for counseling. We filled out all the paperwork, and then he never showed up for the sessions. I told the counselor that I was really scared because we had both grown up in abusive homes that we would end up the same way. The counselor said I should continue to come for myself, but I never went again. Now they have a record of me having gone to the counselor. Sometimes, I wish I weren't so damn honest. They wouldn't know if I had just skipped the bulimic part of the questionnaire. Now I have to go to a facility, but it was okay with me, because I once fasted for almost twenty days, I ate only crackers and soup once a day. So I'll just do what they say. Besides, I could use the peace and quiet--I'll just think of it as a vacation. Yea, that's it...a vacation.

♋

I finally gathered up my things and left the office. I just kept replaying the day's events in my mind. I just couldn't believe it. Then, I felt embarrassed. All these people know what I've been doing to loose weight. And Nicolette will probably tell Afrikka and Simone. I'm definitely not going to answer the phone.

♋

On Friday, I laid in bed all day watching soaps and eating myself into oblivion. I was bingeing and purging more than I had ever, and I felt drunk and dizzy. Several people called me later that evening, including LaRon. I just didn't answer. I tried to get up and exercise on my stairmaster, but I couldn't. I climbed back in bed and changed the channel. I flipped the channel all the way through to the porno station. There was one of those 1-900 commercials on with some big tittied blond woman playing with herself. I don't want to see her ass. I wait a few minutes to see if it is about to go off, and it does, but another one comes on, this time it's called 1-900-big-butt, and these white women are running around sticking their butts out when they could have saved some time and just got a sistah to play the role. They could of called me--I could do it. I get up and look in the mirror and stick my butt out, and grab my tits. Looking all seductive I recite, "call 1-900-BLACK-ASS, and get your monies worth." I licked my tit to give it a personal touch. And then I turn my butt to the mirror and looked at what a man would see. Boy, some lucky man is in for the ride of his life!

When I was little I used to do my favorite commercials in the mirror using a brush for my microphone. I would read the Jergens lotion bottle or Johnson's No More Tears, and pretend I was the woman on the commercial. I loved the ones with a grown-up jingle like the Enjoli woman. I would wait til momma was gone and put on her shoes and one of her pretty necklaces, and then I would pull the neck of my T-shirt down over my shoulders all sexy, and sing into the mirror as if I was making love to it: "I can bring home the bacon, da-da da da da. Fry it up in a pan, and never, ever, let you forget you're a man. 'Cause I'm a woman...with Enjoli." If momma had known I was gyrating and throwing my body like that at eight years old, my ass would have been hers. "You've come a long way, baby," I reminisced of the Virginia Slims commercials while looking in the mirror at the face that now closely resembled the one I'd had as a child.

Then I thought about my jobs and how quickly I had been able to move up the corporate ladder and get opportunities because I was so mature-looking with all that fat. I looked like somebody's momma, and I'm glad I look pretty again, and no one is ever going to take that away from me.

I'm interrupted by the sound of a bed squeeking. I turn to see a woman playing a teenager in a little skirt and a ponytail on the t.v. The guy is trying to finger her, but she won't let him because her parents are in the other room. He finally convinces her by using the old tongue tactics. But I must really be tired cause I fell asleep before they got to the good part.

♋

I spent Saturday running errands and exercising to combat all the stuff I ate yesterday. One of my sorors called to tell me about a party the Omegas were giving at the Hilton, and said she would talk about me so bad if I didn't go.

♋

The sermon today was just what I needed to hear. It felt like Pastor Banks was speaking right to me, which is scary cause I hope he don't know what I've been up to. I cried out to God at the altar prayer asking him to forgive me and telling him that I didn't know what to do now. And something happened to me that has never happen before. I felt all flushed and then I felt as if I was being lifted off the ground. Something said to raise my arms and so I did, really high, and I didn't even feel ashamed. Tears just poured over my face, and created a puddle on my new silk dress, but I didn't care. I just started to jump up and down and screaming something. I don't even remember what I was saying, just that the next thing I was doing was lying on the floor with a lot of people fanning me including sister Jean who got down on the floor and rocked me like a little baby. When she was doing that, I was actually seeing Jesus at my feet, and I got scared and I looked around to see if anybody else saw him, but people were going back to their seats and it was just me an Sister Jean. He didn't look like all the pictures I'd seen, but I just knew it was him. I tried to talk, but he put his finger over his mouth motioning for me to be quiet and then for me to follow him. I think I did follow him, but I don't remember what happened after that I just felt so relaxed and at peace. Then, when it came time for rededication, I needed to go, and I had all these voices in my head. "You don't need to go up there--you're already saved. You live the best you can considering where you came from. If you go up there, you'll have to start being all boring again like you used to be, or worse fat." That last one made it really hard, cause Lord knows the last thing I ever want to be again is fat. But, I just couldn't sit in my seat any longer, it was as if something else was in control, and I didn't mind. I felt so peaceful as I strolled to the front of the church where I had spent many times praying or speaking at one of our events. It all looked different right now, and I finally knew what the old folks mean when they say "you see through new eyes." My sight was crystal clear at that moment and I knew that God had his hands on me, and that I was in for a ride. Whatever happens in this hospital, at least, for the first time in my life, I know I'm not alone.

I wouldn't be able to have visitors anyway for the full two weeks that I would be there. So I just told my family that I was going away on business. I didn't lie...it is *personal* business. I was only allowed to bring clothes and a few other items, so I didn't have much luggage, but when I arrived at the hospital the lady checking me in took what I did have away from me, including my purse and locked it in a miniature cell and didn't give me a key. I felt like I was in prison except it was very comfortable and homey-like. In fact, it wasn't even like a hospital in the part that we were in. There were all kinds of people in here, but mostly white women who looked emaciated. One woman is really huge and she really disgusts me. I hate to look at her, but at least she's trying to get some help. I realized I was going to have to make a conscious effort to be nice.

It looked like some sort of meeting was about to take place because everyone was bringing the chairs that were placed somewhat haphazardly around the room, to one area in the room. I scaled the room to see that there were only about 30-40 women. Some of them looked like absolutely nothing was wrong with them. I'll bet they are saying the same thing about me.

In a few minutes the ladies in the front office came around and stood in the front so that I was sure something was about to happen. I just had no idea what.

Sheila, the lady who checked me in, smiled to me, and I felt a little better.

"Good morning everyone. We have some people to introduce to you today. And we have a couple of people graduating today. We will all go through the morning proceedings together and then we'll have orientation for the new ones and the rest of you can take some free time til lunch. Well, I guess we can just start out with introductions."

Immediately the first lady in the first chair on the right stood up and starting speaking: "I'm Elizabeth E. and I'm a healthy eater."

The next lady stood up when she was finished: "I'm Carolyn and I eat only when I'm hungry."

By the time it came to me I wasn't sure what I was going to say, so I just stood up and something else in me took over. I said, "My name is...."my voice started to quiver a lot... "Da-na."

I sat down quickly before I started to cry. The last lady to stand up was graduating from the program. She had been sexually abused as a child, and had a lot of other problems, too, poor thing. She said the program helped her to overcome her fears and to face change. She said a whole lot of stuff which I daydreamed through and then the whole room swarmed her with hugs and well-wishes. I thought about how nice it would be to be at home in my bed, and I wished I was going with her.

♋

At orientation, they told us that we would be given three meals a day, and that we would be weighed daily for the full two weeks that we were actually on the campus. Then we would be expected to check in with a local group once we left the premises and spend at least eight hours per week in session. There were two other black girls in the orientation, and one of them was sitting right in front of me. She need a perm, but I ain't here to give advice. They told us it was good to get close to people that had been here and find out what it was like to go through the program. The program is very intense, and would include both group sessions and individual counseling sessions. We would also be given something called hypnotherapy which I assume is just hypnotizing us to stop eating so much and start exercising which would not be a problem for me.

I wondered how they were going to fix a lifetime problem in just two weeks, and that's when the hypnotherapist who happens to be the permless black lady in front of me got up and started talking about the hypnosis part of the program. She said that it was totally voluntary that we participate, and that hypnosis had helped her to not only overcome bulimia and lose weight, but to also quit smoking. She looked like she had never known what fat was, and she explained how her abusive background had caused her to continually replay the abuse on herself until her subconscious mind was reprogrammed with hypnosis. She said that ANYONE could be hypnotized. Hypnosis is just a state of mind where we are tuned into our subconscious where our emotions and feelings and life experiences and patterns are stored VS. the conscious mind which is what we use to make everyday decisions. "How many times have you been going home and just completely missed the entire trip..as if you weren't driving, but you know you were. That's an example of what it is like to be under hypnosis--you are just relaxed to the point that you block out what is currently going on around you and focus in on your internal self. Or like when you brush your teeth in the morning..you probably couldn't tell exactly what steps you take to do it or whether you brush the back or front teeth first. That's because you do it on automatic pilot because you've done it so many times..you don't have to think through each step.. it comes from your subconscious mind. Then, she told us that studies show that it takes 14 to 21 days to firmly change your mind which controls your behavior and that is why we would spend 14 days here and then 14 days on outpatient care in which we would be expected to report to a local support group four days out of the week. This would help us to make the transition back to the outside world. Plus we would be allowed to get further therapy if we needed it, but according to Afrolocks, most students didn't need further hypnotherapy. We would also be given tapes to listen to three times a day. Sounds a bit like Jamestown to me, but nothing else has worked for me so I'll give it a try. Besides what other choice do I really have.

When I went in for my first individual session with Ms. Bell--that's the hypnotist, it seemed like any other counseling session. She asked me about myself and my family and she took notes while I summed up my life in about thirty minutes. She asked me some questions about when I thought that I had turned to food as a refuge and I told her about eight. She didn't look surprised. I then told her that I wasn't so sure about this hypnosis, and she took time to explain exactly what was going to happen and assured me that I would be in total control and would know exactly what was going on at all times. I would not say or do anything that was against my will. When she told me that, I felt a little better. Plus, she was very pleasant and really seemed to feel my pain.

I laid in a big recliner chair and she began to hypnotize me. I felt extremely relaxed, like my body was floating on air. I could hear everything she was saying and I didn't feel weird like I thought I would. Then, she started to ask me where I held my anxiety since that was what I told her was a big problem for me.

I said out loud, "In my stomach."

She told me to focus in on the feelings I felt when I feel anxious, and that certainly wasn't hard to do since I've been anxious since I set foot in this place.

"Okay, I want you to go back in time to when you first felt this way. Let your mind just find the connection with the feeling...it knows what to do."

I went back to a time when I was in a Christmas pageant and my mother was helping me to get dressed. She seemed really uptight and I was walking around without my shoes on. My mother popped me on the butt and told me to get in my shoes. But I was nervous so I forgot, and she whipped me in front of all the other little girls. I must have been only four, but I was humiliated and my mother dared me to cry and mess up my makeup. I hadn't remembered it before now, but I could tell by how strongly I felt this pain in my stomach that this seemingly small incident was definitely connected to my anxiety. We kept going back and dealing with the feeling, and each time I felt tension being released from my body that I never thought possible. When it was over, I felt great, unlike regular therapy sessions where I used to go home and cry and eat even more. She told me we would do more sessions when I was ready and I thanked her and asked her about her training. It seems she had started out intending to be a psychotherapist like me, but believed this method to be much more gentle and effective in helping people overcome their problems and start living in the present.

Other sessions with Ms. Bell got even deeper, revealing I had been sexually molested by my father. I could barely believe it. I didn't want to believe it, but there it was right before my very own eyes. He had fondled me and forced me to suck his penis when I was just a toddler, and I had absolutely no memory of it. I was totally disgusted, and she assured me that a little more work would help me to deal with the feeling I was having about even this. I wasn't so sure about that.

By the end of the fourteen days, I was astonished at how free I felt. I knew things about myself that I had never known and for the first time I didn't feel like I had to stuff my feelings down with food. On graduation day, I cried because I was going to miss these people who had impacted my life so greatly in such a short period of time. I was more thankful than words could ever have conveyed, and since I cried through most of my graduation speech which each student was asked to give so that the next group of students could get a 'taste' of what the end was like. I remembered back to when I had started and what things were in my head on that day. I told the new women:

"I've always been afraid of things that were different. In fact, I've spent my whole life trying to fit in. Fit in with my family, with old people, with my friends in school and with my colleagues at work. And now I realize that I should love being different because that is what I am, and what we all are. This program is a bit different, and that really scared me at first. But it is the best thing that has ever happened to me in my life. I know that God sent me here because I would never have come here or have been able to make it throughout this without him. I didn't have a choice--I knew my life was going downhill, I knew that I couldn't continue the way I was going, but I didn't know any other way. Now, I've been reprogrammed to live!"

I went to my seat and as I was about to sit down a couple of the ladies came over to hug me, then Ms. Bell, and before long, nearly everyone was standing right there congratulating me. I felt like I'd just won the Miss Universe pageant.

CHAPTER 17
Hand-Cuffs
♋

Lord, I can not believe that this is happening to us, to her. And they had the nerve to go on her job and arrest her. Luckily, Brad called me as soon as they hauled her off in the police car. She's only been out of the hospital less than two weeks and now this! Candy moved all of her stuff out of Earl's house and into Nicolette's crib her first week back on the job. And now, when she finally feels safe again, she's back in another hell hole. Only it's in a different place this time.

I called Candy first. She wasn't at home. I think Simone talked about her going out of town for a few days with some new man in her life. Temeka is going to pick E.J. up from school and look after him until this is over. Nicolette should be on her way here from work any minute now. I talked to her dad and he assured me that he would get in touch with Nic right away. Dana is no where to be found.

The cops discovered his body this morning when a friend of Earl's found his place with the door wide open. They immediately thought of Simone as their first suspect.

I never would have believed in a million years that I would be trying to help one of my friends get out of jail. And she probably doesn't know I'm here. She declined her one phone call. Why, oh, why did she do that? Now, it makes her look guilty. I just refuse to believe that she could ever kill Earl. Even after all of her talk about Earl and wishing he was dead, I still refuse to believe that she could ever do that to him. Simone don't have the guts to ever kill anybody...I don't think. As much as she hated Earl, especially after he put her in the hospital, I refuse to believe what happened to him had anything to do with her. Maybe...just maybe she could have killed him...No, she wouldn't do it for E.J.'s sake. She wouldn't want E.J. growing up without his mother...*and* his father.

Just then, a man whom I had never seen, but whose face was very familiar, walked through the door and into the dinky waiting area I was in. He was a handsome older gentleman wearing a shirt and tie, and he was coming towards me.

"You must be Afrikka. I'm Nic's..."

"Father...She looks exactly like you. Thank you so much for coming."

"Nic is on her way from the office, but I thought there might be something I could do to assist Simone in this matter, so I came on down."

"Thank you. Lord, knows I don't know what to do."

"Well I've already spoken with Simone and have permission to sit in on any proceedings so that she won't be misrepresented in any way. Right now, they are only questioning her. Let's go on back to the interrogation rooms to see what's going on."

He led the way down a big hallway and into a room with a one way mirror.

"She can't see us, but she knows that there are people on the other side of this wall," Nicolette's father said.

What are they waiting on? Why do they have her sitting in that cold room, alone? 'Simone' I said to myself knowing that she can't hear or see me. But she is looking straight at me as if she, perhaps, feels my presence. Just looking at her right now, I can not tell if she is guilty or not guilty. She is just sitting with so much poise in that chair with both hands folded on top of each other on the table. She even has her legs crossed under the table, as if she's waiting on the President to walk through that door any minute now.

"Nicolette," I whispered as she was coming through the door escorted by Lieutenant Jefferson.

"What's going on? Daddy, I'm so glad you're here!" Nicolette sounded so relieved.

Nic's father halfway acknowledged her, and then got right down to business.

"What's going on here Lieutenant....?"

"Jefferson."

"Right. If Simone needs an attorney, I will represent her."

"I'm sure you will, counselor," Lt. Jefferson was saying as Detective Cruz was walking back through the door. "She may need it."

"Ladies," Lt. Jefferson interrupted, "the only reason I'm allowing you to witness her questioning is because she denied her one phone call, she lives with you," he said pointing to Nicolette, "and she stated that she had no family."

"Did she really kill Earl?" Nicolette asked Lieutenant Jefferson.

"Have a seat. We're going to try to get to the bottom of this," he told us as two other officers walked through the door. "This is Detective Cruz and Detective Hodge."

Detective Cruz was an attractive, hispanic female. She appears too gentle-looking to be a cop and detective Hodge was a good-looking, young black man about my age. He definitely looks like the serious type out of the pair.

"It's a pleasure meeting you," Detective Cruz stuck out her hand and Nicolette and I shook hers back. Then she moved to Nicolette's dad and did the same. The other detective just stood there, overlooked us, and stared at Simone as if he knew her.

"Uhhh..." Nicolette tried to get Detective Hodge's attention to introduce herself, "Do you know her, or something?"

Detective Hodge slowly turned around and looked into her eyes. She smiled back as if those sparkling green eyes of hers somehow stablized his attention now on her.

"As a matter of fact," Detective Hodge finally spoke as he was somehow examining Nicolette, "....I believe I do. We grew up in the same neighborhood. She used to be pretty damn wild in the hood, so I'm definitely not surprised to see her here. It was only a matter of time."

"Alright," Lt. Jefferson butted in, "These folks are here to support her, so let's get down to business. Cruz...you going in?"

"Well..." she was saying until Detective Hodge blirted in.

"I'll go in first," he said.

"This seems like it may be a little personal for Hodge, Lieutenant," Nic's dad said firmly.

"Lieutenant, I haven't seen Simone in fifteen years. She probably won't even remember me."

There was a brief pause. I don't even know if I feel comfortable with him going in there to question, or interrogate her. He seems like he is carrying around some unfinished business about Simone and his past experiences with her. It seems kinda shaky to me.

"Okay...okay," Lt. Jefferson gave in. "But just stick to the basics. Cruz, you go in with him, and let's get to it"

"Like I always do, Lieutenant," Detective Hodge said as he smiled and walked out the door.

Nicolette and I glued our eyes on Simone as Detective Hodge entered the room. He stood at the door for about ten seconds. Simone sat there, still calm, cool, and collected. I don't think she recognizes him, yet. Or, maybe she does and doesn't care.

"What is he doing just staring at her like that?" Nicolette asked as she looked at Lt. Jefferson.

"He does that to every suspect," he answered, "...he studies their reaction to him first. It's one of his many introductory techniques."

We all sat there quietly like we were watching a play. Only, in this play, there are no actors...just real people playing real parts.

"Simone,..." Hodge called her name out as he sat down, "where were you last night?"

"What time?" she asked still calm.

"Between eight and nine."

"At home."

Nicolette looked at me and whispered, "She's lying, Afrikka. She left the house at eight o'clock saying she was going to the studio to practice while I kept E.J."

"Maybe she forgot what time she left," I told her.

"Are you sure you were at home between eight and nine o'clock last night?"

Hodge attacked Simone.

"What...I'm senile now? Of course, I'm sure."

Hodge sat there and stared at Simone...and Simone still sitting cool, calm, and collected in her white, sleek dress like an innocent angel stared back at Hodge with no fear in her voice or face.

"Who do you live with?" Hodge asked.

"A friend of mine," Simone answered.

"Nicolette, perhaps?" he asked.

Simone paused and sighd.

"Yes."

"Well, according to Nicolette, she stated that you left the house at eight o'clock," he said looking at his pad.

"How does he know that?" I asked Nicolette.

"Well," Nicolette admitted, "they told me when I came in that it would help her if I made a statement since she lives with me."

I rolled my eyes at her, and Nic's father scrunched his face, too, to show his disapproval.

"What," she grabbed my arm, "was I supposed to lie. What if she killed Earl? I mean, I put E.J. to bed at nine o'clock and I fell asleep around eleven o'clock....and...she wasn't at home by then."

I know Simone. She wouldn't kill a fly. Not even behind that hardass, headstrong attitude of hers.

"So what," Simone fought back, "I left the house around eight or nine. I don't watch the clock every time I leave the house...do you?"

"I'm not the one who's a suspect here. Let's talk about you. So, where were you?"

"At the studio."

Hodge laughed. I looked at Nicolette and before I could speak she blirted out,"Well, that's what she told me and that's what I told them."

"Simone," Hodge looked away from her, "you lying."

"Oh, you know me, now?"

"I've known you all of your life, remember. Do you not recognize me?"

"Oh, yeah," Simone started to get relaxed. She finally unfolded her hands, leaned back in the chair, and placed her hands in her lap. "How could I forget yo' nerd ass. As much as I enjoyed beating your ass everyday, I could never forget you. I guess you tryin' to prove you 'the Man' now by hiding behind a blue suit, huh? But you know what, it's not working so just give up this macho, bullshit role that you trying to front. Is it suppose to scare me or something? Ohhhhh..."

Simone laughed as Hodge walked toward the wall. She gained her composure and became calm again.

"You wasn't at the studio, so where were you...out looking for some old bastard to scheme on, for old times sake." Hodge said trying to maintain his composure as he leaned back on the table in Simone's face. Simone just smerked and remained totally cool like she did this everyday. Hodge started getting frustrated and yelled, "We checked that out already...so where were you?"

"You tell me since you know everything."

"Simone, I'm trying to make this as simple as I can so we both can get out of here soon....well...at least me, anyway. So answer the question--you wasn't at home, you wasn't at the studio, so where were you?"

Simone sat there. I looked at Nicolette and she shook her shoulders.

"I drove around the city, by myself. Is that a crime?"

"Only if you weren't picking up men along the way and gettin' paid for your services like you used to."

"Fuck you!"

"She used to trick?" Nicolette whispered to me.

"We don't know that for sure," I told Nicolette, "plus, if she did, that was in her past. If I had to go through what she went through growing up I probably would have been worse off or dead. Think about that, Nicolette. How would you have tried to stay alive and survive?"

Nicolette turned her head the other way.

"Oh, come on, Simone. You used to be so good at thinking about or at least coming up with your own aliby, even if it's not true," Hodge threw at her.

"Why is it so important to know where I was last night instead of finding the real killer?" Simone said throwing her hands in the air.

There was a brief pause as both Hodge and Simone stared at each other. Then Hodge walked over to the table and calmly stood in front of it.

"Have you ever wanted to kill Earl?" Hodge questioned Simone.

Simone sighed, looked away and then back into Hodge's eyes.

"Yes...yes...I...I wanted him dead but I could never do it no matter how much he hurt me."

"So," Hodge sat down in the chair, "when was the last time you thought about killing Earl?"

I looked at Nicolette and she looked at me.

"I want to believe she's innocent," Nicolette said to me.

"What's stopping you?" I asked her.

"I don't know," she whispered.

I grabbed her hand and she clinched mine.

"It's been a while," Simone finally answered.

"You mean to tell me that after he beat the shit out of you a couple of weeks ago with a bat, putting you into a coma with a broken arm and ankle that you didn't think about killing his black ass...C'mon, Simone, I know you wanted to kill that sorry, no good mothafucka after that. I know I would have if I were in your place. I mean, I'm sure it's not his first time abusing you. I'm sure he used to rape you, fuck you anytime he wanted, tearing your clothes off...hell...I even heard he made you suck his dick behind the projects we used to live in, before I moved out...and that was a long time ago...and I'm sure it got a hell of a lot worse after that...especially when you started singing in nightclubs. I'm sure he hated to see you get much love by other people. I bet everytime you came home at night he probably wouldn't let you sleep until you satisfied his every wishes whether it was sucking him, fucking him...."

"Tell him to stop!" I screamed at Lt. Jefferson. He just stared at them. And Nicolette's dad stood up like he was about to do something, but then, re-focused his attention back on Simone.

"Alright! Alright!" Simone yelled out. "Yes, I wanted to kill his black ass so that he will never, ever do that shit to me again. Is that what you wanted so fuckin' much to hear?"

Hodge laughed and leaned over in Simone's face.

"So where did you hide the gun?" he asked.

"What gun?" Simone asked.

"The gun you used to kill Earl?"

"What gun?" Simone insisted.

"There is a .38 special registered in your name..and when we found Earl's body in the house, there was no gun. It's missing. And guess what, the bullet we found between Earl's eyes came from a .38."

"So what's that suppose to mean?"

"It meeeans your gun is registered in your name,...it is also missing,...no aliby, so therefore, if you can't show us the gun..."

"I haven't seen that gun in years. I bought that gun for Earl and I never knew where he hid it."

"Oh, I think you did."

"Besides, I have an aliby."

"Oh, now you want to save your ass," Hodge said as he got up from his chair awaiting Simone's answer as he leaned on the table, "so where were you last night?"

Nicolette looked at me.

"Have faith," I told her.

She smiled and continued to hold my hand.

"I was at church," Simone answered.

"Church?" All of us in the room questioned at the same time.

"Church?" Hodge questioned himself. "What church?"

Simone paused.

"First Baptist on Memorial."

"I'll check this out," Nic's dad said as he opened up the door.

Detective Cruz followed him.

"Good job," Lt. Jefferson said behind her as she closed the door behind her.

At that moment, I knew my intuition about the whereabouts of Simone last night was right. I think Nicolette is starting to feel the same. At least, I hoped.

"What were you doing in church?" Hodge asked her.

"What do most people do in church?" Simone fought back.

"I thought you would never go back to church after what your grandfather did to you."

"He has nothing to do with my religious beliefs."

"Ha! Ha! Grandfather molests granddaughter in church making her perform repeated sex acts as a child over a number of years and causes granddaughter to experience severe maladjustment problems in her personal life--theft, and a little prostitution, along with the other problems she has had with a missing father and a drug addicted mother...brothers...and sisters, so she meets a young man who serves as her personal saviour but she finds that he, too, gives her the same treatment her grandfather gave her and she couldn't take it anymore so, she murders the man in cold blood as an escape from killing the real perpetrator, her grandfather, instead."

Simone sat there as tears rolled from her eyes. But somehow, she remained, still, calm, cool, and collected. There was a long period of silence in the room as neither Detective Hodge nor Simone attempted to speak.

"Poor kid," Lt. Jefferson said. "It's a wonder she made it out herself."

"Simone never told us about her grandfather," Nicolette said to me.

"Would you?" I asked her.

"My, God," Nicolette grabbed me and hugged me beginning to cry, "she should have killed her grandfather, instead."

I didn't hug her back. For some reason, I don't want to be a rescuer anymore.

"Simone didn't kill anybody," I reassured Nicolette.

"Dad," Nicolette looked toward her father, "what did you find out?"

"We have to let her go," Cruz looked at Lt. Jefferson.

"Under what circumstance?" Lt. Jefferson asked.

Nicolette's dad started in: "She was at the church altar until about eleven o'clock last night talking to ...God...Pastor Evans witnessed because he was head of the Bible Study class there last night in the same congregation where Simone was praying. Plus, we got a lead from a witness who said they saw Ivey Stow leave Earl's house around nine o'clock last night. Neighbors called in a few minutes ago from visiting some relatives since early morning saying that Earl has been out of town for a couple of weeks after what happened behind Simone and that he just got back in town a day or two ago. Perhaps Mr. Stow may have been hard up for some dope Earl was selling and didn't want to pay up. Neighbors also said that some thugs had been coming to Earl's house everyday since he's been gone. Maybe he owed them some money, or even drugs and that's why he skipped town."

"Damn, Earl," Nic said looking at his picture in the newspaper. "Sorry 'bout your luck."

So that's why we haven't heard from Earl and why he hadn't been trying to get in contact with Simone, or even E.J. Maybe Earl was in some serious trouble with a couple of no good drug dealers.

"Hey, is that the same kid who just got out of prison for that big drug bust that was made a few years back?" Nicolette's father asked.

"Yeah, that's the same crack-head kid," Lt. Jefferson answered. "Cruz, go in get Hodge out and prepare the paperwork for Simone's release." Cruz left the room. "Girls, I apologize for any inconvenience but I'm sure you know..." he looked at Nicolette's dad "...we were just doing our job."

♋

I sat on the sofa at Nicolette's house not knowing what to say, how to feel, or what to think. Simone sat near the fireplace staring into the chimney. And, Nicolette, was in the kitchen looking for something to eat. On the way to Nicolette's house, Simone rode with me, and Nicolette drove by herself because Robert had called her on her cellular phone and, as always, she wanted to talk to him in private. Her father said he had to go back to his office for some last minute touches he has to finish up for a case he defends in the morning. Nicolette walked back in the room with a bowl of fruit which she tried to share with Simone and I, but neither one of us wanted to eat, let alone had the desire to eat at this moment.

"Simone...what are you feeling?" I asked her.

Simone didn't turn around to answer. She sat there as if she didn't hear the question. Maybe she didn't. Maybe she is in her own little world now and is afraid to come out. Nicolette sat beside her in a chair and looked at me, then at her.

"I really don't know what to feel right now," she finally answered.

We sat there for a brief moment. Nicolette sat her bowl on the floor beside her chair. She leaned back and looked intensely at Simone.

"Simone...," Nicolette began, "...it's quite normal to feel scared...sad....confused...angry, and...and even lonely."

I can't believe Nicolette said that. I mean, all of those feelings she named hit right on the nose of what I'm feeling right now--for Simone. Maybe, just maybe, Simone feels those same emotions Nicolette just named. But if she is, she definitely is not showing it. Maybe Nicolette is feeling those feelings, too. Naw. She's a therapist intern. Of course. She is an academically experienced psychoanalyst.

"You're right, Nic," Simone turned around, looked down and said, "I am scared. Scared of knowing what could have happened to me, and even E.J., if we were in that house with Earl...and afraid that our lives could have been taken so easily, so quickly, too. I'm sad. Not so sad that Earl is dead, but unhappy because now E.J has to grow up without a father, and even though he wasn't 'Father of the Year', at least, E.J. could have said that he knew his father. I'm angry at Detective Hodge because I don't understand why he still has this personal vendetta against me, and I don't understand why my childhood has anything to do with my well-being now. I'm angry, too, because I'm lonely, and I'm lonely because I can't find satisfaction within myself. All of my life, I thought Earl would give me the satisfaction I needed to live and be, you know, happy, not just a sexual satisfaction but an inner personal gratification. And when he couldn't give me that, I turned to music. And you know what? Music has helped to find that inner peace in my soul, with the help of God's grace. Still, today I have come to the conclusion that even music is not the key to soul satisfaction."

"Satisfaction," Nicolette smiled, appearing to have an answer. "I'm sure there's some man who can hit the spot that music ain't getting."

"Nicolette, I don't think Simone is talking about that kind of satisfaction," I told her. "I'm sure she means something a little bit deeper."

"I do. See, Nicolette," Simone looked at her, "ideally, when most people think of a satisfaction, they think about the body...and how it can be stimulated. But, that's instantaneous gratification that is sexual and temporary. But, I've been praying a lot lately and it's amazing, especially coming from someone with my history, but God has revealed to me that we do have a 'G' Spot..." Nicolette's eyes perked up, "but it's the place where we are one with God...a Gift Spot...and not a center for self-gratification. What we're all really looking for God has already instilled in us, it is just up to us to search within ourselves to find it. And the only way to do that is through the Creator, himself."

We all sat there as if, somehow, Simone had just had a spiritual awakening. Then I started to think about me. Where can I find my 'gift' and what is it?

"I can't see how a person can find their ' G ' spot, from the way you describe it Simone, without having a man, " Nicolette spoke out, "because to me, only a man can satisfy my needs. I know you have to pray for personal satisfaction, in fact, Robert talks about that all the time. But I honestly think that God has given me that through Robert, because he is the first person who has sincerely and honestly satisfied me. I have even gone to church with him, and I know you won't believe this, but we haven't even had sex..."

"You're not understanding me, Nic," Simone looked at her, "true enough, Robert is satisfying you physically because he's, ideally, what you want a man to look like. He's satisfying you emotionally because he's feeding you what you want to hear. He's satisfying you mentally because he's quite intelligent, and therefore, capable of holding a conversation. And, soon enough, you'll know that he can satisfy you sexually, because we all know that if he doesn't you would not be around long."

"You don't know that... " Nicolette smiled from ear to ear, "I think Robert has helped me to find myself in every way that's possible!"

I sat there actually agreeing to Nicolette's statement because that is exactly what Simone just said.

"No," Simone blirted out. "You left the ultimate satisfaction out."

"What is it?" I asked curiously.

"Spirituality," Simone whispered to the both of us.

No one said a word. Not even Nicolette.

"Of course, you can find any man in the world who can give you emotional, mental, physical, and sexual gratification, or satisfaction," Simone added, "but in order for any relationship to be complete, in order for any relationship to endure, it has to have spiritual power. That is, the vital and animating force of the soul. That is the part of us which encompasses all of our deepest feelings. It's our heart and mind working together which gives us real meaning, and significance, and when we learn to balance these two can we find that deep part of ourselves. It's the only force that can hold any relationship together--whether it's family, friendship or companion. And spirituality is something that you have to possess and should also be a quality to look for in others because it bonds two or more people together forever. It is the main quality that completes the spectrum of the self. Think about your past relationships--not just with a man, but with family or friends, and think of a time when that relationship unfolded and think about why."

We each sat there and just thought to ourselves.

"When I think about me and Earl," Simone thought, "sure enough from the beginning he gave me satisfaction emotionally, sexually, mentally and physically but you know why it didn't last?"

"Because throughout that entire time you two were together..." I thought, "I would say that your relationship started to deteriorate because God was not the center of either of your lives. It's like you guys were feeding off each other for personal gratification and satisfaction but after a while, because you lacked the spiritual bond, it just didn't work."

There was a brief pause as we all tried to figure this thing out.

"Right," Nicolette stepped in, "and when you became stuck what else is there to do besides corrupt one another. And neither one of you could satisfy each other any longer, so there was nothing else to do besides attack each others' souls. ....That's deep, Simone, I would have never thought of it that way. That makes me think about Dana...and why she may be so hard on herself...because we all was thinking she was happy on the outside but...but her soul was...well, I guess she never got in touch with that side of herself."

"Finding that intense place inside of you that makes you tick is not something you can find overnight, conduct research on, or study...it takes time, patience, and faith, and also your willingness to believe in and love yourself. Because when that happens, the whole world will see it in your eyes and no one, I mean no one, can abuse you physically, mentally, emotionally, or sexually because of the strong love you have toward your spiritual self," Simone concluded.

I sat there and began to think about my past relationships and I think Nicolette was, too, visualizing back to hers. All of this time, I always felt that I was lonely, even with all of the people I meet on a daily basis, all of the friends that I have, and my wonderful career, I still often feel empty on the inside. All of my life, I have been trying to satisfy others thinking that by doing what I thought was the moral thing to do, I would fill this empty void that I have; when this whole time, the person I've been missing out on satisfying is me. And if I can't satisfy myself, totally, how can I satisfy others, wholeheartedly and truthfully. I've never let any one become attached to me because I always feel like they are going to leave me... and that's the same kind of anxiety and hurt I experienced when my parents separated when I was young. God, I fear that same anxiety now...and it's preventing me from being physically and emotionally attached to others. That's why I'll probably never get married. I fear getting so attached to someone, and it not working out. Then, we would have to separate, like my parents did to me. They don't even know what a divorce does to a child and all of the insecurities I carry around every day hiding from others. No one knows this hidden self and I wouldn't want my children to experience my pain....as I lay in my bed thinking about what I've learned today, and what I hope to accomplish in my future. *Lord, please, I'm begging you to give me the strength to help me let that part of myself go, the part that I've been holding on to all of my life, in order for me to become the total person you always meant me to be.*

Afrikka,
On a spiritually, awakening night

♋

"Simone, girl, what you cooking-up in here," I said loudly since Lil Earl was watching his cartoons at the loudest volume level on the T.V.

Simone didn't respond; she just kept right on flipping pancakes and doing whatever else she was doing in there. There were three places set at the table in the breakfast nook, so I just sat down at one of them and started to rub the sleep from my eyes.

"Simone, what you gon' wear to the funeral?"

Simone still didn't say a word. She came and sat the pancakes she'd been preparing on the table. Then she flipped the eggs in the frying pan and served them right out of the pan. I love my eggs right out of the pan, and Simone can really cook some food. I'm surprised I haven't gained ten pounds with her around here, cause she cooks almost everyday. She just gets in here in this kitchen and gets to humming or singing, while me and lil Earl play the new Super Nintendo I bought him. And the next thing I know a full course meal is on the table. And she likes for us to sit at the table and say grace and have dinner conversation and all. I'm not so used to that--I usually eat by myself, in the car or something, but I must admit it's nice to have someone to eat with. In fact, the only time I ever do cook is when I have a boyfriend. Roselda says it is important for a man to know his woman can throw down in the kitchen; so she taught me how to cook a steak, how to roast a chicken, and to make simple veggies like baked potatoes, green beans, and corn. I actually have perfected these simple meals over the last two years, and you know, Roselda is right, it works like a charm everytime! Even

Robert thinks I'm a great cook--I guess he hasn't noticed that I always cook the same thing. Men are so easy.

"E.J. get your little butt up from that T.V., wash your hands, and be at this table in less than a minute!....and don't let me have to say it again!" Simone finally says.

Her tone is very forceful and I can tell that she isn't in the mood for any crap. So, I just sit there staring at those delicious pancakes, and before I knew it Simone took her shoe off and sailed it through the kitchen, over the bar, and into the living room at lil' Earl. He immediately cut off the T.V., and sulked into the bathroom. I just sit there motionless like the sibling of a mother on the warpath...I'm not about to change the wrath to my direction. Lil' Earl has been in the bathroom for a long time, and I could tell that Simone was getting tired of waiting on him. Everything is on the table now, and Simone is about to sit down. So I get up and go after E.J. before Simone kills him.

"E.J., can I come in and wash my hands?" I said.

E.J. cracked the door so I could come in. It didn't look like he was washing his hands at all. In fact, he's sitting on the toilet with both of his hands under his chin. So, I just ignore him and start washing my hands. I had to step over him to get to the towel to dry my hands, he didn't make a sound, nor did he move. I can tell that he's upset, but I don't know what to say...I've never counseled a child. But, I decided I'd better say something before the wrath of Simone comes down on him for not coming to the table when she told him to. "E.J., sweetie, you know your mama gets upset when you let the food get cold. ....You'd better get out there."

"I ain't hungry."

When I looked at E.J. I could see all of the fear and anger in his little body. His eyes were full of emotion that he didn't know how to express. My heart collapsed as I felt his pain, knowing the silent years ahead of him with only one living parent. Tears came to my eyes, and I sat down on the edge of the bathtub right in front of him. I looked at him intently, not knowing exactly what needed to be said, but just wanting to be there....in the way no one was there for me. I was only three years old, but I can still remember waking up and crying for her and her not being there. I remember no one knew exactly what to say or do...they just shifted me from one person to the next like a misplaced doll.

Lil' Earl didn't look at me, he just continued to stare at the ground as tears formed and dropped right out of his eye on to the black rug around the toilet. Instinctively, I got on my knees in front of him and put my arms around him. He touched the top of his head on my shoulder...and I could feel his body shaking and quivering.

"It's okay to cry, honey...it's okay to feel sad," I heard myself say. That must have been like opening the flood gates because he started to sob so heavily and deeply that I, too, just had to let go and cry loudly. I picked little Earl up and sat him on my lap, and we sat there for a long time just crying and rocking...rocking and crying. It was something we both needed so much. I wish someone would have done this for me, years ago, and then I wouldn't be so messed up about my mother's death. But then again, maybe I wouldn't have been able to be here for E.J. the way I am right now. Who knows? I just feel so relieved and so grateful that I could be here for him.

I looked up and noticed Simone in the doorway, leaning on the door seal; she smiled at me with tears in her eyes and then turned and went away. I just kept on holding E.J. as if my life depended on it. I had been so angry...and in many ways I still am, with my father for not knowing how to help me, and for being too wrapped up in his own pain, that he didn't even seem to notice mine. Everyone around me seemed to be looking at me all pathetic like I was a lost puppy. I heard people whispering about me...about my mom being dead. I always felt so alone...so damned alone. And nothing and no one has ever filled that void in my heart. I don't want E.J. to have to feel alone like that--I wish I could hold him in my arms forever, and protect his little heart from pain. I wish I could be there when he needs a man to talk to or when he scores a touchdown and looks for his dad in the audience or when he falls in love for the first time and feels so confused...but I can't. I'm doing all I can right now though to let him know that he is not alone. That someone is here for him...that someone understands, and maybe, somehow that's enough.

When lil' Earl and I finally emerged from the bathroom, the food was still on the table--untouched, and Simone was nowhere to be found. It was getting close to time for the funeral, so I told E.J. to go put his clothes on since neither of us had an appetite anymore. I started putting away the food, and then I figured I should help him pick out something to wear. Simone had already left his clothes out on the bed, and E.J. was taking his clothes off. I smiled at him.

"You okay?" I said as cheerfully as possible under the circumstances.

He knodded yes and I smiled again, closed the door behind me.

I finished putting away the food and Simone was still gone, so I went upstairs to start putting my own clothes on. This time, I noticed Simone outside on the terrace, because the sheer curtains were blowing up from the wind outside. I don't think I can handle another scene like the one with E.J., so I yell out to her, "Simone, we only have about two and a half hours before the funeral starts, so you'd better start getting dressed. Simone turned around and leaned back on the banister. She took the cigarette she was smoking out of her mouth, and stomped it out, then kicked it off the terrace. She came back through the sheers looking like a diva even in her robe.

"I didn't know you smoked," I said.

"I don't, but I used to...I just felt the urge to today...you know."

I just smiled at her, and continued to look for the panty hose I just bought on yesterday, "Where in the world did I put'm?" I said out loud while looking around the room with my hands on my hips.

"If you're looking for your stockings, they on the sofa downstairs," Simone said as she exited my room.

"How did they get down there?"

"That's where you left them when we came in last night. You want me to get them for you."

"Would you?"

Simone dissappeared and brought the pantyhose right back up. I felt like I needed to say something to her about E.J., but I don't like to butt in with how people raise their kids.

Simone looked at me funny, and then said, "Thanks for being there for E.J., he really loves you. I think he has a crush on you..." Now why in the world would she say that. "...he can't stop talking about you all the time: 'Aunt Nic bought me this...' and 'Aunt Nic let me ride in her car' and 'Aunt Nic is so great', I'm sure it meant a lot to him to have you be there for him right now...Lord knows I haven't been exactly sympathetic."

"Thanks, Simone, but I really can't take any credit since E.J. has helped me waaay more than I have him."

Simone sat on my bed, and I did too, reluctantly cause I don't want to get all emotional again. But, then again, I guess it's just going to be one of those days. "Having him around has helped me to relive some of my childhood since I really feel I got cheated out of a lot of it, in boarding schools, and living with different relatives when my dad was away. I was always trying to be a grown-up so that I could escape my gruesome childhood, and now I realize how much I missed." Simone smiled as if she understood.

"Girl, I guess we all have something to complain about, no matter what our lives look like from the outside."

"If I had a quarter for all the times I've cried for my mother, how lonely I've felt, how isolated from my peers...Man, I'd be rich."

"You are rich!"

"Yea, but I mean having my own money."

"I know what you mean," Simone got up and started singing, "Mama may have and Papa may have. But, God bless the child who's got his own!"

Boy that girl can sing.

"Please talk to E.J., Simone. I know you've got a lot going on right now too, but he really needs you. I know--I've been there."

"I know, Nic. I just don't know what to say...my feelings are so confused. I'm angry, but I'm hurt. I'm happy, but I'm lonely. There's just so much going on inside my head right now that I don't know what to say to him."

"How about that...kids are people too, they're just little people, and what we model to them is the way they learn to handle tough situations. That's why I always run from stress, I learned it from my dad. We just never talked about the hard stuff, and ignored it hoping it would go away." Simone was really listening intently. "I remember that I was confused about how to feel and act too...I just didn't know what to do. So if you tell him that, I'm sure he'll understand even bettter than you think. Besides, E.J. is a very smart kid. Sometimes I wonder if he really is your son," I joked.

"I do too. His teachers keep talking about how exceptional he is and I'm wondering where he got that from," she smiled.

Then it was quiet for a moment and I asked, "Are you sure you're going to be okay to sing today? I know I wouldn't--funerals give me the creeps."

"Girl, when you been there as many times as I have, it ain't nothing but a thang. Besides you know singing is the best way that I express myself, especially at times like this."

"Well, we better get dressed before people start showing up."

"Yea, I'm gonna check on E.J."

"I'll be in the shower, so would you get the phone," I said removing my pj's.

"I'd rather just let the machine get it, if you don't mind."

"That's cool," I said as I turned on the water.

I haven't been to a funeral in years, and I wouldn't be going to this one if I didn't love Simone and E.J. so much. I just hate them. Everybody whining and crying over someone when it is much too late for the person to know how much they care. So pointless. I think I'm going to be cremated, and save them some time and energy.

♋

I daydreamed through most of the funeral while Robert twirled my hair around his fingers with the hand he had rested around my shoulder. I sat right behind E.J. and Simone who was sitting between her two sisters. Some of the guys from the club were right next to me and Afrikka on the other side of Robert and Ed. We are like one big family, and I really love being this close to my friends. I daydreamed about me and Robert being married and inviting everyone over for dinner. We would have some beautiful kids...a head full of hair and big brown eyes like Robert's.

Simone sang *"I Won't Complain,"* which she explained to everyone, had been Earl's favorite song when they both went to her grandfather's church as teenagers. I'd never heard that song before, but after Simone sang it, I felt as if it were my very own anthem. Simone has a way of making words and notes turn into soul-stirring rhythms.

♋

At the gravesite I couldn't keep my eyes off of lil' Earl. I felt so sorry for him. Robert held my hand and I wondered if he could feel me shaking. I also noticed that Earl's family wasn't very cordial with Simone. He had a couple of sisters and a bunch of nieces and nephews. None of them looked alike, and they were not nearly as well-behaved as E.J.

Lil' Earl hadn't shed one tear throughout the entire ceremony. He just had a familiarly empty look on his face. Nothing else about this whole thing was even remotely sad to me, but E.J.'s expression kept tying into my own pain.

When it was finally time to leave the gravesite, people were so busy deciding who would take which flowers, and giving directions to Earl's mom's, whose house everybody was going to, that nobody noticed lil' Earl and Simone sitting by the gravesite holding one another. But I did. I wanted to go over, but I decided they might need some time alone. As I walked away in the distance holding Robert's hand, I heard

Simone's voice gently singing, and I turned to see her and E.J. rocking from side to side. I could tell by the shaking of their bodies that he was really crying and she was too. I think it was the most beautiful sight I've ever seen.

CHAPTER 18
Strip Tease
☞

Gosh it feels good to be home! I'm still overwhelmed by what just happened to me. I can't believe I just totally blocked out large parts of my life. I learned about this stuff in school but it all seemed kind of like getting AIDS-- something that happens to someone else. I'm not sure what to say to my family now that I know so much. My friends are probably mad that I haven't returned their phone calls.

I decided before I did anything to just sit down and relax a minute. I noticed all the newspapers that I had brought in stacked on top of the T.V. and I go to breeze through them and throw them out instead. I don't want anything negative invading my space right now.

Rinng!

Rinnggg!

"Hello," I said without checking the I.D.

"Dana!" It was Afrikka. "Girl, where in the world have you been. I have been so concerned about you. Nobody seemed to know exactly where you were. Nic said you were on vacation from work, but when I saw your brother the other day, he said you were on a business trip. So, I started getting a little concerned. Are you okay?"

"Yes and no."

"What does that mean?"

"Well, yes, I'm okay right this minute, but I feel like I've just stepped out of a time warp," I said sounding different even to myself.

"Where have you been?"

"I.. I was away at a retreat of sorts....it's kind of a long story."

"Well, do you not want to talk about it?"

"No, that's not it. I can talk about it. I'm just not sure what to say." There was a bit of silence, then I said, "it's really deep."

"Well, Dana, I know you've been going through a lot, but you haven't really shared it with me, and I respect your right to privacy. But you should know by now that I'm here to listen if you need anything."

"Oh, Afrikka, I know...it's just the kind of stuff I'm going through right now, I'm not so sure that you would understand--I know I don't. Except I have no choice because it's my life."

"Then doesn't it make sense that as your friend, I have no choice either except to support you in whatever way you need. Sometimes I feel you really shut not only me, but everybody out and try to just handle everything by yourself. That's not fair to you or others, Dana, cause it's through our pain that our relationships grow and develop. And it's like you're saying you don't trust our friendship to withstand your pain. Whatever it is that's going on, it's a part of you and, therefore, it is a part of our relationship anyway."

"I never thought about it like that. Thanks for being concerned. I've always felt like I should be there for others, and that my problems would work themselves out. I've actually been harboring a lot of anger towards God because my life is such a mess after all I do for others, you know? I'd started to feel like nothing good ever happened to me, and you know what?"

"What?"

"That's exactly what started happening--nothing good. But it didn't have anything to do with God, it was my belief that bad things would happen that made them happen."

"What changed all that?"

"Well, for the last two weeks I was in an eating disorders clinic, so that I could clean out my system of all the mental, physical and emotional damage I've been doing to it."

"Oh, Dana! Why didn't you tell me??!!"

"Because I didn't want to make an even bigger deal out of it than it already was. And, well..I wasn't so sure you guys would understand. I mean..none of ya'll are like me. I have some *real* problems..the kind that don't just go away from talking about it or having dinner with a friend. You know what I mean?"

"Dana, you of all people should know that it doesn't matter how major or minor the problem is to others, but how it effects you is what matters. Would you like me to come over and maybe we can have some tea and just chat?"

Afrikka has always been so caring and so understanding.

"I really would like that, but later. I'm just so drained right now that I think what I need most is sleep."

"Okay, I understand. How about later on about six o'clock?" I looked at the clock and it was 12:45. That gives me plenty of time.

"Okay."

"I'll see you then."

"Bye."

"Goodbye."

I put one of my hypnosis tapes into the tapeplayer and listened to it to help me relax and to continue to feed my subconscious mind my new needs. When I woke up it was 4:30. I guess I was sleepier than I thought. Now I felt hungry, and that is definitely a good feeling these days. In the center, we learned about eating as a natural response to the bodies physical and *not* emotional needs. Somewhere along the way for most of us who struggle with our weight, we got the signals confused.

My mind flashed back to being a kid in the hood. I was always a pretty healthy kid, but that was considered a good thing back then. Whenever something bad was going on around the house, we had lots of sweets in the house. Mom liked baking and would spend hours in the kitchen to herself just making cookies and pies and cakes. I could smell the aroma from just thinking about it. Sometimes she would take them to church or work, and sometimes she would give them to neighbors or family members. But mostly, we would just eat them. There was always something--strawberry muffins, sock-it-to-me cake, banana pudding, or my favorites: chess pie and pineapple upside-down cake. I quickly developed a keen sweet-tooth.

And we always had ice cream. I loved ice cream, and mom used to use it to get me to do things for her like "honey, don't you want to rub mommies' feet? I bought some ice cream today." Or, "sweetie, why don't you go outside and play. And when you come in we'll have some ice cream." We would celebrate together with ice cream and the dessert on the day when I made straight A's, or led the school play, or got first chair in the band UIL competition.

I smiled as I thought about the joy those times brought me. It's funny then, that I thought it was the sweets that gave me the gratification I was looking for, when it was actually the love and attention from my mother that made it so great.

I popped a Healthy Choice meal that had been in the freezer quite a while from the looks of the frost on it, into the microwave. I'm really hungry, so while I'm waiting I look for a snack. There's all kind of stuff in the cabinet, from cookies to popcorn to potato chips. Without even thinking about it, I pulled a trash bag out of the pantry and dumped all that stuff in the bag. I don't even want to see it anymore. It is not that it tempts me--I just don't need it..don't want it in my life. I'm better than this.

The microwave buzzer went off, and I stirred up the creamy fettucini, shut the door and turned it back on. I went right back to my task, going through all the cabinets and tossing out those foods that weren't worthy of entering my body.

"Now that's definitely a change in thought," I said aloud recognizing my progress. The buzzer went off again and I got the aromatic food and took it to the table. I said a prayer of thanks for the food as well as my family, friends and health, and then begin to dig in. Wow, this tastes really great! I thought to myself. As I sat there enjoying my meal instead of feeling enslaved by it, the phone rang. The phone rang again--I'll just let it go to voicemail.

Later that evening I visited with Afrikka who had never actually been to my apartment. We didn't even talk about me. We just relaxed and watched *Friday*, one of my favorite movies. Later on, before bed, I wrote in my journal:

Now, this is the life--eating exactly what I want, when I'm hungry for it and until I'm full. You know, when they told us we could eat anything we wanted, visions of cakes, pies, and all kinds of sugary sweets danced in my head, but it's funny that now that I have a choice and all the taboos are gone, what I really want is now green beans or chicken or an apple. I never, ever thought that I would crave those kinds of foods...I guess anything is possible if you believe.

April 12 at 9:00 pm

By the end of the week I'd gone back to work, started attending the support meetings and listened to my reinforcement tapes at least twice a day. I felt so strong and more committed to anything than I've ever been in my life.

As was expected, I'm gaining weight, and that is the only scary part. Sometimes it feels like I just won't be able to stop gaining and that I'll balloon up to two hundred pounds. But, that ain't nothing but the devil--he knows that if I believe that that I will automatically make it happen no matter what I do on the outside to keep myself slim. So I just keep reminding myself that my body will even out, that the gain is just in response to all the damage I've done to my body and metabolism. At some point, my body will stop feeling like I'm going to go back to starving it at any moment and stop holding the fat. Until that time I allow myself to be a little obsessive about exercise so I won't freak out or give up or anything like that.

On Saturday night, I went out to a club all by myself something I never would have done before my treatment. It was kind of weird at first not having anyone to talk to, just sitting there all by myself. Then, this nice guy came and sat next to me, and offered to buy me a drink. I started to look around and see who he was talking to, but instead I just smiled and declined.

"My name is Desmond," he said and extended his hand for me to shake.

He has nice hands, and until that moment, I hadn't noticed, but he has beautiful skin and a nice, warm smile. Something in me said watch out, you *are* in a club. Then another part of me said, no limitations, no expectations, just have fun. I smiled and thought of Afrikka. I danced all night and had a great time. I even got a few phone numbers.

I ran into LaRon who came in about midnight. He looked better than ever. He acted like he didn't see me, and at first I was going to pretend that I didn't see him either. But, I felt pretty good so later on I saw him standing amidst a pack of females and I just went over and told him I wanted him to dance with me. I just walked on the floor and there he was right behind me when I turned around to dance. Now this positive thinking is the bomb!! We danced for a while, and then I didn't see him until I was about to leave. He almost stepped on the girl's toe who was trying to talk to him as he was trying to talk to me. I just kept walking out the door, and when he caught up with me all winded, he asked was I leaving.

"No I'm going to refill my drank in the car, negro."

"Okay, Miss Comedy."

"Well, you look so nice you should be careful walking out by yourself."

"With all these half naked women out here to get with, I know these brothas ain't even thinking 'bout me."

"You know that's not true. Look at those guys over there hanging out in the parking lot. They was just waiting for you to get closer to them to start trying to put they mac on. And, several guys asked me who you were tonight."

"For real??"

"Yea."

It was quiet for a minute. I guess LaRon was trying to think of a way to get me to stay or to get to go home with me from the look in his eyes. I don't feel sorry for him though...I'm not going to help him find the words. I just stand there with a smile and a sparkle in my eyes, and let him dig his own hole.

"Well, I've got a new crib. It's just a lil somin', but a brotha is comin up, you know," he said.

"That's great."

It was getting pretty awkward and I was feeling pretty tired from all that dancing. So I decided to let him out of the noose.

"I had a great time. Thanks for walking me out. I'm really tired."

"Yea..anytime."

I got into my car, and just as I was about to close the door he said, "You know, Dana, I never got to take you to that dinner we planned, so I still owe you."

"Oh, you don't owe me anything, but I'll take you up on the dinner. Call me sometime."

"Ah-ight."

Even his ghetto voice was sexy to me, but it was funny that somehow this whole thing felt suddenly like my relationship with food--as long as it was forbidden, I was killing myself to get it, but as soon as I let myself go to enjoy it, I find I really don't even like some of the foods I ate the most. LaRon is sweet, but I deserve so much more.

"Have a good night, LaRon," I said with a sexy wink, enjoying every iota of this moment, absorbing the very thought of being desired by this man while secretly knowing the thrill was gone.

CHAPTER 19
Treasure Hunt

Robert gave me a key to his apartment while he is away for the week so that I can keep an eye on the place. I'm really tempted to go over there and go through his things looking for dirt on him, but I keep thinking about the last time I thought I was going to bust somebody. So I just go over and make sure everything is okay and leave quickly before I'm tempted.

He's been an angel. He's almost too good to be true. And my dad always says that anything that seems too good to be true, probably is. But then again, Daddy has been single nearly twenty-five years. If I went without for that long, I'd be a bit delirious too.

Robert is the best thing that has ever happened to me. It is like we belong together. He hates fraternity shit and I think sororities are for insecure people. He can only sleep on linen sheets and so do I. He loves politics and I love to debate. He likes Chinese and I live for Chinese food. God, I can think of very few things that we aren't in agreement on. And when we aren't in agreement on something, we laugh at each other because we end up almost arguing over who said they would give in first. He is definitely the catch of the century--and I can't believe he's all mine. Finally, someone worthy.

There is a big carwash right next to the apartments where my baby lives and when I drove up at Robert's apartments on Friday, the day he was due back, there were some real nice looking guys outside washing their cars. They were listening to some really loud rap music and all I could hear was cursing. A couple of them started whistling across the street and trying to get my attention. I waved and smiled back.

"You need some help with those groceries, miss lady," one said as he crossed the walkway that divided the apartment from the car wash.

"Uh...no thanks, I've got it," as I leaned over and picked up the two bags on the floor in the back seat of my vette. I had to really reach to get them because I'd had to stuff them down real hard to keep them from flying up since I had the top down.

"Well, maybe I can just walk you to your door."

Okay, you're cute, but don't push it.

"I don't think my boyfriend would like that."

"Shiit! If I had a woman like you I'd be carrying her and the groceries in the house."

I smiled and walked off, starting to get a little anxious to get inside.

"That's a real nice ride you got," he said and kept walking behind me as if he wasn't going to leave.

"Thanks," I mumbled, wishing Robert were here now.

"What model is this? '67?"

"'69, I think"

"Really? Is it your boyfriend's car?"

None of your damn business is what I wanted to say, but I've really been trying to be a little nicer with guys so I don't get cursed out all the time..

"Listen, I'm kinda in a hurry. Nice meeting you." I said, hoping he would get the message.

"So...uh...how can a brotha get in touch with a sista like you."

I guess he's deaf, so I'm gonna play like I'm deaf too.

"Oh," he said, his tone getting really aggressive. He caught up with me and jumped right in front of me. "You can't answer a brotha?"

I just walked briskly around him and dashed to the stairway as quickly as I could. As I neared the stairs, I called out to Robert as if he was in the apartment waiting on me to get there. The guy stopped at the bottom of the stairs, and just watched as I went inside. I didn't even turn around to see if he was still there. I just sensed he was up to no good, so I closed the door as quickly as I could. I was really scared and I didn't want them to try and hit Robert over the head or something as he came in. So, I called him on his cell phone. He didn't answer so I left a rather shaky message. "Robert, honey, I.. I am at your apartment and there are these guys at the carwash across the street who were flirting with me. I hope I'm not being paranoid, but I felt like..like he was stalking me or something. Please call or hurry home."

Just then, I remembered that I hadn't turned on my alarm, but I'm definitely not going back out there to do it.

The phone rang and it was Robert.

"Hey baby. I miss you."

"I miss you too. I'm so glad you called me back. There are..."

"Did you call me? Oh I guess we did it again. I just couldn't wait another minute to hear your voice. I'm on the plane still."

"Robert." I said reflecting that something was wrong.

"What, baby? Is everything okay?"

"I'm fine, there were just these guy over at the car wash who kind of got me upset."

"What did they do?" he sounded really concerned.

"Well, one of them just came over and followed me to the door. At first I just thought that he was flirting and I didn't take him too seriously, but then I felt like he was up to something."

"We will be landing any minute and I'll be home. Just keep the doors locked and I'll be right there. Okay?"

"Okay, honey, I'm probably just being a bit paranoid."

"Well, you're doing the right thing...you'd rather play it safe, especially with hard heads."

"I'm sure I'll be fine. You've already made me feel much, much better. And I'm going to show you how much I appreciate it when you get home."

"Hummmnn, what are you doing over there?"

"You'll see. Just get home fast."

By the time I got off the phone, I was walking by the window and noticed my car wasn't in the spot where I thought I'd left it. I looked again to see if I was seeing things. I looked on the other side, just in case I was dreaming. My car is not there. Surely, no one would steal it in broad daylight. This is ridiculous. Where is my car? No one else has a key, but my dad and he is in New York. I just talked to him today.

"My God, those damn hoods got my car," I said out loud to help the other parts of me that refused to believe this to know it was reality.

I called the police and they came right over.

"I thought this was a pretty nice neighborhood. Can't you do something to keep people like that away?" I said infuriated by the inconvenience of the whole thing.

"Miss, this happens all over town, no matter where you are."

"That's not true. I don't even have to lock my doors out where I live."

"Ma'am, if you don't lock your doors you could really be putting yourself in great danger and I suggest that you not do that no matter where you are."

After getting all the information, the officers had to leave. I was still feeling pretty shaken up, but they assured me that they would do everything possible to get my car back.

As I was seeing the policemen out, Robert was coming up and saw all the commotion. I guess it really scared him cause he jumped out of his car in two seconds and ran to me. "What's going on? Are you okay?"

"They stole my car."

"Who did?"

"Those guys from the car wash."

"Are you okay?"

"I'm fine. It has just been an unbelievable day."

"Oh, baby. I'm so sorry," he said giving me a big bear hug. We held each other for an extra long time, then he said, "Let me bring my stuff in and I'll give you a massage."

"You want some help?"

"No. You just sit here and relax. I've got it."

Robert finished bringing in his things, and came over and sat next to me.

"I was going to save this for later, but I thought it might cheer you up," he said handing me a flat gold box.

Inside was the bill that completed my rare bills collection that my dad had started for me when I was a baby.

"Oh Robert! Where did you find this? I've been looking for this forever." I kissed him all over his face, and he smiled so big.

He looked absolutely wonderful, and I was just noticing because of all the commotion.

"You got a tan, honey. It looks great. ..I'd planned to have dinner cooked for you, but I.."

"Thanks for thinking of me, but under the circumstances I'm not too hungry anyway. After you called me and told me what happened, I just couldn't relax. I almost didn't wait for my luggage. I just wanted to be here with you, to hold you and comfort you. Then, when I drove up and saw the police here, I almost died." By now he was holding my hand and looking me straight in the eye. "If anything ever happened to you I don't know what I'd do--I might go crazy."

"I'm okay, I'm just too mad about my car. My dad went all the way to California to get me that vette when I turned sixteen. He had always wanted a '69 vette when he was growing up...it is kinda the only thing we've really done together...and it still has the original paint, and has never been wrecked. I don't know what I'm going to tell him," I said looking down and starting to get upset again. I didn't want to cry. "I mean it is just a car, but it meant so much to me because my dad..." my voice trailed off and I just couldn't shake the tears.

I felt so silly for crying, but Robert just put his arms around me so gently and tenderly that I felt like it was where I was always meant to be. I couldn't help just letting it all out. In between tears, I told Robert how silly I felt for crying.

He said, "Would God have made tears if he didn't mean for us to use them?"

"But...but...I jus...don't want you...sniff, to think I'm a big baby."

"But you are a big baby," he looked down at me smiling, "...my baby." He looked into my eyes and I had to look away cause this shit is getting a bit too deep for me. He reached out with one of his hands and turned my face to meet his. "Nicolette, there was a time when I would have been so afraid of this...of us. But, all I could think about all week was you. I missed you so much, that in one meeting I almost walked out." I started getting fidgetty cause this kind of romance is so real, and so intense. I just don't know how to take it. "Nic what I'm trying to say is..."

Please don't say it...not yet...please. "Nicolette," he said to get my attention back from the Twilight Zone, "I'm in love with you. I have been since I met you. ...God, I hope this doesn't scare you away...but I just have to let you know, because it is only getting stronger."

Damn, what do I say? I'm just not good with this romantic stuff. I think I love him too, but I just can't tell him...can I?

"Robert, I...I...," he put his finger over my mouth. "You don't have to say anything, Nicolette. I just needed to let you know how I am feeling. This is weird for me--I've never been so open with a woman so soon, but sometimes you just know it's different. You know?"

"Yea," I said looking deep into his eyes, and suddenly not feeling afraid anymore.

We kissed and it was more than explosive. I was excited instantaneously. He picked me up and carried me to his bedroom where we kissed a lot more and a lot slower. It was going so slowly, that I wanted to just rip his clothes off and jump on top of him, but I just let him lead. After about ten minutes of just kissing, I was so wet, he could of dived right in. He took off my shirt and massaged me and teased me one layer at a time. I was on fire. He caressed me so gingerly, and the look on his face was such that I could barely look at him..it was like he was glowing. It must have taken a full hour before we were both totally unclothed. And then it was on!

♋

The next morning when I woke up next to him, I just watched him sleeping. I couldn't believe this same gentle sleeper had just turned my body inside out last night and into the morning. I had to *tell* him I was tired for him to stop. I think we were both a little buck wild after waiting so long. Cause as tired as I am right now, I want some more!

The phone rang, and Robert reached over me to answer it.

"Hello," his voice vibrated through my body, "uh, yes it is. Hold on just one second."

"Hello," I said surprised to be receiving a phone call here. "Yes sir."

It was the police and they had found my car all stripped down in an alley early this morning. I had to go down to the pound to claim it. Robert went with me.

"I can't believe this shit," I said as angry as ever when I saw my 1969 corvette all carved up and pitted out. "Why don't people just buy their own stuff and leave other people's alone."

I had to call the insurance company and have an adjuster come out and look at it. The guy said it would be better to just total it and start from scratch.

"They were probably just kids, out for a joy ride. It's really not that bad, baby. Plus, I know a few people who can fix it up for you just like new...."

"I don't want it fixed up..." I interrupted, "I wanted it just like it was."

I didn't say a word after that. I was just so mad, and how am I going to tell my father. He really loves this car, too. We arranged for a tow truck to take my car to the junk yard. I said goodbye to Roxane, that is what I named my car when I first got it, and walked away. Then he took me shopping and to a movie to get my mind off of things.

Robert was particularly quiet, but I wasn't really in the mood to talk very much anyway. I finally asked if he was okay, and said that he was, but that he just had a lot of stuff to do. So he dropped me off at home, and asked me if I wanted to go to church with him. I told him I wasn't sure, but that I would call him later and let him know if I could. The truth is I don't know about going to church with a man. I read somewhere, I think Essence, that when you go to church with someone it is like a sign that the relationship is getting pretty serious. Plus, Robert is very involved in his church, and I'm not so sure what to do in a church--I would hate to embarass him. I mean the only times I've ever been to church was when my grandmother died, and of course, when my mom died. But I don't even really remember those times. And then again in high school whenever I spent the night with Becky, who was my best friend, and we went with her parents a couple of times. And then again, in college, I went with my roommate, Brianna, who is Catholic, and I actually kind of liked it because they had everything except the sermon written down so that you could follow along if you wanted to. All those times were okay, but I really didn't know anybody, and I didn't have to be concerned about what might happen because I wasn't going to see any of those people again anyway. Now with Robert, not only could I potentially embarass myself, but him too, and I would never want to do that. So I decided to call him before I went to bed and tell him I couldn't make it.

 Ring!
 "Hello."
 "Hey girl. This Dana. I need to ask you a favor."
 "What is it?"
 "Well this guy I met asked me to go on a skiing trip with him and you know I don't have the slightest idea about skiing--what to wear and what to do. He says he'll teach me, which is fine with me. Still, I don't have any of the stuff you're supposed to wear, and I was wondering if you could help out?"
 "Sure! You know you're in luck because I almost gave my gear to the Salvation Army last summer, but something told me to keep it a little longer. You can have all of it! And I'll show you how to put it all together. When is your trip and who is this new guy?"
 "Oh, nobody important, just a good friend from my support group."

"He must be at least a little important, I know you don't just go travelling with any old body."

"Well, when you talk about all of your personal business with people like in these group therapy sessions, you get to know each other and trust each other quite a bit. You know that from work."

"Yea... so when's the trip?"

The trip is not for two months, but before I tell him yes, I just wanted to make sure I could get the necessary equipment, so if I just happen to break my neck or something, at least I can do it in style!"

"Girl you missing some sense. But, yea, you..uh probably want to come over and try some of that stuff on. You know you might want to do that before you call him back, because most of those clothes items are sizes 6 and 8..." I said trying not to offend her--I mean she has lost a lot of weight, but some of that stuff was tight on me even.

"That should be fine. Most of my suits are sixes and eights, but I'll come by this weekend to try them on anyway, just in case."

"Dana, you have really lost some weight. I remember when 14's were fitting you tight, and you hated trying on clothes."

"Well I've lost a lot more than weight, thanks to the hypnotherapy."

"Wait a minute, I thought you said there were no black people in your group."

"I did."

"Oh!!"

"Oh what?"

"So you all fine now, so you going to the flip side."

"What is that supposed to mean? He's just a nice guy and a very good friend. You know how I am, if he was more than that I wouldn't even think about taking a trip like this with him--that might be too tempting. Besides, I'm not attracted to him that way, I'm just having fun meeting and enjoying people for who they are on the inside and not on the outside because I really appreciate it when people see me that way."

"Yea, well be careful cause some white people still think black rubs off."

"Girl, who you telling? Remember, I'm the one from the hood. ..."

My phone beeped and I asked Dana to hold for a minute while I checked to see who was on the other line.

"Hey you."

"Hi baby. I'm on the other line with Dana. What's up?"

"You know what's up," Robert said in a seductive tone.

"Oh, so now you want to be horny."

"Nah...I don't want to be horny...I want to be inside of you."

"Oooo you bad boy. What happened to my little church boy?"

"You turned me out. And speaking of church..."

"Uhh. Let me finish up with Dana and I'll call you right back," I interrupted.

"I'll be waiting."

"Okay. I'll call you right back," I clicked back over to Dana.

"That was.."

"Robert. Girl, who else calls you these days? Ya'll getting a little close, don't you think?"

"Not too close for me. That man gives me a high that's inexplicable!"

"Oo-oh. Sounds like somebody's getting sprung."

"What does that mean?"

"Oh it just means you are head-over-heels for somebody."

"Well that's definitely true! I mean there's just something about Robert that makes me just.... silly, like a school girl with her first admirer. He's romantic, and creative, and *passionate*..."

"Humm do I smell love in the air or is it just that he finally hit it?"

"BOTH!!" Nicolette screamed out like she was cumming at that very moment.

"So when was you gon' tell me? What's up with that?"

"It just happened last night, and girl my car was stolen."

"While ya'll was doing it!"

"No, before he even came home. See, I was at Robert's place early to cook dinner before he got home from the airport."

"*You* cookin'--it *is* serious."

"Well, anyway, these thugs across the street at the car wash stole it and stripped it down and it looked horrible. The insurance adjuster suggested that I total it, so I did. I don't know how I'm gonna tell my dad...at least it wasn't my fault."

"How do you know who stole it...did you see them?"

"Well, not exactly...but there were just these thuggish-looking guys that were flirting with me when I got there...they were listening to loud nasty rap music, and one of'm came over and started flirting and being real aggressive with me...they just made me feel uncomfortable...you know how those kind of guys can be."

"Well, you know, I sometimes listen to rap music, and that doesn't mean I would steal your car, Nic."

"I know, Dana. I didn't mean it like that. You know, how I normally treat guys when I'm not interested, well I was very nice and everything--I just got a bad vibe from those guys, and it had nothing to do with the music or what they look like--I just know they did it!"

"Uh..well..I'm sorry about your car. I know how special it was to you, and I'd be pissed off too, but could you get back to Robert for a minute."

"Girl, I'm still speechless!"

"So what happened to his celibacy vow?"

"He already talking about getting some more just now when he called!"

"I guess you just turned a brotha out...ain't nothing wrong with that!"

"Well, he had said that one of the reasons why celibacy was such a good choice for him was because he is a feen. When he was getting it, he said he had to have it every night, and sistahs just couldn't keep up."

"Well you two make a perfect match."

"Quit trippin'."

"You know I'm telling the truth."

"Yea, well he worked it all night long, and I was the one who got tired first. He's soo sensitive and gentle, yet he knows when to hit it hard. True skill."

"Well you need to find out if he has a friend and hook a sistah up."

"Girl, all the ones I've seen are short or married, and I know you don't go that route. But I'll be looking out for you. Tomorrow we're going to his church...I think."

"What do you mean 'I think'?"

"Well, he invited me to come earlier and I'm not real sure if I want to."

"What!?! Is this the same in-love woman I was just talking to? Girl you got a good black man, why wouldn't you want to go to church with him?" Damn, Nicolette is lucky.

"Dana, you know I rarely go to church. What if I do something stupid and embarass him or something?"

"Like what?"

"I don't know...like drink from the wrong glass or get lost in the bible trying to find the scripture."

"My bible has all the books labelled, so you can borrow it if you like, and tomorrow is not the first Sunday of the month, so unless he's Catholic, I doubt you will be taking communion."

"What if they ask me to stand up and tell if I've been baptized and all that stuff."

"Didn't Robert tell me he attends Mt. Olive Baptist Church?"

"Yea, that sounds right."

"Well don't worry about it, you won't be required to say a word. I've visited there many times, and I've even thought about joining there except I've been at my church since I was young and they helped me through so much, I just couldn't leave....they're like a second family to me. But, if I did, I'd be over there quick. It is a real friendly, home-like atmosphere even though the membership is pretty large. And that Pastor Haney really know how to preach the Word so that you can not only understand it, but apply it to everyday situations. The congregation is pretty young and there are a lot of singles there. I think you'll really like it."

I gave a big sigh of relief. "Okay, okay! You sound like their church cheerleader. I'll go, but answer one more thing for me."

"What?"

"What if God gets mad and breaks me and Robert up because he is too good for me?"

"Nicolette? How can you say that? I thought you were in love with this man."

"I am Dana, but I feel like I'm pulling him down. He's so strong, and I am so weak. I don't know a thing about God or religion."

"Well, to me that makes you a lot stronger that some people I know who claim to know the Bible backwards and forwards. At least you realize your weaknesses, and now, you can do something about them. Why do you think God put Robert into your life? You surely haven't ever even thought about it when I've asked you to go to church with me."

"Maybe you're right."

"It doesn't matter whether *I'm* right or not. Why don't you ask God what you should do?"

"What do you mean?"

"I mean just ask him... Right now, if you want to."

The phone was dead silent. I didn't know what to do. I've never said a prayer on my own, and I surely didn't think I'd say my first one over the phone.

"Nic, are you there?"

"Yea, I'm here....and see this is what I mean. It probably seems stupid to someone like you who practically grew up in the church..."

"I didn't start going to church regularly until I was in high school, Nicolette. I realized even then that there was more to life than what was going on around me. So me and my older sister started going to church together. And when I was in college, I would call her sometimes when I needed a lift, and we would both get down on our knees right over the phone, and we would pray and cry together sometimes for hours. We were so close because of those times, and until she moved so far away, we kept that up even in the good times when we just wanted to thank God for something wonderful he did. ....Would you like it if we did that now? I mean you don't have to say anything if you don't want to. I'll do the praying, you just be there in spirit, and then when I have something I need to pray about maybe you can return the favor."

"Okay," I said, still feeling a bit uneasy.

"You ready?"

"I guess so."

"Dear God:

First of all, I would just like to thank you for sending Nicolette into my life, and for our friendship that has grown so much, and that I deeply treasure. Then, Father, I would like to ask that you would cleanse both of us of any sin so that we can be worthy to call upon you and so that nothing will get in the way of us communicating with you, Father. We come asking that you just lay your hand on Nicolette's heart, and let her know that you are there to listen anytime she wants to talk, and in any way she wants to say it. Father, I know you would not have put Robert and Nic together if it was not in your plan. Help Nic to see her part in your plan, and your desire for her life. Help her to to find in you what she believes she lacks in herself. Give her peace and confidence as she goes forward. Thank you again for answering my prayers, and thank you for sticking with me through my recovery. Amen."

"Thank you Dana. I really do feel much more relaxed about this whole thing. Maybe I should call you and pray again in the morning."

"You can if you need to, but if I don't get my butt in the bed, I won't even be able to get up myself."

"Thanks again, Dana. You know you my girl.. Goodnight."

"Goodnight."

♋

Robert picked me up a ten o'clock sharp, so that we would have plenty of time to get there since I live all the way on the other side of town from the church. I was a little nervous, and Robert asked me if I was okay. I decided not to tell him that I was nervous until we left church cause it seems to me like when people keep asking me if I'm okay, I feel worse.

Dana was right, this church feels real comfortable. I did have to stand up when they called for visitors--I felt Robert's arm nudging me a little, but I didn't have to say a word, just like Dana said. The people were really friendly, too. Everybody, even Robert got up and went to speak to the people who stood up as visitors. Robert spoke to a lot of other people who seemed to be members, too. He introduced me to a couple of ladies, who gave me that 'who are you' eye and several guys, that he says he knows from the Men's Ministry. They all seemed so close, and it made you feel right at home like you could have taken off your shoes and noone would have complained.

The scripture was written in the program, so I had already found it and read it by the time the preacher called for everyone to read it together. Robert put his arm around me, and read along with me from my bible, I guess since I obviously had already found it. The sermon was from Romans 5:3-11 which talks about how when bad things happen to us, it helps us to become strong and patient. I thought about my car. This pastor is really funny and he really does help to apply the words to everyday life. I was actually enjoying the sermon, and then he started talking about the young singles who come to him to ask about sex and what they should do about their urges to 'do it'. He called it "biology versus theology", and he had everybody standing up and waving their hands, but I just sat there feeling like he was talking directly to me. Robert was looking pretty stiff too, but he didn't look over at me not one time. God, I feel so ashamed about pulling him down, while he's trying to get close to God, and do the right thing. I don't deserve him. Just as I said that I remembered praying with Dana, and how she'd asked God to help me with that. I tuned back into the sermon. The preacher told us how it is through faith and persistence to do the 'will of God' that we would find that 'real' love that we were looking for, if we just wait and ask God for patience to do so. But otherwise, when we try to 'make love' it don't work, cause love can't be made, it can only be given and only through God. Those words were truly powerful, and even though at the end of the sermon, Robert was standing and clapping, I could sense that the message had touched him too.

After we spoke to lots of people, and he introduced me to nearly the entire church, including his pastor, we finally left. It was really quiet on the way home. Robert asked if I would like to get something to eat, and I said no. Really I was starving, but I just wanted to go home because I didn't know what to say. I just sat there looking out the window until we were almost at my place. Then, I looked over at Robert, who looked to be deep in thought, and I looked back at the window and we both let out a great big sigh at the exact same time. I looked back at him, and this time he was lookin' at me too. So I started to speak, "I felt...

I stopped because Robert was saying the same words I was. He stopped too. There was a pause and I started again, "I think..." We'd done it again! I smiled, and he did too.

"You go fir..." Man we did it again!

He grabbed my hand and we just giggled and giggled like two little kids.

When we got to my place, Robert turned off the motor and we just sat there looking into one another's eyes. I couldn't stand it--I had to look away. Robert reached over and turned my face to meet his. He looked deep into my eyes and gave me a very long deep sensual kiss. I was thankful the seats are separate in his Explorer cause if we had been touching there would have been some major flames.

"Robert, I'd better go."

"Why?"

I sighed, and he looked at me as if he knew what I was thinking.

"Robert, I don't want to make you do something you might regret."

"First of all," he smiled and his big eyes twinkled, "I'm a grown man, and any decision I make that effects my life and my well-being is totally up to me...and, second, I did just what I wanted to the other night...and I don't know about you but I don't regret one minute of it."

I looked puzzled.

"See, Nicolette, I know what I did was wrong, and I even asked God to forgive me that very night, but that's the great thing about God...He's not like us, if we ask him for something, if it is in accordance with his will and his plan for our lives, he will give it to us."

"So what about your vow of celibacy?"

"Well, I can't say I feel good about breaking it, but I actually felt worse about the thought that I had disrespected you."

"Disrespected me??!"

"Yes, by sleeping with you before we get married."

It was quiet. I didn't know what to say. I'd never been so flattered, and I'm not sure if it is because he felt he had disrespected me or because he has obviously considered marrying me.

"But I wanted you too."

"I know that, but I'm supposed to be the leader in the relationship, and how could I help you and lead you if I myself am weak."

It was quiet again. I'm usually pretty good at figuring out where things are going between me and a man, but I sure am lost this time.

"Nicolette, baby, I want you to know that what we did... that making love to you was very real and very intense for me..."

"Me too."

"But I didn't just do it because I wanted to, I truly wanted to please you, because I really have come to care about you...in fact, we just had this kind of connection from day one. I don't want that to stop."

"Neither do I."

"Then let's just put the past behind us, and go on from here."

"It's gonna be pretty hard not to..."

"Uhmm let's not think about that right now...let's just take it one step at a time."

"Okay, then. Could the first step be to get some food...I'm starving?"

"You know I am too!"

♋

I had to get a rental car for a while, and I got a new vette. It wasn't so bad. It had a turbo engine and could really go, so it'll do til I find another car. Robert agreed to look with me on Saturday, since my dad is still out of town. But when Saturday morning rolled around Robert had some emergency to take care of, so I was on my own. I started to pout, but then I figured that wasn't going to get me anywhere. So I just went out and started looking.

I went to the nearest vette dealer. The one I used to go to, to get my car serviced. They know me here, and as soon as I drove up in the rented vette, Bob the service guy notices me. "Hi, how are ya today? Did you have an accident in Roxane?"

"No," I said sullenly, "she was stolen and totaled."

"Oh, I'm sorry to hear that. So you're looking for a new car today, huh?"

"Yes, and I've never had to look before. This is my first time."

"Well, hey let me introduce you to someone who I know will take care of you. Just a second."

He went away for a minute and came back with John, a tall, dark, handsome white guy. He has one of the most honest faces, I've ever seen. I wonder if he practices in the mirror or something.

He took me straight to the classics which were inside on the showroom floor. They had a baby blue one that looked a lot like Roxane except it was a '72. He offered to let me drive it, and I didn't really want to, but he just insisted. So he got the keys and after he drove it out of the showroom, he gave them to me. I got inside and it was really nice. He took my license and handed me a tape that said listen to me. I popped the tape in and drove off.

"Hello, Princess," a familiar voice said, "it's your knight in shining armor and I'm about to take you on a ride." Oh what will they think of next?! "Nicolette, if you haven't caught the voice by now, it's me--Robert." I vaguely heard the tape say as I was checking out the dash board.

"What??...Robert! What in the world!"

"Calm down, now, sweetheart. Just keep driving, and I'm going to tell you what to do. Okay?"

I just stared at the tape player and looked so confused.

"Okay, you want to know what this is all about, well I'm going to be your tour guide today, even though I couldn't be with you. I want you to go to the Mobil gas station on Pearson street and go to the ATM machine. Turn this tape off now and wait for your next instructions."

There was a pause and then, he said, "Stop the tape, Nic," as if he knew I hadn't done it.

I drove into the Mobil and sat in the parking lot feeling very strange. I decided to turn the tape on to see what was the next thing I was supposed to do. It played for a few seconds and then it said, "Okay, Nicolette, you should be in the store by now and not listening to this tape. So just trust me and play along."

Damn. I looked around to see if anyone was watching me and got out of the car. I went to the ATM machine and just stood there. Then I noticed a small white teddy bear sitting on the side with a note on it. The note said, "take me to the country club with a smile, and your grandmother's locket."

"My grandmother's locket, what is this all about? Robert, are you in here?" I said out loud.

The guy at the cash register said, "you're to go to the country club smiling and wearing your grandmom's locket."

"What about the car?"

He shrugged, and repeated himself, "Smile, and wear your grandmom's locket to the country club."

"Okaaay?!? This is getting very weird."

When I got back in the car, and started going again, I kept waiting for the tape to say something, but it didn't. I was wearing my grandmother's locket as usual, so I just went straight to the country club which is about ten minutes away. About halfway there, the tape kicks in again and scares me to death, "Nic, you should be almost to the country club by now. Don't worry about the car, okay?"

"Okay, dear. Whatever you say," I said sarcastically, since I'm obviously not in control of anything.

When I got to the Club, I was just going to park in front and go in and see what was there for me, but as I was getting out, Kevin, the guy who parks the cars asked for the keys. I tried to explain to him that I was just going to run in for a minute, but he insisted on taking my keys. Then, he handed me a note that was rolled up like a little scroll with a ribbon around it. It said:

Roses are Red, and Violets are Blue.

I can't write poetry, but I sure do love you.

Go in the lobby and wait by the centerpiece.

So I went inside and waited by the centerpiece. People kept looking at me and I felt like everybody around me knew what was happening except me. Before long, a dark-haired woman dressed in a pink coat came over toward me looking toward my breast. I looked down and noticed that she was looking at my locket. Then, she gave me a robe and a towel and said put this on and wait in room 10. So I did.

Then two women and a man came in and worked me over...massaging me and then waxing me from head to toe. God, this feels so good. Robert is too sweet!

When they were finished I was put back in the car and given another note that read:

Lettuce is green, and Beets are red

Next on the list is to work on the head

Next stop, Paradise Salon. See Shelle.

I smiled and headed over to the salon. Shelle is my new hair stylist and she's in on this. She can't hold water, so I know she'll tell me what the hell is going on. But sike, he's gotten to her too, because she wouldn't say a word, and it was abnormally quiet in the shop. People kept whispering and giggling as if I didn't notice them.

When I left there finally after three hours of hair drying and mani- and pedicuring, I was exhausted and needed a nap. This was fun, but now I'm getting tired. I should call him and see if I can take a break. I love this, but something about the beauty shop just wears me out. I asked Shelle if she had anything for me. She didn't, so I wonder what I'm supposed to do next. I went to the car, and when I got to it there was a white rose on the windshield with another tape attached. I got in the car and popped the tape in quickly.

"Hey you, you must be getting a little wired by now, so go to the Westin Hotel now and rest for a while and I'll see you there at eight."

There was nothing else on the tape, so I went straight to the hotel. I can't believe he knows me so well in just six months. I'll bet this is our anniversary celebration. Yea, that's it, it's our six months anniversary celebration, I said to myself as I snuggled into the soft warm bed at the hotel. I was awakened by a knock at the door at seven o'clock on the nose. Oh my God, it's Robert, I thought. I jumped up and went to the door.

It was a bellman and he handed me a piece of luggage that looked like mine, but I'm still halfway asleep so I don't know what is really going on.

"Do you know where Robert is?" I asked him. He handed me a long garment bag.

"No ma'am. I was just told to deliver this to room 1410, I'm sorry."

"Oh, that's okay. Let me get you something," I said heading for my purse. But when I got back he was gone. Now I know something fishy is going on--a bellman that doesn't wait for a tip. The bag *is* mine, and inside it are all kinds of makeup, jewelry and tidbits from my vanity area. There are some cute new shoes, I put all that in the bathroom and go over and look out the window. It is getting dark now and the view from this window is spectacular.

I lay the garment bag on the bed and unzipped it. It is the baddest dress I'd ever seen. I pulled it out and looked at it.

God, this man is the bomb! I can't believe this, we even have the exact same taste in clothes.

I took off my clothes and put the dress on. It is so beautiful and it fits just perfect. He must have consulted Afrikka for this. It is a straight red dress with a sweetheart neck line and a slit up the front. It shows all my curves, the muscles in my back and arms, and it even makes it look like I have a booty! I'd better take a shower and get ready!

Wow! I look great. My hair is still tight. The front is swept up away from my face with one little curl spiralling down in front of my eye. And the back is hanging on my shoulders.

By the time I get my jewelry and makeup on it is almost 8:00. I'm so excited. I can't wait to see him and thank him for a wonderful day. I sit on the bed to get relaxed, but I'm too pumped and I don't want to wrinkle my gown. So I get up and pace around the room a little, getting so anxious.

The phone rings and I almost jump out of my skin.

"Yes. This is Nicolette....Downstairs where?....okay... okay....yes...I'll be right there."

I headed downstairs as quickly as I could. I went to the front door as instructed, and my mouth dropped. I couldn't believe my eyes. No...no...I'm dreaming this! My car is totaled, I sent it to the pound last week. I ran out to Roxane and Robert was sitting in her with all these silvery blue balloons just smiling so handsomely in a bad ass tux.

I leaned over and peaked in to make sure I wasn't dreaming. Everything looked exactly the same. I could hardly believe it! He must've known from the look in my eye that I was struggling to believe all this.

"Yes...It's the REAL Roxane," he started rapping. "Roxanne, Roxanne, uh-uh, I want to be your man, uh-uh."

I ran around to the driver's side and gave him a big hug and a kiss that curled my toes.

"You are the greatest!!! God, I love you!" I said before I knew it.

He just looked at me and said "Well, don't you want to take a ride."

"Yes, but not with Roxane."

"Oh...it's like that!"

"Unh-huh."

"Well, I just have one more thing for you." He looked very serious. And I just stared at him while he got down on his knee and extended a large diamond in my face. "Nicolette, I know I've only known you for six months, but I've never felt something was so right in all my life..." He had tears in his eyes, and for the first time in my life I just couldn't hold mine back for one second. "...I ...love you! and I want to wake up to you everyday for the rest of my life as Mrs. Nicolette Shoderaux....Will you marry me?"

By now, people were gathering from everywhere. I looked up briefly, and it was as if time stood still. I knew without a doubt that this was right.

"Yes....yes." I said dropping more tears on Robert.

He removed the ring from the box and placed it on my finger. There were cheers even on the inside of the hotel as we walked through the crowd to the most perfect dinner I have ever been fed. God, I love him.

CHAPTER 20
Freak Nic
♋

"Who is she calling now?" Dana asked me as if I knew.

"I don't know," I told her as I was checking off a 'Things to Do' list.

"Do you need me to do anything, Afrikka?" Dana offered.

"Naaahh. Just rest, honey, 'cause you gonna need all of your energy tonight," I told her.

We both sat there listening to the T.V. But Simone was talking so loud on the telephone that we couldn't hear what was going to happen next on *The Young and the Restless*.

Well, I guess our own lives are so exciting that we no longer need soap operas.

"Can you slam my phone down any harder," I told Simone as she practically smashed the receiver on the hook.

"Damn, Simone, what's up with ya," Dana laughed at the goofy dance Simone was doing.

Simone kept dancing and smiling until she threw herself on the floor next to the T.V. I just ignored her because I knew she had something up her sleeve. Plus, I was into this soap opera now and I had no time for Simone at this moment.

"What the hell is wrong with you?!" I yelled at Simone 'cause she turned the TV off. "You must wanna get yo ass kicked!"

Dana laughed and when I gave her this evil look, she stopped.

"Check it..." Simone began, "I got the finest, blackest, biggest dick mothafuckas for Nic's party tonight!"

"Who'd you get?" Dana seemed anxious to know.

"You horney...ain't you, Dana?" Simone asked her.

"Oh, like you ain't," Dana came back. "You probably cut a deal to fuck after the party or something knowing you Simone."

"Girl, I thought you knew--you wanna join us?" she grinned.

"Who'd you get, Simone?" I interrupted them cause they both know they ain't gon' do shit. Now I wanted to know.

"I got 'take-a-look at my dick here'--Turbo in the house," Simone spoke.

Dana and I looked at each other.

"You getting warm," Dana told her as I smiled at the thought of that big penis Turbo got women talking about around town.

"I got sexy, 'slap my booty anytime'--Seduction, in the house," Simone continued.

"You getting warmer," I said 'cause I heard about how he seduces women just by watching the way his moves his muscles on every part of his body...and even that part that we aren't allowed to see.

"And last, but not least, I got that smooth skin, 'wax my ass all night'--Mr....."

"...Clean!!!" Dana and I screamed to the top of our lungs.

"...in the hiz-zouse," Simone finished.

"I heard he was the Bomb on stage," Dana whispered staring in space.

"Me, too," I added, "...and I've never seen him before."

"Well, this is going to be the best bachelorette party that anyone can ever attend," Simone smiled as she was peeping out my tapes from my movie collection.

All of a sudden Simone started laughing that same old laugh again. What could be so...the Bomb...this time? Damn, I hope it's not what I think it is. I hope she hasn't found...

"Afrikka?" she called my name as I was trying to play it off by picking up my notepad of my 'Things-to-Do' list. "What is...'In Search of a Big Dick'...about?"

I was so embarrassed because I'm letting a side of myself show that I never wanted to reveal. What was I to say? How am I suppose to explain this.

"What?" I was thinking of something to say. "Oh, that's a movie I taped over and forgot to put another label on it."

Dana and Simone actually looked at me like they believed me. I wasn't about to confess that I had been watching porno flicks to substitute for my absentee sex life. It's not like I'm addicted or anything. I practically forgot it was under there anyway.

"Oh..." I remembered, "...one of you guys come with me to pick up some last minute stuff from Parties to Go."

"I'm gonna stay here and catch up on my sleep," Dana immediately responded as she layed herself across my sofa right after I hopped up putting a pillow under her head at the same time.

"I'll go," Simone agreed. "But we've got to go pick up E.J. from over Candy's house so that I could drop him off at the babysitter's house tonight in order for Candy to come to the party tonight."

"No problem," I told her grabbing my purse at the same time. "But as long as you drive my car 'cause I'm sick of driving right about now."

"Well, just use me then," Simone laughed as we headed out of the door.

After about ten minutes I realized that I left the Things-To-Do list sitting on the coffee table. I took my cellular phone out to call Dana because there was no way I was going to remember everything on that list.

"Dana?" I asked because it didn't sound like her answering my phone at my house.

"It's me," she responded.

"Look, girl..." I began, "...I left the Things-To-Do list on the table in front of you....do you see it?"

As she was looking for it I could have sworn that I heard my tape playing in the background. Nah...I know she didn't pop that tape in...or did she.

"I got it," she returned back to the phone.

"Call off that list to me if you will?" I asked her.

As she was calling off the list and as I was writing those items to my new list, I heard moans and groans in the background. She was listening to *In Search of a Big Dick*. I can't believe this. Dana thank she slick. That's why her horny ass didn't want to come with us...talking about she had to catch up on her sleep...like she had been hanging out all night or something.

"Dana, what are you watching?" I asked her after she called out the last item.

"I'll talk to you later," she said as she hung up in my face.

"Is something wrong?" Simone asked me.

I must have had this strange and surprising look on my face like Dana was doing something wrong.

"...oh...oh...nothing," I threw out afraid I would give myself away, and in a way I really don't care, I just know that Simone would give me a hard ass time about it. "...Dana just sounded real tired."

"She just need a big dick," Simone laughed. "Well, we're here."

How ironic, I thought to myself.

♋

I cannot believe that this day has finally arrived. In less than twenty-four hours I will be a married woman. Me. Of all people...married. I pulled the newspaper out of my purse and looked at the exclusive article that had been placed about my wedding today. These people are more interested in making money off of dad's popularity with this Versace case than publicizing my wedding, but Afrikka said we should take advantage of it, so I did. We invited a representative from each of the five main television stations, plus someone from Ebony, Jet, and Essence, and a couple of fashion media people that Afrikka wanted to invite to get some exposure for her wedding creations.

The article talks about how much money everything costs and how my dad is sparing no expense for my wedding. It also talks about all the politicians and famous people we know who will be there tomorrow. I guess I should be all excited about that stuff, but all I can really think about is Robert. We decided not to take our honeymoon until after this semester since I will be graduating then. That way, not only will it be my graduation present, but also a wedding gift all wrapped up in one. So this weekend we are just going to spend our pre-honeymoon in Cancun before our seven day cruise to wherever Robert plans to surprise me with this summer. The paper just mentions the Cancun trip as our honeymoon, and I'm glad they won't know about our real trip because I'll be damned if I want *anybody* disrupting *my* honeymoon.

Aaahh....finally, my ultimate dream has arrived, and with Afrikka's help everything is put together so perfectly and in just a few months time. It's a miracle we got everything done so fast, but like Robert says, "When God does things, it doesn't take a long time." And now I have accomplished all of my goals. Well, having three kids and a tiger will come very soon, I'm sure.

"Nic," Simone was yelling through the door, "what are you doing in there? There are at least fifteen horny-ass women out here desperately waiting for you to come out so I can let these big-dick mothafuckas in the room."

I opened the door slowly.

"Uhh, can a lady have some privacy before her wedding day," I told Simone, as I closed the bathroom door behind me, "and I wouldn't go in there just yet if I were you."

"Nasty ass," she said scrunching up her nose and pushing me toward the living room.

The family rehearsal dinner we had earlier was the bomb. Ed knew of this catering place around the corner from the church that specialized in the best soul food in town. Damn, that sweet potato pie for dessert was so good I wanted to slap the shit out the chef. He better be glad that he didn't deliver the food because I would have, for real.

Since Robert and I are the only children and we both come from single parent, affluent homes, I'm sure our parents are going to spoil us on our wedding day. My dad met Robert and fell in love with him instantly, but I never met Robert's mom in person. She lives on the coast and is always as busy as Afrikka with her own chain of boutiques, so we never got a chance to visit each other. However, we talked on the phone at least twice a week and I just knew during that time she fell in love with me, too. Besides, I was engaged one day and almost married just a few months later, so of course time flew by before I knew it. She just got in town today and I was so excited about meeting her. But, at the dinner she didn't seem quite pleased when she saw me. She was acting kind of stand-offish, and she left the dinner early and headed back to her room. Robert reassured me that I was overexaggerating and that she was extremely tired from her long flight and the hectic week she'd had. I'm sure that he was right.

It was nice of Afrikka, with her coordinating my wedding and all, to also help Dana to put my bachelorette party together. This suite is perfectly decorated with the finest foods and drinks, candles, and other paraphanelia. And there's a cake made like a penis with light-brown chocolate icing and a little squirt of white icing at the tip--only Simone would have come up with something like this. It even has balls with darker chocolate icing in little spirals that look like hair.

Afrikka brought about six of her co-workers and close friends whom I've met previously at her job or through Ed. Simone invited her sister, Candy, and Temeka. Dana came with one of her sorors. I invited a few of my classmates and some people from work. Ed's sisters, Ashia and Tracia, who are just like sisters to Robert and whom I've become close to in these past few months are in the house. And of course, Roselda, and I was surprised when she showed up because she doesn't usually feel too comfortable hanging out with us young folks and partying, but she said she wouldn't miss it for the world. I didn't want too many people at my party because I want to have the strippers all to myself. And Simone claimed to have gotten the best one's in town--Mr. Clean, Turbo, and Seduction.

"I need dick in my life....I need dick in my life....I need dick in my life," I was singing to the beat of this song rubbing my hands against Mr. Clean's nice, big, round, fat ass. No wonder they call him Mr. Clean--his body is so beautiful without any scars, marks or blemishes and he is oh, so smooth, "I need some dick, I need some dick, I need some..."

"Simone," Temeka tapped me on my shoulder, "It's my turn. You been humpin' and bumpin' Mr. Clean a little bit too long. You got to share the dick. Remember, it ain't no fun if yo' homies can't have none."

"Alright...a-ight...a-ight," I gave in, "Mr. Clean, I will be back. Here's a few dollars that should tie me over til next time."

I stuffed about eleven dollars down his 'G' string. Hey, and he was well worth it. I looked over at Nic and her nerdy, selfish ass was sitting in a chair watching Turbo give her a, what do the men call it except it is now reversed, a 'lap dance'.

She just sittin' there like a little child not knowing what to do with that big, baldheaded mandingo.

"Nic," I walked over to her, "why are you sittin' there like some little nerd?"

"What am I suppose to be doing?" she asked. "He's doing his job and I'm suppose to watch, right?"

"How much money you got on you?" I asked her.

"Simone, if you need to borrow some...."

"Nic, I don't need to borrow no damn money," I cut her off, "have you ever been to a strip club."

"No," she answered.

"Have you ever been somewhere and seen niggas strip?" I asked.

"No," she answered.

"Damn, girl," I whispered, surprised, "you have been sheltered all of yo' life. You missing out."

I grabbed Nic from her chair and sat down in her place.

"I forgot to tell you guys that before we planned this," she told me.

"Oh, that's a-okay," I pushed her out of the way while I started feeling on Turbo's chest.

"I guess I'll go and see if everybody's having a great time," Nic responded.

I waved her off and started workin' this body.

Damn, I came in here just to get a refill of Absolute and vodka and they have to nerve to have food spread out all over the table. Well, I ate a little at the rehersal dinner and I was too full to have dessert. There was a time when I would stuff myself even if I was full, but today at the rehearsal I didn't and felt good about it, too. But...these hot wings look too damn good to pass up. Naw, I'll just have a slice of cake like I said and be through with it.

"Dana," I heard my name being called from around the corner. It was Afrikka, "see, you and I think alike, don't we?"

"Yeah," I said, "after watching and dancing with those fine bodies out there, especially Seduction, I developed a sweet tooth all of a sudden."

"You ain't lying," she added, "My sweet tooth developed when Mr. Clean flipped and landed head first into my co-worker, Tara's pussy wishing he would have landed into mine. And you should have seen how Robert's cousin, Tracia, was trying to take her place."

We both laughed hysterically.

"So what's taking you so long to cut the cake," Afrikka looked at me, "it's not like this is Nicolette's wedding cake, girl."

"I know," I told her, "I can't believe my best friend is getting married. I am so happy for her, too. I know Robert will make a great husband."

Afrikka looked at me and smiled.

"Me, too," she said, "I just knew that at the age of thirty I would be married, and look at me...I'm thirty and planning the wedding I always dreamed of having for someone else. But, I'm happy with myself now, more than ever because I know deep down, the Lord will let my day shine real soon. I don't know exactly when,"Afrikka laughed, "but I know that it's gonna happen soon."

The phone rang in the kitchen. We both looked at each other trying to figure out which one of us is going to answer it.

"I'll get it," Afrikka volunteered, "Hello...Ed?..I thought you was at Robert's bachelor party...what?...okay...hold on while I go in the bedroom...Dana, I've got to take this call...something happened with one of my accounts...hang this phone up when you hear me pick it up in the room..."

Afrikka gave me the phone. She seemed a little bit concerned.

"Hey, Ed...yeah...I'm having the time of my life...I'm not going to tell you what we're doing...oh...you got it Afrikka?...you, too, Ed...bye."

I hung up the phone. I looked at the cake and realized that I no longer have an appetite for that chocolate cake. My appetite is now back in full force for Seduction. I yelled out heading back into the living room.

"My cheeks are about to meet your cheeks, Cheeks."

♋

I hope Nicolette doesn't get mad at me for not socializing with her guests. I'm suppose to be the coordinator and I'm laying in bed sick to my stomach after what Ed just told me. I worked hard for that account and now it's gone. I've never lost an account before and this one would have made sure that I was taken care of for the rest of my life. Why today?

"Afrikka," Nicolette was walking through the door, "why aren't you kicking it out there? Simone just taught me the ropes of how to handle a stripper. She gave me a whip, and you should have seen how me and Turbo was clowning together on my first lesson."

"I just finished talking to Ed...something happened with one of my accounts and I'm suppose to meet Ed at midnight so he can give me the full details," I told her.

"Tonight?" she questioned me, "Are you not going to be tired after this?"

"No," I shook my head, "I need to know what happened with my account, tonight. You know how I am."

"Yeah," she whispered, "I understand. Just make sure when I come to your house at ten o'clock in the morning for you to make me look all beautiful and all, that you're bright-eyed and bushy-tailed, okay?"

I smiled. The phone rang.

"I'll get it," I said. "It's probably for me again."

"No, it's Robert. I just paged him from my mobile 'cause I was feeling guilty about what Simone was about to make me do to Mr. Clean," Nicolette grabbed the phone, "Hey, sweetheart....you having fun?...You are?...okay...okay..stop playing with me...what?...at nine o'clock in the morning?...why?...okay, honey..don't do anything I wouldn't do...bye...have fun... smack! smack!..."

She makes me sick.

"Is something wrong?" I asked Nicolette.

"No," she looked irritated, "it's just that my father and his mother want to meet with us in the morning to talk to us before the wedding. So if I'm a little late coming to your house, don't panic."

"Don't sound so disgusted," I suggested, "this is the last time you will be you're father's little girl and Robert a mama's boy...so you know, they want to have an intimate, last time parent-to-child talk."

"I know," she pouted, "my dad will probably get on my nerves as usual. But you know what, these last couple of months he has been spending more time with me than ever before."

"That's because he's about to lose his little girl..." I paused, "...to some man whose gonna take advantage of her."

We both laughed.

"I'm proud of you, girl," I hugged her.

She looked at me.

"I've been meaning to tell you this," she said, "you deserve everything that I have because you have been so good to me. Thanks for being a friend. I don't know what I would have done without you."

I smiled.

"Get outta here," I punched her, "go back and show those fine bunches of balls what you can do."

She hopped up, kissed me on the cheek, and ran out of the room. What I wouldn't do to be in her place right now.

♋

Ed and I agreed to meet at my place since he had been drinking, and my place was much closer to him than the hotel or his place. I rushed to get home hoping to make it there before he did. My place is a mess because of all the wedding stuff that is stashed there, and even though Ed and I have definitely seen each other on some bad days, I don't even want him to see my place looking like it is. Maybe I'm just fussin' over nothin'. I'm really concerned about my Macy's account. They are one of the biggest client's I've got, and if they drop me, I'm going to have a whole lot of reorganizing and hussling to do to meet my goals for the year...hell, to pay the bills.

I wonder what could have happened. I know that sales weren't down because they just re-ordered a whole new full-figured lot. I just can't imagine what could be wrong. Oh God! maybe we sent the wrong shipment and they didn't let me know. Or maybe the swatches we sent weren't the same color, or worse, quality of fabric. Either way, they should have just let me know and I would have gotten it taken care of immediately. I mean I've been working with them for a whole year and a half now--you would think they would have that much confidence in me! After I literally crawled on my hands and knees to get this account...they can not do this to me!

I was really getting myself all worked up. I was getting all shaky. Thank God I'm almost there.

As I pulled into the garage area, I noticed Ed standing in front of my place looking sullen, and actually kind of sexy. I shook my head, and focused in on the account as I screeched on the brakes to keep from crashing into the wall, and jumped out of my dark blue Legend.

Ed was at the garage doorway by now, and following me into the house. "By the way you driving, it looks like I wasn't the only one drinking."

"I haven't had a thing, but I could use a drink."

"What?! I haven't ever seen *you* drink."

"Well, there's a first time for everything."

"Oh, Afrikka, I keep telling you not to get yourself all worked up, worrying about things you can't change. I started not to even call you, but under the circumstances I knew you would have had a fit if I didn't."

"You damned right! Ed, this isn't just a job, this my whole life."

"Who you telling? Don't you think I got just as much riding on this as you do?"

"Yea, Ed...I'm sorry for snapping at you...will you tell me exactly what was said?" I sat down cause I just felt terrible.

"Well first of all, Alan from the Marketing division called a couple of times for you this morning. On the third time, I insisted that he share any pertinent information with me, since I wasn't sure if you were going to make it in or not."

"I was getting things together for the wedding...I knew I should have called in and let you know...I didn't think anything like this would happen."

"Anyway," Ed looked at me all serious, "they are reorganizing the whole ladies department from sportswear to the accessories, and they are going to keep us for the fall, but they are going to be under new management and are going to go with some new lines for the spring. I called a friend of mine over there to see what exactly was going on. She couldn't talk over the phone, so we met for lunch downtown.."

"Who is this? I didn't know you had a friend at Macy's, that sure would have been helpful information two years ago when I was begging them for that damn account."

"Just listen. Okay?" Ed just looked at me trying to be compassionate, but I really was making that hard for him with my attitude. I just can't help it. I feel so frustrated right now. "So, we met and she told me that they do this all the time in order to shuffle around the contracts and keep a good mix of trendy merchandise on the floor. A couple of the large manufacturers are coming out with new knockoff lines they want to try out, and you know the little guys like us get shifted for those big merchandisers--it's all politics. But as good as your stuff is, and as fast as it is catching on, it's even a good chance we may be able to get back in in the summer, or as early as March. We just got to be patient and persistent. And I'm willing to bust my butt pulling in a few new contracts. As far as I'm concerned, this is just a challenge..we were starting to get a bit too comfortable anyway. This'll make us hungry again, like when we started out. Whadaya say, boss!"

My mind was a million light years away. Ed looked at me for a while, I guess waiting on a response. I just sat there motionless, looking at him, but in another world. Finally, Ed said, "Afrikka those strippers must have you still going."

"Huh?" I said, still not tuned into to Ed's words.
"Girl, you got something on your mind?"
"Not really."
"Come on now Afrikka, you been preoccupied for days now, but I just hadn't said anything...I thought it was the wedding plans. What's *really* going on?!"

Wedding. The word wedding brought me back to reality. I had been spending all this time and energy on Nic's wedding, and neglecting my own life. Hoping maybe God would notice how good I've been...how unselfish...how caring...and give me what I need. But I just realized, in this very moment, that it doesn't happen that way. You can lose everything you once valued as much as life itself in a matter of minutes, and at this moment I don't even care about that anymore. I'm about to be thirty years old, and all I got is this damn company, and I don't even control that! It is so clear...so, so, clear right now what I need most in my life is what I fear and fight most. But I give up, I surrender, right now.

"Afrikka??" Ed looked really worried.
"I'm just tired, Ed."
"That face says more than just tired..."
"No, it doesn't," I punched Ed in the stomach, which is my way of letting him know I was okay and most of all, that I didn't want to talk about it anymore. "We got a long day ahead of us tomorrow, let's go to bed."

Ed grabbed his keys off of the mirror stand by the door where he always puts them. When I heard the keys, I turned around and said, "And where do you think you are going?"
"Home.??"
"Unh-uh, Mister. You've been drinking, so this is your last stop unless you want me to call a cab."
"I'll be fine...I made it over here didn't I?"

I took the key off of his extended finger and put it back on the stand. I just turned around and pointed to the sleeper sofa Ed has spent many a night on.

He gave in and started pulling out the couch. I went to get him some linens, and when I came back he was standing there with his shirt off and hand out waiting on the linens.

I helped him put the sheets on and Ed said, "Did you see how good *my girl* looked?"

"You know, I told her she's looking younger and younger everytime I see her. Those poor waiters couldn't even concentrate for trying to look at your mama. I told her I can't get no attention with her around!"

"I told you about how my friends used to be trying to mack on my mama when she would come up to the school."

"And yo' daddy is as crazy as ever."

"Did he ask you when we are going to get married again?"

"Oh, not only did he ask me when the wedding was going to be, he introduced me to several people as his future daughter-in-law."

"The old man just won't quit, will he. I've told him many a time that we're *just* business partners. You know, a man and a woman can't be just friends in this world without everyone trying to push them together."

"Well, you can't blame the man for trying to get him some grandchildren. I've just started expecting that from your family--it's kinda cute."

We finished putting the covers on the couch, and Ed sat down to take off his shoes. I just had to comment, "I see you been working on those feet."

"Yea, I love that gel you bought me...Let me go ahead and put in an order for some more this Christmas."

"You don't have to wait til Christmas, cause friends don't let friends walk around with crusty feet," I cracked.

"Thank you, mama," Ed cracked back, looking so ridiculously sexy in just his slacks.

"That's foxy mama to you," I said heading into the back to change into some pj's since I sorta had company.

"Gon' Foxy Brown," Ed laughed, "but you got on a few too many clothes for the role, I think."

"Well, what do you suggest I take off first," I said coming out of the bathroom in a long, black, silk nightgown, the only one I own, and looked at Ed with intensity. Ed looked back totally caught off guard. And then he snapped his fingers in front of my face and said:

"Girl, you *are* tired. You over here dreaming I'm Jamal or somebody. You better go get that vibrator you been telling me about."

"Oh, you want to use it!??"

"Oooo Afrikka, I'm scared of you....You go to a bachelorette party and come back turned out!"

"Nah. I ain't into looking at or playing with nothing that ain't mine to take home," I said sitting down on the edge of the sofa bed. I slyly turned my head to watch as Ed, who is on the other side of the bed, slowly removes his pants and folds them neatly over the back of the loveseat. He is so meticulous.

"I hear you. Watching those little young girls at Rob's deal made me think of my little sisters strutting around at the beach when they first got what they considered a figure. Now they are all grown up and Ashia is nearly married."

"I know. Casey right?" I said, and Ed nodded his head yes. "She talks about him all the time. I thought she was going to break down and recite *Casey at the Bat* at one point."

Ed slipped into the bed and under the covers, and I was leaning back on one arm while we talked.

"So, she told you he plays for the Braves," Ed slid the arm that was supporting me out further until I was lying flat on the bed.

"Told me, I'm trying remember his jersey number." Since I was lying down now anyway, thanks to Ed, I scooted up and made myself comfortable.

"Yea, she's pretty sold on the brotha. He seems crazy about her too. I just hope he know he is going to have to give up his "other" life...the one he doesn't tell her about. The partying, the booze, women..."

"Now what makes you think he's into all that."

"We grew up together...I know the nig...I mean brother. Besides, that nigga broke one of the cardinal rules--NEVER DATE YOUR FRIEND'S SISTER. Rob and I have both already had a little talk with him."

"Do I sense a bit of big brother protection?"

"Absolutely. I didn't raise those girls up right for some knucklehead to come along and hurt their feelings."

"Uhh, who died and made you their daddy?"

"Oh they would rather have me checking up on them and telling Dad what's up with these brothas, than to have Dad doing it himself cause my dad is ruthless. One time one of my sisters, I think it was Ashia, was dating this weird dude...called himself Panther, and had a big, black panther with green eyes tatooed on his arm."

"Sounds scary."

"Worse than scary. Anyway, he came over to take Ashia to some party wearing this pimp hat and I thought my dad was going to come unglued. He told him to go get a haircut, and come back without the hat in less than an hour or he couldn't take her out."

"Oh my God! What did your sister say?"

"Oh she knew better than to cross Daddy with her lip, so she went and told Mama. Mama took Daddy in their room, and they were in there for a while, and when they came out, all I know is that Daddy was in a much better mood."

"Well, what happened to the boy?"

"He came back with a hair cut in thirty minutes!"

"Man, your dad is tough, but unfortunately not nearly as tough or crazy as mine."

"Oh yeah?"

"My dad used to follow me around all night when I started dating. He would also run police reports on my male friends, even if I wasn't really even dating them."

"Has he run one on me?"

"I wouldn't doubt it." I was getting tired and I could tell that Ed wasn't exactly winding down. He loved to tell stories about him and Robert when they were little kids. Some of them I'd heard hundreds of times, but they just seemed so real, so animated, that I enjoyed them each time he told them. Robert and Ed have such a close relationship; they're more like brothers than cousins. Robert practically lived with Ed's family while his mother was getting her business going. And some people actually started to believe the lie they told about them being brothers, since Ed's parents spent time checking on both of them in school. Ed had once told me that at one point he'd gotten jealous of all the attention his dad, who'd been a pro football player himself, gave to Robert, who turned out to be one of the leading rushers in the state in high school with a 3.6 GPA. I knew so much about Robert that when I first met him, I walked right up to him in the airport and said, "You must be Robert!".

I looked over Ed's shoulder at the clock on the wall, and it was near two o'clock. I snuggled a little closer to him. He wrapped his arm around me and kept telling me some of the childhood stories about him and Robert...like the time they got the whippin of their life for setting a mattress on fire, and how they would shoot their bee-bee guns at the neighbor's cat. Bad ass...no wonder he's so calm now...he's still worn out from his mischievous youth. He says it wasn't nothing for the two of them to get three whippins a day. Now that's ridiculous....

I must have dozed off because when I woke up, Ed was talking about high school, and how he would sneak out or sneak girls in almost every night. Then he told me about the time he got busted with one of the substitute teachers in the physical science lab's storage closet. I couldn't believe Ed had done some of the crazy things he had done, it really makes me wonder what he does when he's not around me, or maybe he's just outgrown that stuff. I wanted to ask, but I wasn't sure I wanted to know. So I just listened as he went on to talk about his college escapades including his first and only real girlfriend whom I'd heard about many times before. It seems she was the only girl on campus that nobody could 'get with', and he finally captured her heart only to find out a year later that she was dating two other guys, on other campuses, seriously too. After that, Ed didn't date anyone seriously for years, and when he finally started to do so again, women just seemed "too superficial--not one real sistah..." I heard him say.

I must have dozed off again cause when I woke up, I had my back to Ed and he had his arm draped over my waist. At first I thought I was dreaming, and then I felt his warm breath hitting my neck and going straight down my back. I felt a familiar tingle all over my body, and I peeked to see if he was sleeping. He was. I shifted my now rigid body just slightly to get comfortable again. I must have awakened Ed because this time when I looked up and over my shoulder Ed was staring right back at me. Our eyes locked on each other for a strange, but comfortable moment. It was like we were communicating without saying a word. Ed closed his eyes and went right back to sleep. I flipped over on my tummy. Then I thought to myself, at moments like this, I sure am glad I'm not a man cause I would definitely be on hard right now. I folded my arms around my pillow and listened to Ed breathing deep and rhythmically as I forced myself to go back to sleep.

CHAPTER 21
Ass-Out
♋

I can't believe he waited until the morning of our wedding day to do this to me. And the nerve of him to tell me in front of her. I should have known that something was fishy. That's why he never wanted to talk about his past. Every time I would ask him to tell me about their relationship, and how I was like and not like her, he ignored me or made up some sorry excuse to not talk about her. He also never showed me a picture of her, so I used to look in the mirror and visualize how she could have looked to me. He knew I wanted to know more about his first love. It became sort of a hidden obsession that has constantly been on my mind these last couple of months.

"Get the hell out my way!"

These no driving bastards gonna make me late to Afrikka's house. It's close to eleven o'clock and she probably thinks I'm fooling around. Boy, if she only knew. I can't wait to tell her what I just found out. I would hate to have to call off this wedding that she worked so hard to organize. But, I've got to. I don't have a choice. That sorry bastard has driven me to it. I mean, there is no way that I can marry him now, now that the secret is out. MEN AIN'T SHIT!!! I should have known that this was too good to be true. Why did he do this to me? I never did anything to him. I don't deserve this type of treatment. I never hurt him--ever. I thought we had a bond that no one could ever break. Fuck men!...to hell with all of them. Maybe I should become a lesbian after this. ...I have tried so hard to get him to talk about her. If he would have just told me the truth, I would have understood. It would have never led to this. All of this could have been avoided. But, now he has fucked everything up. My life, my heart, my mind, and even my soul. I had faith in him, and now he has fucked it all up. Damn him!!! Damn, his soul!!!

"Damn, Nicolette!" Afrikka yelled at me as she opened the door, "did you have to knock so hard?"

I stood there and gave her this real evil but sad look. Maybe because I was feeling angry and hurt at the same time.

"Nicolette..." she lowered her voice, "I haven't seen that face in months. Has something happened?" Afrikka said, as she stepped outside on the steps with me, and pulled the door closed right behind her.

I stood there as if something was preventing me from moving. Everything, I mean everything that I put into this relationship was gone in less than ten minutes. I've never trusted anyone the way I trusted him. He was my life. After thinking about it all, I don' t have the words to explain how I feel right now. My entire identity has changed. Now, I've lost my sense of self, and how I used to see and think about myself. And if I could find the words to explain this..this 'unthinkable'...I wouldn't even have the energy to let it out. As I stand here facing Afrikka, I feel an urge to just cry. That's the only way I can release all of my pain right now.

"Nicolette," Afrikka grabbed me, "come in...what's the matter...please, girl, you've got to tell me...it's killing me to see you this way."

Afrikka's townhouse looked on the inside, the way I *feel* on the inside. Her sofa bed was pulled out, and the covers were all over the floor. I just stood there numb while she cleared a chair of some of the material she used for the bridesmaids' dresses. I stared at the fabric that she seemed to be moving in slow motion.

I finally got the energy to place my worthless body in the chair. Then Afrikka dissappeared for a few minutes while I sat there feeling like someone has taken all of the life out of me.

Why couldn't he have told me this yesterday when he saw her again for the first time after so...so many years. He never cared about how I would have felt if I found out. How selfish can he be. Now, I can no longer trust any man, anymore. Especially after putting my faith in the man I loved and trusted all of this time.

My senses must be coming back to me because I thought I recognized a male voice coming from the back, but I figured it was the T.V. Afrikka reappeared in a minute carrying a mug with the words "Pretty Moody Sister" with an accent on the P.M.S. part. She offered it to me, and I took it hoping it was cyanide laced with toxins from the gutter. It was some of Afrikka's wonderful herbal tea. I took a sip, and then let out a huge sigh. I felt a mild sense that things would be okay. Then I heard another noise coming from the back room, and I looked at Afrikka.

"Uhhh, that's Ed leaving out the back door." I shook my head and took another big gulp of the warm medicinal tea. Afrikka must have sensed my curiosity cause she explained, "it's chamomile to calm your nerves," she paused and smiled warmly at me. I broke out into tears, and she hugged me for what seemed the longest time.

When I was able to talk, I told her everything from front to finish. After repeating the tragic news that had been given to me, and now to Afrikka, we both sat there not knowing what to say or do. The wedding is just a few hours away. What am I supposed to do? I once thought that I had all of the answers to all of my problems, and now I am faced with something I can not change, and I don't have a clue what to do about it? It used to be so easy to tell my clients in therapy that what they thought was a huge issue actually wasn't. It occured to me now that I lacked empathy with them because I never took the time to tune into *their* world and realize that what *they* thought was a problem, *was* a problem in their eyes. And it doesn't really matter what anyone else thinks. But I...I am so damned judgemental, and now here I am facing the same fire I helped to build in the lives of so many others. Something deep inside me was telling me that I have to reap what I have been sewing for so many years. Now, it's my turn to suffer. I felt sad, but at the same time I felt relieved, like things were happening just as they should.

That thought really pissed me off. How could I think that way? Now I'm even turning against myself!

Afrikka looked at me and smiled so assuredly I could have slapped her for being so calm and focused. How could she smile at a time like this? There could not possibly be a solution to this. There is no way out except to cancel the wedding.

"What?" I asked her revealing my disgust with her disposition. "What are you thinking? What can I do?"

"Simone is singing in your wedding, right?" she asked.

"Right," I told her.

"Dana is your maid of honor?"

"Yes."

"Robert's cousins are two of your bridesmaids?"

"Yeah."

"I'm your coordinator and one of your maids, too?"

"Uh-huh."

"Ed, Desmond, and Robert's best friend, Michael, are the groomsmen?"

"Yes, yes, Afrikka. So, what's the point?"

"And my family, Dana's family, even Temeka and Candy are coming to see you get married?"

"So?" I wasn't getting what Afrikka was trying to say, and her suspenseful building, was making me even more frustrated. "I don't understand."

"Well, you have an audience of all of your closest friends, your friends' friends and family and, of course...a beautiful outside, garden wedding in your backyard with a gazebo to top it off...the finest foods and drinks money can buy... with the baddest wedding dress and bridesmaids' dresses created and made by the one and only - Styles from Afrikka...and to top it all off, Kenny Lattimore singing '*For*

You' at your sit-down dinner reception and dance..." she was going on and on and on.

"What are you trying to say?" I had to cut her off.

"Does Robert, your dad, and his mom think you guys are still getting married?" Afrikka asked.

I paused.

"As far as I know," I sighed, "...everyone is going to meet me at the house, dressed, and in their places to see this tragic wedding go on."

"Perfect," she picked up the phone, "I'm gonna try and catch Ed on his car phone and tell him what's going on, and my idea about what to do."

"You mean..." I looked at her believing she had just lost her mind, "you want me to marry him after all of this?"

"Well," she said with the phone to her ear waiting for Ed to answer, "everybody is still going to play their parts, in fact, we're going to have so much fun, just like we planned....cause like they say 'the show must go on!' "

♋

I can't believe Afrikka has me doing this. She got all the bridal party together to explain exactly what was about to take place. She broke the news so gracefully that everyone just sat there stunned and didn't even ask questions. Now, everybody is in place and ready to walk down the isle.

The colors are lime green and silver--two of my favorite summer colors. I love bright colors. They always seem to make me cheerful, and my attitude could certainly use some cheering up right now.

The bridesmaid's are wearing a double-layer, empire-style slip dress in a soft lime green. The lower layer is a soft flowing silk, while the upper layer is chiffon. They look so feminine and the dresses flatter everyone's figures. Their strappy criss-cross, tie-up-the-front, square-heeled sandals by Evan Piccone are in a silver satin fabric. We bought the shoes as is and didn't even have to dye them because they matched the silver kufu and veil that each girl would be wearing until the bride removed hers. Each bridesmaid will carry a bouquet of fresh, long-stem, silver roses flown in from Tyler, Texas-- the rose capitol of the world, wrapped with lime twine bows. In fact, this whole place looked like the rose bowl the last time I saw it earlier today. There were florists everywhere adding all kinds of exotic flowers especially white roses and azaleas to every inch of the grounds making it look like a garden.

Everyone looks so beautiful in their dresses. Especially Dana--that lime looks great on her caramel brown skin! Then again, with the kind of beauty Dana has, she could look great no matter what she is wearing. She is such a wonderful, delightful person to be around. So beautiful, and yet so caring...the ultimate black woman. Dana has been running around making sure everything is in place and everybody is comfortable this whole week. When I need someone to talk to, she is always there. When I need a favor, she never hesitates. And when I need some support, she is my personal cheerleader. But I, on the other hand, was always selfish when it came to Dana. It was always my way or no way, at all. Deep down, on the inside, I have always envied Dana because she is the kind of person I've always wanted to be, but couldn't. She has so many positive qualities that she doesn't even know she possesses. I can't believe I didn't see what was going on with her. I guess I just never took the time to understand what she was going through. I overlooked all of the pain she was suffering. All of the signs were there but, no, I was too selfish...I was so blind. And it wasn't that I couldn't see...I didn't want to see. And after all we've been through, here she is, right in my corner.

"Are you guys ready in there?" Dana asked banging on my door that leads through the back yard and straight down the wedding isle. The wedding had started on time just as I wanted.
"Get the bridesmaids in place," Afrikka told her cracking the door and peeking out, " make sure everybody is in place...tell them to start the music... and Nicolette and I will be out in a second."
"Okay," Dana said as she ran out of sight.
"You can do this, " Afrikka reassured me.
I just smiled not knowing what to say.
"If you say so," I finally responded.
We covered our heads and got in our places.
When I got to the door and looked out I couldn't believe my eyes, Afrikka had made this place into a fairy tale.... there were lime and silver fabrics draping the aisle from the back to the front. The fabric was attached by a huge bowknot to stilted candle holders which held long silver electric candles surrounded by a delicately fluted huricane crystal globe. Each stood about seven feet high, and lead down the long aisle right to the elevated gazebo. It is still quite bright outside and the candles are set to come on at dusk along with all the other lights that have been added to this scene to make it light up like Christmas around here. There are also about twenty huge exotic vases on tripod stands that are as tall as I am. They have identical flower arrangements in them with some kinds of flowers that I have never seen before,

but they are lime green, and other colors, elaborately displayed with those long spirally twigs.

I can't believe the number of people who showed up. Afrikka even called up a bunch of media folks today that we had previously cut from the guest list, so there were even more than we'd expected. Fortunately, Afrikka knew to plan for more than expected, 'just in case' she says. I felt even more nervous when she suggested that we add more media coverage--I guess because I just don't want everyone in the world to know what happened. But, Afrikka says if you try to hide things that that makes people even more interested in finding out about it--and then if they can't dig up dirt, they will just lie. I really just don't want to ruin my dad's reputation, and Robert...I wish this whole thing had never happened....I wish..oh, Nicolette, not now...I just can't think about this right now....

    I am waiting for the bridesmaids to walk down the isle, it looks as if the whole world has come to see my disaster, and it feels like it's going to take a lifetime to get to that gazebo. I just can't believe that I am going through with this....My God, is that Simone singing? That *is* Simone. She is singing *Inseperable* in a sultry jazzy style that clearly reveals her gospel roots. Everyone in the house is misty-eyed....including me. She sounds like an angel pouring her heart out to the world.

    Her beautiful voice soothed my mind just like it does when we are at home, and I just reflected on what a blessing it has been to have Simone living in the house with me. I asked her to move in to help her get away from her past and start trying to make a better life for her and E. J., but the truth is that I have been the one receiving help from her tremendous spirit. Our friendship has brought me so much peace...that I take for granted. She's used this time wisely to become in tune with who she is and where she is going, yet I never offered to listen to her suggestions or her advice--her problems or her concerns. I am so stubborn and want to find out things on my own. She is always saying that she prays for me on a daily basis, but I never asked why or even what specific things she prayed about for me. I was so into making Robert my life that I sometimes forgot that Simone was even around.

Simone never complains when I act like a spoiled brat, and she never gets impatient with me when I make mistakes. She just says, "It's all good." And even though I was there for her when she was down and out, I can be pretty judmental and self-righteous, so I know I was hard to live with. Still, she was always there for me, even if it was just to listen. She always listens to me...

As I get closer to the altar, now and turn to look at Afrikka, I think about all that she has done for me. If I had to choose a role model, it would definitely be Afrikka. Afrikka is the strongest sista I have ever met in my life. She doesn't allow any obstacle to stand in her way. She attacks the issue at hand and goes about her business like it never existed. She has taught me that in life there are consequences of every behavior that we choose, and when you are confronted with a consequence that you don't like or disagree with that brings you distress and pain, accept it, so it won't happen again. Then, just let it become another book on your shelf. Afrikka believes that there are no such things as mistakes, only lessons, and that each lesson is simply an opportunity for growth, that prepares us for something still to come in our ever unfolding lives. After today, I will always take these thoughts to heart.

When Afrikka told me that she had been saving a dress for her wedding that she'd been working on since she started her business, there was no way that I was thinking she was gonna let it be *my* wedding dress. She hadn't even completely finished the whole thing, but insisted that if I liked it, I could consider it my wedding gift. I was astonished by her unselfishness. She put every bit of her pride and creativity into it. It is the baddest, most imaginative wedding dress I have ever seen! First of all, it is silver in a handwoven silk fabric with a natural texture to it. Afrikka had it flown in from Zimbobway, and the fabric is just perfect for the dress, which is a two-piece with a column-style top that stops just below the waist barely revealing the belly button. The upper half of the top is shaped like an upside down 'V' which the rigdes go horizontally into a sterling silver band that forms a necklace which serves to hold the top up in front and in back. The bodice is fitted also except the stripes go vertically on the bodice to define the waist. The skirt is made of the same fabric, but looks somewhat like a wrap skirt because of the way the lines meet to form an oval in the front. Afrikka said that it was like the African dress where the woman took fabric and wrapped herself around the hips with it like a towel when you get out of the shower. It is elegantly form-fitting all the way down to just above the ankles where it swings slightly out into a gradual a-line bottom sort of like a fish-tail but smoother. This elegant draping bottom gives way to a floor-length train reminiscent of movie stars of the 40's. In the front where the skirt scoops below the belly-button is a tiny silver chain with three lime-colored jewels in the shape of triangles, representing 'peace, prosperity, and procreation'. This delicate chain goes from one hip to the other to accent the barely open midriff.

Afrikka even went to the trouble of having the dress annointed by some older lady that she knows. The Kuffi headpiece which leans outward on the top to create a 'V' shape effect attaches to a full floor-length, silver tulle veil that covers the complete face in the front, and flows down the back like a crown. The kuffi is accented by triangular, lime green gemstones that line the top and bottom of the elegant African headpiece. I've never seen anything like it, and Afrikka said it would be good advertising for her business since she wasn't so sure when or if she was ever going to get married, and because of all the media attention we're getting since my dad worked on the Versace murder case.

Well, here we are, finally making it to the altar. I'm glad Afrikka talked me into doing this. I am so proud of her. It's not so bad after all. She has made the right decision. She always does. My heart is pounding so hard against my chest. I hope I don't pass out. Everyone is quiet. I look up and see Malik standing at a podium on the side of the gazebo that is covered with more white roses and azaleas. He smiled at me and begin to recite a beautiful poem:

I looked and looked
but could not find
the love that was
meant to be mine

I was searching for a love
that is real and true
I looked all around
But I didn't see you

I called out to God
in despair

Where is he, Lord?
I can't find him anywhere

A voice from far away
called out to me in the night
I couldn't see the way
so I went right
Into the arms
of this man I know
Who inspires me, guides me
And loves me so

Now what I thought
would never begin
Has brought me
To this perfect end

Cause here I am
about to wed

my soul, my heart
my lover, my friend

Malik's words soaked even deeper into me than ever before. I thought I really knew what love is...now I'm not so sure.

As I look around, I find myself not listening to Pastor Evans. The time is going so fast, and the sun is going down and there is a beautiful full moon replacing it in the eastern sky behind the gazebo. I feel overwhelmed with emotion..I wish I could be writing what I feel right now. The scent from the thousands of fresh flowers encapsulates me. I just keep watching the moon, and the water falling from the two huge, imported, seraphim water fall sculptures. I wish I could stay here in the beauty of this moment for the rest of my life. The clear, smooth flow of the water down the arm and over the body of the sculpture, lets me know that I am still alive..that this is really happening.

When I finally tuned back in Rev. Evans was saying, "...you may now kiss the bride." We all pulled back our veils...Ed leaned over and gave Afrikka the biggest wedding kiss I have ever seen...there were cameras flashing everywhere. And with the sun sinking below the horizon, the electric candles and outside lighting Afrikka had slaved to get just right, kicked in, and lit up the moment, right on time. There was not a dry eye in the house, as Ed and Afrikka embraced each other. Then, Ed looked into Afrikka's eyes and went for a second kiss. When they finally came up for air, everyone was cheering and clapping. From where I was, right next to the gazebo, I could see the tears in Afrikka's eyes. I read Ed's lips as he said to her, "You've just made me the happiest man in the world...I love you." Then Ed, too had tears in his eyes. The whole thing was like a scene from some old Billy Dee Williams movie. So I guess Afrikka once again was right...the show had to go on, and *that* it did.

I let the tears that had welled up in my eyes fall now, and my life was, for a moment, not a concern. I felt as much joy for Afrikka as if it were me being married, and I experienced, right then, what love is all about--letting go.

CHAPTER 22
Fortitude
♋

Lord, Father God in heaven, it's me again, Simone. Thank you for changing my life just like you said you would. Thank you for giving me the strength to accept the things I cannot change, and the courage to change the things I could have changed a looong time ago. You showed how niggas in this record industry are full of crap. And that what fulfills my needs, and not wants, is and has always been--fashion.

I know now that you have sent so many blessings through the people in my life. Like E.J. showed me I can love a man. And Afrikka showed me I can trust again, and believe in myself. And the angel from the hospital, Lord, nobody else may believe me, but I know it was real. Even Earl helped me to see how trying to ignore my pain only elevated it. I just hate that he was smuggling drugs on the side and ruining people's lives.

I am so blessed today with my own place, around people who care about themselves and the community. Luckily, Earl had some common sense to take out life insurance on himself while he was working at UPS. I guess he was thinking about E.J. just in case something happened to him. That $100,000 sure paid off. You've given me and E.J. a whole new start, such as using some of that money to put E.J. in a private performing arts school. Maybe he can grow up and be the next Picasso. And, of course, I just can't thank you enough for the scholarship that Afrikka helped me to get to go to the Fashion and Art Institute. Today is my first day of class, and it has been a looong time since I was in school, but I know you haven't brought me this far to turn back on me now. So I'm going to trust you to carry me through. Fashion has always been my heart, and now I'm just going to do it. I'm not afraid of anything anymore, including myself. And I don't need to hide behind men or fame or money or music or anything else.

God, continue to work on me and keep me dedicated to the church and your work. I promise you I will always use my talent to minister to others in song if you will just continue to hold me up when I'm falling down--and I know you will. Be there for my friend tonight as she embarks on a new part of her life, and exposes herself to the world through the talent you have given her.

Amen.

♋

Dear Diary,

Today, I finally finished putting the wedding scrapbook together. Well, there's still a couple more things, but basically it's finished. I never dreamed it would have been the way it was. I didn't know if Ed felt the same way...I didn't know if...all I knew was that I loved Ed and I wanted him to be my husband. It was weird but everything just felt so right, and fell right into place. It couldn't have been more perfect if I had planned it myself....Then, I guess I did!

Consequently, the publicity turned out even better than I thought.. It actually made national news because evidently, there had never been such a wedding day switch. And the neat thing is that they thought that it was planned, so Nicolette didn't have to say a thing. I got so much business from the wedding that I hired Simone to work with us since we really need someone who already knows the administrative end of the company so that Ed can focus on marketing, and me on the creative. She's a great help to the company, and she's so inspirational, and it's like having our own Anita Baker in the office. Even Macy's was calling me and trying to get my line back after all the wedding reviews came out. And I've gotten hundreds of requests for wedding coordination. Who knows? maybe I'll start another company, but not right now. I'm still adjusting to my new life.

That's why it has been a couple of months since I've written.

Married life is so different from what I expected. Ed and I really thought we spent a lot of time together before, but now we really spend a lot of time...just hanging out and enjoying one another. We have both put aside a lot of our worrisome, workaholic ways, and come to enjoy the best part of life--love.

This is the first time since we have been married that I have had time to myself. Well, I better enjoy it before he gets back from his fraternity convention... It's not that I don't miss him, cause believe me I do. It's just nice to have some solitary time for myself. It's funny, but when I was single, I just didn't appreciate quiet time like I should have. Now I can't do some of the things I used to like just get up and walk around the house naked. Well, I could, but that causes too much confusion with Ed on the prowl--he such an animal. I can't believe his sexual appetite, but I love it!!

*I also still struggle to believe how this whole thing came together. Something just clicked in me that night before Nic's wedding...I mean **my** wedding (that really takes some getting used to), and I felt totally different about Ed. It just happened, and he felt it, too. I guess some part of me knew all along that Ed was my soulmate, but I was too busy trying to help others with their fears, that I overlooked my own. Ed has helped me to see that and so much more. He is my best friend, and I'm so lucky, no...blessed, to have him in my life.*

Gotta go now, I'm running off to Nic's little thing tonight. It won't be months before you hear from me again.

Afrikka,
...still honeymooning

♋

I've finally got it! Now I understand! All this time, I've been afraid of the sexual part of me. Afraid that it would get out of my control (like my appetite did.) That's why I was afraid to be thin--I know or at least I think I will attract a great deal of men and I'm not sure how to handle that. That's why I liked **The Rules** *so much because I have no idea how to have a healthy relationship whether sexual or not. And I know that the more I allow myself to become who I really am, the more choices I'll have to make relationally.*

I remember walking across the street with my mom in about the third or fourth grade, and she was telling me how I was going to be a knockout, and that they were going to have to be cautious with me. I remember feeling flattered, yet somewhat alarmed at the thought that so many guys might be interested in me. I developed a guard which is still standing to this day--keeping me from meeting men and then keeping me from being close to them once I do.

The young me was so proud, and so free, and quite sexually aware. She knows what types of sexual advances are not appropriate. She learned to dissociate and not deal with them, but she still remembers being nothing more than a sex object for her own father's pleasure. Somehow I believe he even knew that it was wrong because of her outrage at what was being done to her. It was wrong. He was wrong! She is not to blame. Her body and nothing about her is to blame. She was only a child and no matter how mature she was, she couldn't protect herself. In fact, it was his job to protect her then! Now he's been fired by me--he never was and never will be capable of being her protector or the families' protector for that matter. A weak little boy still throwing rocks and looking for an easy way out. I know he didn't know how this would effect me--he probably didn't think I'd ever remember. I'm going to be the protector now--me and my real father, God. He is going to help me listen to Him and keep away from bums like LaRon out to leech on good God-fearing women. I don't know why, but until now I haven't really been angry about this whole thing. And I know I haven't really accessed all my rage and anger, but Oh! I'm going to. And then, there's momma-- Ms. Innocent (PSYCHE) I don't care how many times she says she didn't know, I still say she was an accomplice because she was not strong enough herself to stand on her own two feet and deliver. She took the easy way out, and she would never admit it, but the first man she had any attachment/attraction for she clamped down on him like a starving church woman always does. I'm so pissed off at the Christian church for denying sexuality--the way to life itself. By denying its existence we've done exactly the opposite of what was desired--turned it into a taboo and thus, a marketing tool. If men can pretend that women don't have legs, then they can pretend it is not rape to tear them apart and stick their own guilt, pride and anger into women. What the hell is going on in these backward churches? It is everywhere and it is total injustice. Women are more than just bodies looking to be filled. We are strong, proud, intelligent (we made them think they were getting the best of us so they would leave us alone--we played dead, but we are NOT dead--quite the contrary.

    I AM ALIVE! I AM SEXUAL!
    I AM OKAY JUST LIKE THIS!
    I AM DEPENDABLE AND INDEPENDENT!
    I HAVE ME! I AM ME! AND
    GOD I'M PROUD--I AM BEAUTIFUL.

*I AM EXPRESSIVE. I AM BOLD. I AM CARING.
I AM IN TOUCH WITH MY NEEDS
(Ahh! that one feels good!)
I AM NECESSARY. I AM SENSITIVE, ANALYTICAL
AND EMOTIONAL. I AM GLAD I'M ME!*

Nic and I are closer than ever. She actually opens up and shares her feelings, and I feel like I have someone that I can truly identify with since our situations are similar. In II Corinthians, Paul talks about how we suffer so that we can help others through similar pain. Now, I truly understand those words, because helping her has helped me to see that I don't need to help someone to feel worthwhile, but it is a blessing to give without looking for anything in return. And after getting through tonight Nic is really going to be a whole new woman.
    August 29 at 5:30

♋

    "Well, Nicolette, I haven't seen you in two weeks," my therapist said interrupting my daydream, "how have you been?"
    "Well, first of all, Robert and I are talking again, and I'm happy that we will still be able to be friends after all this. But, it is just hard to accept the fact that he is my brother. Deep down, I still love him as if he wasn't. I know it will take time...."
    "Second, Dad and I haven't talked much since the wedding and I've moved out into my own place. That morning, at the pre-wedding meeting, Dad swore that he didn't know Robert's mom was his ex-wife until he saw her. If he

wasn't so busy into *his* career he probably would have known before the wedding was even planned...or immediately after. Her name was right there, written on the wedding invitations but...nooo...he didn't bother to look at them before we sent them out. I still remember that morning as if it was yesterday. I was sitting there, holding Robert's hand. Then, his mother so coldly blirted, " your whore mother was white and you are their female bastard child." I don't remember the details that occurred after that scene...just vague images of my dad, Robert, and his mother going at it. I also remember lots of tears...a lot of hurt...a lot of pain and suffering...and more tears..."

"And I'm really glad I put off graduation for a semester, so I could truly focus in on getting to know myself. I'm still confused about a lot of things. Finding out that my mom was really my dad's white mistress, and that Robert's mom was his wife before she caught him cheating with his secretary--my mom, has changed my feelings about life, my dad...just everything. I don't blame Robert's mom for leaving my dad with his stubborn non-emotional ass. How could he dare conceive another child while his wife was pregnant? The worst part is that my mom and my dad never even got married--they were shackin'...as much as daddy hates it when other people do that--heaven forbid I try a stunt like that. That's when the divorce came between my dad and Robert's mother, and Robert's mother moved to the other side of the country to raise Robert, without my dad's help of course, and my dad never saw Robert again, until we met. I don't know whether to hate her or him for what they did--I just know I' m still pissed off and I may never forgive either one of them."

"Robert's mother has really made this transition easier for me, by opening her heart to me at this time. She called me up shortly after the incident to apologize, and offer her ear for listening. At first I was so angry at her for calling me a bastard, cause that wasn't even my fault. Then I realized I really can't blame her, she'd had all that anger bottled in for so many years, and she just let it go, and I probably would have done something ten times worse. We've talked a couple of times, because I had so many questions and things I needed to have clarified, and since my dad wants to play dumb, I just called her up. She is a real strong sistah, and actually she's quite warm. But, most of all, she really understands what it is like to be caught up in a lie with my father."

"The funny thing about this whole mess is that I still sometimes can't believe it's all true. I feel like I'm having a nightmare that I'm on the Ricki Lake show, and that I'll wake up and be normal again. I never thought something like this would happen to *me*. But that just ain't happening. And I don't know whether to cry because of what I lost, or to rejoice because of what I've gained. I do know one thing, I have so much more sympathy and compassion for others than I ever thought I possibly could, and getting therapy has helped me to deal with all of this waaay better than I know I would have on my own."

"Another thing that's really helped is getting my own place. My girlfriends helped me move out last week. I know it's gonna be a struggle with all the other things I have going on, but it's worth it for the peace of mind I have."

"After I threatened to never speak to him again, my dad finally showed me a picture of my mother. And you know, all along I thought I was a little black girl caught in a white woman's body, but really I am a PROUD, STRONG, BLACK WOMAN."

♋

I can't believe that this is really happening. I am sitting at the Soul Coffee Cafe watching Malik Akbar only this time it is my turn. Dana is the reason I am here today. I knew I was missing my manuscript but I had so many things going on in my life at that time, I forgot that it was even gone. But she knew that poetry has always been my true talent. Secretly, she has been working with Malik this whole time while I was in therapy, gathering my best works, getting it copywritten, and now published. And she worked day and night with Malik setting up a brief booksigning tour to market his newly released novel, *Barking at the Moon*, and my collection of poems entitled, *Mood Swings*, at different cities throughout the country. I sit here, with Dana at my side holding my hand, and Afrikka and Simone to my left, I look back and recognize Robert hiding against the back wall. I notice a couple of my co-workers and a few of my classmates present in the audience. As I look to the other side, I couldn't help but see Roselda in a bright, red dress looking like a Spanish Queen.

Malik Akbar came to a conclusion in his speech and I knew he was about to introduce me... "... I will now introduce to you a young lady who I met over a year ago...in this same cafe...only at that time she was not aware of her full potential. But I saw her recite her poem... and on that day I knew that she would soon become the rising star she is today. It is a pleasure and an honor to introduce to you at this time, the author of *Mood Swings*, reciting her soon-to-be most memorable poem...audience, put your hands together for Nicolette. "

As I listened to the applause the audience is giving me, I immediately look up knowing God is always by my side. And as I am on the search for my 'self', he is the footsteps I always imagined by my side every step of the way. As I stand here, giving thanks to Malik, and my friends...I notice my father creeping through the door and slowly making his way over to Robert.

" I also give thanks to my family," I spoke as the audience listened while acknowledging the people I named by pointing them out at the same time, " for without them, I would not be here today--my godmother, Roselda, my brother, Robert....and...and my father. "

I saw a smile in my father's face as if he has realized that this is now the beginning of our future - again. And as he hugged my brother, I really believe that maybe...just maybe we can be the family I never got to have.

" I dedicate this poem to my brother, Robert, " I told the audience, " it...it is entitled *Finding the 'G' Spot* and it goes like this...

Last night while trying to find it
We was pumpin' and grindin'.
I screamed out: "Oh! Jeee-sus!"
"You coming" he sighed.
"No, baby, ...I arrived."

How many times you asked yo'self:
Isn't there more to it than this?
Where's the bomb, the spot, the lick?
Well, I found it.
When I let go, and let God
Finally the Right One,
Uhh-Huh.

When I learned to pray
The way
I know how to hit
My clit
When I need the shhhh......
No words compliment,
The true commitment,
Of the Arms strong enough to lift your soul.
Eyes that see you,
And lips that say you
The most beautiful one in the world--
    the way you always wanted to hear it.
With hands that caress yo' ass--
When you 'bout to fall on it!

And hung--I thought you knew--on Calvary.
He's yo' boy, yo'dog and yo' gee,
And it's all free,
When you find your G-..O-D.

ABOUT THE AUTHOR

If I had to describe Marchella in one word, it would be an extremely difficult task. An extrovert, she is full of life and positive energy. You will find this one-of-kind sister most interested in people and social activities, sharing her recently-acquired knowledge and wisdom on naturalistic healing. I have to admit, though, that her detailed, deep thought and meditated behaviors contributed much particularly toward the ending process of writing our book. Many a days, I would watch Marchella contemplate in isolation over the scene of a rough draft which she was not quite satisfied with, then, after her added touches, the masterpiece soon followed. Writing this book for two months with Marchella was filled with many highs and lows but somehow, we always found a way to overcome our obstacles, balancing both positive and negative energies, while getting the job done at the same time.

Rarely would you catch Marchella in a bad mood. If you find yourself feeling down, she will pick you up. Her lovely personality is just a reflection of her inner beauty. When I first met this talented, spiritual human being, I found myself desiring the same ambitious goals she possessed. At the same time, she is as highly motivated as I am. On any day you will find this creative creature exploring a new book, discovering an ancient mystery, rearranging her closet, or organizing a social gathering. She can be goofy and intelligent; she procrastinates but will eventually get the job done; she is an optimist, a serious perfectionist, a soul-seeker, assertive....I can go on and on. So if I had to describe Marchella in one word, it would be...Versatile.

Written with many praises by,
Jwaundace

ABOUT THE AUTHOR

Jwaundace is a creative jewel...without whom I would still be planning to write a book. Her patience and persistence urged me through this entire process and taught me a lot about myself in the meantime. To Jwaundace, I am eternally grateful for her spirit of giving and her energy for life. As natural as grass, and as earthy as fresh, red, clay dirt, Jwaundace utilized every strength of her character to highlight and energize mine so that we could quickly see this project to the end. Her bright smile and perky personality wins the heart of everyone she meets. Jwaundace inspired me in everyway--mentally, spiritually, physically, and emotionally. She is so grounded and so aware that I had to constantly check myself to make sure that I was on the ball. Thank you for enduring with me through this fun, but challenging project. And thank you for being a role model for women everywhere!

just one dance... (for Jwaundace)

Writer and warrior whose weapons weaken wrestlers and wraps wounded
Willing to weather womanhood, winning wholeness with works, not wants
Walking without wander or waging wars within
Watch whose wings will widen when winter-winds whistle
A white elephant in whose womb await wacky wit and wide-eyed wisdom
A window worth watching; her warm waves wax the world wonderful
A weeping waterfall which washes the way worthy with well-done writings!

Written with much love by,
Marchella

Jwaundace Belcher has a B.A. in Psychology from Grambling State University and a M.A. in Psychological Counseling from Dallas Baptist University. She is a therapist, an educator, a poet, and an actress.

Marchella Bell has a B.A. in Marketing from Texas A&M and will soon complete her M.A. in Psychological Counseling from Dallas Baptist University. She is a certified hypnotherapist, an orator, a poet, and a singer.

For inquiries or requests for public appearances, seminars or book signing engagements, please write to:
Another BOMB Production
2480 Briarcliff Road #166
Atlanta, Georgia 30329
404-219-4205

To place individual book orders call 800-309-8321